EXCELLENCE IN EDUCATION

Excellence in Education

EDITED BY John N. Mangieri

Texas Christian University Press · Fort Worth

Library of Congress Cataloging in Publication Data

Main entry under title:

Excellence in education.

  Bibliography: p.
  1. Education—United States—Addresses, essays,
lectures. I. Mangieri, John N.
LA210.E88 1985   370'.973   85-50539
ISBN 0-87565-020-1

Contents

To Francis T. Borkowski, John A. Masla, and Arnold J. Moore
for their friendship, guidance, and support

The Challenge of Attaining Excellence

John N. Mangieri

Recently, at a meeting of educators, I asked the question: "In order for a school or school district to attain excellence, what conditions must exist within it?" Eight general conditions were cited most frequently by my sample group of educators:

1) a rigorous curriculum,
2) competent teachers,
3) effectiveness characteristics,
4) testing to "prove" the students have learned essentials,
5) meaningful citizen support and positive parental involvement,
6) adequate financing,
7) strong discipline, and
8) commitment to traditional values.

Do you agree with all of these conditions? Are there others which you would have added to this list? Would you have excluded some from the list?

Later, I shared the eight conditions with two groups of community members and posed the preceding two questions to them, adding a second dimension to my informal research. These noneducators agreed generally with the eight conditions. Some individuals added new items to the list, while others took exception to some of the existing items. However, the number of changes was quite small. Both groups apparently believed that the existence of the eight conditions could result in excellence in education in a school or school district.

My informal study had a third dimension. I then asked these same groups to explain precisely how the schools should implement these conditions.

Curriculum

What is a rigorous curriculum? Presumably, it is one which challenges students intellectually and academically. All students receive instruction in the language arts, mathematics, science, and the social sciences, and students perform well on standardized state and national tests in these areas. When questioned, the groups gave a hearty endorsement to the preceding explanation of a rigorous curriculum.

Very different beliefs were expressed when other curricular issues were presented. Should all students be expected to master the same curriculum? "Yes," responded some. If a high school degree is to mean something, they argued, then everyone who has completed twelve years of schooling should know the same general things. Others disagreed, arguing that students differ in ability. Students of less ability will be challenged by a curriculum emphasizing the basics while the more able students should receive greater challenges.

What subjects beyond basics constitute the curriculum? Once again, there was widespread disagreement. Are the fine arts a basic or a luxury in a rigorous curriculum? Should foreign language study be required for all students? If so, which language(s) should be offered? How many years of study should be required? If foreign language study should not be required for all students, who is required to study language . . . and who is not?

The two curricular areas which generated the most heated arguments were physical education and vocational/technical education. Should physical education be a mandatory part of a school's curriculum? Some argue "yes," claiming that health and fitness are indispensable to other facets of life. A contrary viewpoint was expressed by others who argue that play should not provide academic credit. Physical education, they said, has no role in a rigorous curriculum.

With regard to the role of vocational and technical education in a rigorous curriculum, once again a difference of opinion emerged. Proponents argued that schools must prepare students for the world of work. This is especially true for less able students, and training received at school may help them assume a job upon completion of high school. Others argued technical and vocational education are not rigorous. They suggested that students merely take such courses to avoid difficult subjects; even if one completes such courses, it means little because the courses utilize old-fashioned equipment and prepare persons for careers in which there are no real personnel needs.

Teachers

The two groups of community members were shown the characteristics of excellent teachers compiled by Tschudin (1978), the criteria for identifying master teachers suggested by Easterly (1983), and the Florida State University (1979–80) skills, ideas, and strategies related to teaching. These lists were chosen because they are representative of the criteria presently being discussed in the literature. The groups were asked two questions regarding these three listings: first, which of the three do you feel sets forth the criteria for determining competent teachers? (more than one list could be selected); second, which elements of the lists are not in keeping with your concept of a competent teacher?

No list was favored by a majority. In fact, as data from my second question revealed, there was widespread disagreement as to the definition of a competent teacher. Principally, the divergence of opinion focused upon whether such a teacher was strong in subject matter knowledge or was student-oriented.

The "either-or" dichotomy had another interesting caveat to it.

When it was suggested a teacher could be both, the groups agreed that could indeed be true. However, the overwhelming majority rejected such a premise as being "unrealistic" and true only in rare instances.

The community groups also expressed somewhat surprising viewpoints regarding two other matters. As to whether persons preparing to become teachers should be trained in schools of education or in the liberal arts, no preference was expressed. One person summarized the group's viewpoint quite well: "I don't care how teachers are trained. What is important is that they can teach our students well!"

Teacher competency testing was another matter raised with the groups. These testing devices, usually administered by a state department of education, focus upon general knowledge—mathematics, reading, writing—and knowledge in one's area of teaching. The two groups favored the administration of such measures not only to those preparing to become teachers but also to those who currently teach. There was also a strong conviction that capable individuals who have lost their enthusiasm for teaching should either be revitalized or terminated. They felt school administrators were not making this happen on a regular enough basis.

The final major issue with which the group was confronted was quality of students choosing teaching as a profession. The following statement by Dunne (1984) was shared with the group:

> At root, the problem is one of deployment of talent in the United States. As the number of young people declines, the occupational competition for the most talented of our nation's youth increases. This competition clearly exists at the post-secondary level, where colleges vie for their share of the most academically able; it culminates with the career choices students form in college and pursue after graduation. In this competitive effort to garner a fair share of the ever-smaller talent pool, there is a clear loser: It is public education. Fewer and fewer of the young and gifted choose to become certified

4

teachers. And there is no apparent end to this downward spiral.

No feasible solutions to remedy this situation were offered by the group.

Effectiveness Indicators

In recent years, a plethora of material has been written on the attributes of quality schools or school districts. For example, Kappa Delta Pi initiated its "Good Schools Project" in which some of the organization's members "tried to understand and promote excellence and scholarship in education by studying good schools across America" (Frymier et al., 1984). In so-called effective schooling research, five factors were cited as being indicative of such schools: "(1) the principal's leadership and attention to the quality of instruction; (2) a pervasive and broadly understood instructional focus; (3) an orderly, safe climate conducive to teaching and learning; (4) teaching behaviors that convey the expectation that all students are expected to obtain at least minimum mastery; and (5) the use of measures of pupil achievement as the basis for program evaluation" (Edmonds, 1982).

Also, a summary was provided of the recommendation offered by Boyer (1983) in the book, *High School: A Report on Secondary Education in America*. The groups were asked their feelings as to the efficacy of Boyer's suggested actions. The two groups of non-educators strongly endorsed both the effective schooling research and Boyer's recommendations. They indicated their willingness to support the implementation of activities consistent with the previously cited guidelines.

Testing

When the two community groups were presented with testing as a condition of excellent schools, they conveyed a variety of divergent viewpoints. Some strongly, and vocally, endorsed this assertion. They contended that schools needed high standards and that competency testing was a means of assuring that standards were being attained by students. Others supported the need for competency tests (or some comparable measure) as a diagnostic device, so that students who are deficient in certain segments of schooling can be identified and given special help. Neither side expressed a willingness to adopt a more conciliatory stance.

Another issue raised with these two lay groups concerned the cost of testing. If tests are used as competency measures, students who fail to attain a minimum score must be retaught the material upon which the test was based. If the devices are used as diagnostic measures, students who receive poor scores on the tests are presumed to be deficient in the areas tested. These students should then receive special help or remediation. In either instance—whether the test is for competency or is diagnostic in nature—there will be an associated personnel cost as students repeat a grade or subject.

Only about one quarter of the two community groups expressed a willingness to devote more school resources to meet this need. Approximately half the people felt schools should become "more efficient" and "eliminate the fat"; the cost of testing could then be borne from these savings. The overwhelming majority of these groups opposed testing if it meant increased costs for taxpayers. The remaining quarter of the persons opposed this form of testing for a myriad of reasons.

One final dimension of the testing issue was discussed: What should be assessed? The two community groups were remarkably consistent when this question was initially posed. Phrases such as "the basics," "what's important," and "the things a person needs to know to function in our society" were voiced. I asked for more specific meanings for the preceding phrases.

There was general agreement as to what should be tested in the elementary grades—reading, the language arts, mathematics, and to a lesser degree, social studies. Science was *not* mentioned, since according to participants, this subject became important at the secondary school level.

At the secondary school level, English, mathematics, science, and social studies were the areas the groups felt should be tested.

However, sharp differences existed among these groups as to how difficult the tests should be. Some felt the tests should be relatively low level in content to assure a basic knowledge on the part of the students. Others felt they should be demanding, to motivate educators to upgrade curricula of schools and the quality of teaching. Still others argued for a middle ground between these two viewpoints, with tests neither easy nor too hard.

Citizen Support and Parental Involvement

Every person in the two groups *strongly* supported the importance of meaningful citizen support and positive parental involvement in the schools.

The two groups of noneducators were shown a list of parental involvement activities compiled by Mangieri and Demos (1984) which includes the following:

1) parent tutors in classrooms
2) parent tutors at home
3) parent suggests education plans
4) parent recommends disciplinary procedures
5) parent visits classroom
6) parent attends conference
7) parent requests parent groups
8) parent participates in parent groups
9) parent calls at home
10) parent recommends curriculum content
11) parent attends PTA
12) parent requests home visits
13) parent assists in field trips
14) parent organizes parent meetings
15) parent participates in appraisal and review
16) parent hires a tutor
17) parent teaches reading at home
18) parent attends Board of Education meetings
19) parent informs teacher about illness
20) parent informs teacher about behavior problems

21) parent reviews data at home
22) parent asks for test results
23) parent asks to see school records
24) parent brings a friend to conferences
25) parent takes notes in conferences

In the Mangieri and Demos study, eight items were cited by educators as roles which *should be* taken by parents relative to schools: "parent tutors at home," "parent attends conference," "parent attends PTA," "parent teaches reading at home," "parent informs teacher about illness," "parent informs teacher about behavior problems," "parent asks for test results," and "parent takes notes in conferences."

The two community groups did not feel all eight of the preceding were significant if the goal of meaningful citizen support and positive parental involvement was to be realized in the schools. They endorsed five of the eight items but felt the remaining three items— "parent attends conference," "parent teaches reading at home," and "parent takes notes in conferences"—were not crucial. Different opinions were offered as to which of the other items were important. "Visiting classrooms" and "attending Board of Education meetings" were mentioned most frequently by the two noneducator groups.

So, although educators and noneducators concur as to the importance of meaningful citizen support and positive parental involvement in the schools, they differ as to how this is to occur.

Financing

In order for a school or school district to achieve excellence, it is imperative that it be adequately financed. I asked the educators if the schools in which they were employed were adequately financed. About 90 percent of my sample replied "No" to this question. When the same question was asked of the two groups of noneducators, about 80 percent said "Yes."

In "The 16th Annual Gallup Poll of the Public's Attitudes toward the Public Schools" (1984), there are several items which reflect upon financing public education. On the subject of tax increases to support the public schools, the participants in the study were asked: "Suppose the local public schools said they needed much more money. As you feel at this time, would you vote to raise taxes for this purpose, or would you vote against raising taxes for this purpose?" Forty-one percent of the sample were for a raise in taxes, 47 percent were against a raise in taxes, and 12 percent indicated an undecided response. Although other items could be cited, this example probably best illustrates the difficulty of school financing. Educators generally feel schools need more revenue upon which to operate; noneducators, especially community members who do not have school-age children, feel schools are adequately financed.

State governments provide a great deal of funding to finance education, but in many states, high unemployment, loss of revenue, and decreased population have made budgetary cuts a necessity. As a consequence, local communities are not able to rely upon the state for increased funding for schools.

In some states, reallocation processes, with overall total funding remaining approximately the same, have been proposed. Generally, these attempts have not been successful. As one can imagine, those who would receive additional funding favor the revised funding allocation, while those losing money oppose the plan. As a result, a political stalemate occurs, and the reallocation proposals are doomed to failure.

With the current interest in education, some states (Texas, 1984; South Carolina, 1984) have launched bold new plans for the support and financing of schools. Local communities in these states receive aid from the state to provide quality education to students.

Strong Discipline

In the same Gallup Poll cited in the prior section, the participants were asked the following question: "How serious a problem would you say discipline is in the public schools in the community—very serious, fairly serious, not too serious, or not at all serious?" Thirty-four percent answered "very serious," 34 percent responded "fairly serious," 22 percent felt it was "not too serious," 4 percent indicated "not at all serious," and 6 percent had "no opinion" (1984).

Educators as well as the noneducators in my study felt schools must maintain strong discipline if optimal learning is to occur in them. The educators emphasized that *wanting* strong discipline in schools and *having* it exist are two different matters. Frequently, parents want strong discipline until it affects one of their children. Then these supporters of strong discipline became adversaries of the educators. Educators also felt that any measure used to enforce discipline (paddling, suspension, staying after school, etc.) would be challenged by parents.

Neither of the two lay groups questioned agreed with the educators' view about lack of support for discipline enforcement. However, in "off the record" conversations with members of two different school boards, the educators' perception that parents undermine school discipline policies was affirmed. These people told stories of telephone calls in which the parents disagreed with the actions taken by school officials in disciplinary matters, hearings before the school board to appeal disciplinary actions, and threats of litigation.

Educators and noneducators both agree that strong discipline is an essential ingredient of excellent schools. How schools are going to achieve it is clearly a source of difficulty.

Traditional Values

Schools are viewed by many as a vital element of a democracy. They teach not only skills essential to democracy—reading and writing—but also beliefs and attitudes which foster democracy. Hence, in excellent schools, there is a commitment to traditional values.

Most citizens would support teaching traditional values to students. However, it is not easy to define "traditional values."

Should the schools teach sex education to all students? If so, at what grade level should what content be taught? What should be taught about birth control? Abortion? If some aspects of sex education are voluntary rather than mandatory, how will schools know that their students have the same knowledge and values regarding sex education?

Should prayer be permitted in the public schools? From what faiths should these prayers be drawn? Should prayers from all religions be said in the schools? If your answer to the preceding is "Yes," would you be willing to have all faiths' prayers read in school? Should prayer in the school be voluntary? If so, how can schools be assured that traditional values regarding religion are being developed by schools?

In virtually every area which could fall under the values rubric, comparable controversial issues exist. Espoused values such as honesty, citizenship, compassion, and loyalty are difficult to teach in a direct manner. In addition, concerns emerge when one conjures examples of these traits. For example, justice is a premise which most Americans endorse. However, anyone who has read Plato's *The Republic* realizes that individuals have very different concepts of justice. Does justice occur fairly in our legal system? That question would probably yield markedly different responses from members of a community.

Borsch (1984) recently discussed the difficulty of helping university students learn more about values and ethics. Although he was speaking about higher education, Borsch's viewpoint is applicable to elementary and secondary education. He said: "Few educators would disagree with the general idea that helping students develop an awareness of values and ethics is desirable. The difficulty at most of our universities is in agreeing on the specifics. There are many factors at work in the modern university which, whether conscious or unconscious, make it difficult even to sustain conversation of the subject."

Observations

Are conditions for attaining excellence in schools unrealistic? In the main, the eight conditions cited by the educators would be generally supported by other comparable groups, although individual items might vary from group to group.

What about the two groups of noneducators? Were they either so liberal, conservative, or confused that it was impossible to reach consensus with them regarding any issue? No. In fact, the two groups, in my judgment, were fairly typical of citizens in many of America's communities.

Since I conducted my original research with these groups, I have repeated segments of the process with others. The result? Although people generally endorse the general principle, there is great difference of opinion when one probes deeper. For example, the dialogue pertaining to a rigorous curriculum was almost identical in later discussions with noneducators. Individuals want schools to be challenging, vibrant institutions, but they hold widely divergent viewpoints as to how schools are to achieve this.

Does this lack of consensus mean that excellence in schools is an unattainable goal? To this question, I would emphatically respond, "No."

America's educational system is the beneficiary of our democratic society as well as the recipient of its at times burdensome modus operandi. Schools exist because they are perceived to be integral to the ideals of our society. Citizens support schools because education is vital to the economic, social, and political well-being of our country.

In a democracy, citizens have a right to speak freely, and with regard to schools, they amply avail themselves of this opportunity. In doing so, a community frequently provides educators with a set of contradictions. Although educators and laymen endorse the conditions of excellent schools, they hold contrasting viewpoints relative to the attainment of these standards. If a school is to be responsive to its community's wishes, how can it reconcile these contrasting viewpoints? Does this difference imply a hopeless situation for America's educators in their quests for excellent schools? Again, I would respond, "No." America's schools can become appreciably better in the years ahead. Educators have available to them a corpus of research which provides clear strategies for improvement. Some of the policies and procedures derived from research will be difficult to implement. An increased cost may be affixed to these educational reforms. And, of course, probably none of the recommended actions will be endorsed by all or even most of a given community. In short, excellent schools can occur from implementation of bold educational initiatives and the support of strong and dedicated educational leaders.

About This Book

In the remainder of this book, eight chapers deal with the theme of excellence in education. Each chapter considers an aspect of education and is written by an author selected for recognized expertise in the area addressed by the respective chapter. The authors present the obstacles inhibiting excellence in their particular dimension of education and then conclude with feasible recommendations and strategies for achieving that excellence.

Excellence can be realized in our nation's schools. It will not come easily, nor will there be unanimity of opinion as schools seek to revise policies, curricula, etc., to accomplish this end. But excellence can become a reality, rather than an abstraction, for America's educational system.

The contributors to this book are both realistic and optimistic about education. They are candid about the problems facing us and realistic about possible solutions based upon research or proven practice.

Finally, you may note that differing points of view or contrasting strategies may be suggested regarding a particular issue. This should not be perceived as a limitation of the book. By presenting more than a single perspective, the reader is afforded a wider array of options as potential "solutions" to an educational problem.

On the wall of my office is a sign. It bears the words: "Lead, Follow, or Get Out of The Way." These words could well be applied to those who impede the changes necessary for excellence to occur in our schools.

As Sizer (1984) has said: "Inspiration, hunger: these are the qualities that drive good schools. The best we educational planners can do is to create the most likely conditions for them to flourish, and then get out of their way."

References and Bibliography

Borsch, F. 1984. It's often difficult helping students learn more about values and ethics. *The Chronicle of Higher Education* (September 5), 104.

Boyer, E. 1983. *High School: A Report on Secondary Education in America*. New York: Harper & Row.

Dunne, F. 1984. Liberal arts colleges and teacher quality. *American Educator* (Fall), 18–21.

Easterly, J. 1983. Profiles of excellence—The master teacher. Association of Teacher Educators, Orlando, Fla., January 31.

Edmonds, R. 1982. Programs of school improvement: An overview. *Educational Leadership* (December), 4–11.

Florida State University. 1979–80. Evaluation of teacher preparation program. Tallahassee, Fla: College of Education.

Frymier, J., and others. 1984. *One Hundred Good Schools*. West Lafayette, Ind.: Kappa Delta Pi Press.

Gallup, G. 1984. The 16th annual Gallup poll of the public's attitudes toward the public schools. *Phi Delta Kappan* (September), 23–38.

Mangieri, J., and E. Demos. 1984. The frequency and importance of parent involvement: The perspective of educators. Unpublished paper.

Sizer, T. 1984. *Horace's Compromise*. Boston: Houghton Mifflin Company.

South Carolina. Educational Improvement Law. October 1984.

Texas House Bill 72. Summer 1984.

Tschudin, R. 1978. The secrets of A+ teaching. *Instructor* (September), 66–75.

Common Ground

Ernest L. Boyer

All societies, argued John Locke, are bound together by a tacit social contract, a compact among individuals who cede a portion of their autonomy for what is defined as the greater good. In exchange for this concession, every citizen expects certain services, specified protections, and agreed-upon rights and freedoms.

The contract is a pliant one. In most societies, it seems to move first in one direction, then another. When too great an emphasis is placed on group relationships, individuals feel herded, smothered, and restrained. They lament the lack of privacy and the intrusions of social obligations; they demand more opportunity to express their individuality and "be themselves." In contrast, when the pendulum swings strongly toward individualism and independence, people are apt to feel alone, isolated in an apathetic and uncaring world. In response, they move in the opposite direction, seeking to renew ties with their fellow human beings.

Accepting this Lockean view, I suggest that at these times, when social bonds are weakened, special attention must be given to those educational objectives appropriate to all students—to the social contract in education.

The perennial tension between the individual and the community is mirrored in the school curriculum. Certain courses of study and various activities acknowledge individualism—the right of each person to act independently and make personal choices. Here the student, within limits, is permitted to decide what he or she wants to study or how he or she will live.

But is there a portion of the student's program rooted in the belief that individualism, while essential, is not sufficient? Where do we show that the individual also shares significant relationships with a larger community? What parts of the school curriculum affirm our connectedness? Are there educational tools we can use in our search for renewal of the frayed social compact? Is there an education common to all people?

The State of Affairs

In preparing *High School* (1983), our report on secondary education in America, we looked at the education laws in all fifty states. We discovered a numbing hodgepodge of rules and regulations. In the state of California, the education code is four volumes and 3,700 pages long, and in New York, it takes five volumes and 4,000 pages to print the education law.

More troublesome are the vague and wide-ranging mandates the states have imposed on public education. Many of these requirements are pushed by special-interest groups. Frequently, they trivialize the mission of public education and, therefore, are rarely taken seriously by schools. Here is a sampling of what state laws say the schools should do:

> **Idaho:** "The school programs shall be organized to meet the needs of all pupils, the community, and to fulfill the stated objectives of the school."
> **Mississippi:** The purpose of education is "to provide appropriate learning experiences to promote the optimum growth and development of youth and adults throughout life."
> **Oregon:** "Each individual will have the opportunity to develop to the best of his or her ability the knowledge, skills, and attitudes necessary to function as an individual . . . a

learner . . . a producer . . . a citizen . . . a consumer . . . and a family member."

Maine: The public schools must teach virtue and morality for not less than one-half hour per week. This includes "principles of morality and justice and a sacred regard for truth, love of country, humanity, a universal benevolence, sobriety, industry and frugality, chastity, moderation and temperance, and all other virtues that ornament human society."

California: "Each teacher shall endeavor to impress upon the minds of the pupils the principles of morality, truth, justice, patriotism, and a true comprehension of the rights, duties, and dignity of American citizenship, including kindness toward domestic pets and the humane treatment of living creatures, to teach them to avoid idleness, profanity, and falsehood, and to instruct them in manners and morals and the principles of a free government."

Illinois: All graduates are required by law "to have had adequate instruction in honesty, justice, moral courage, humane education, (and) safety education."

Arizona: A half-unit course is required on the "Essentials and Benefits of the Free Enterprise System."

Rhode Island: "Provision must be made for instruction in physiology and hygiene, with special reference to the effects of alcoholic liquors, stimulants, and narcotics on the human system."

Wisconsin: "Every public school shall provide instruction in kindness to and the habits, usefulness, and importance of animals and birds, and the best methods of protecting, preserving and caring for all animal and bird life." And in what can only be described as enthusiastic local boosterism, Wisconsin also requires that every public and private elementary and high school give instruction in "the true and comparative vitamin content and food and health values of dairy products and their importance for human diet."

The American school is a microcosm of the community of which it is a part. Increasingly we expect the school to do what the home and community and church have not been able to accomplish. Schools receive not only well-nurtured, well-motivated students, but they also are called upon to educate children who come out of the deepest pockets of poverty, youngsters from single parent households where often even that single parent is not available to them. Schools are expected to function successfully in communities wrenched by crime and immobilized by despair. What does America want education to accomplish? Frankly, we want it all.

One of the teachers we interviewed during our investigations for *High School* summed it up when she said: "We have to be social workers and psychiatrists, doctors and counselors, hall monitors and referees. I hardly have time to be an English teacher as well." While educators in remote conference rooms often talk of abstract situations, this teacher was trying to deal with the real world of her classroom.

Preschool programs may become universal soon, kindergarten children may be kept in school until 5 P.M., and a year-round calendar of instruction may be introduced. It is not that these innovations have been judged to be pedagogically essential but that parents are working and need babysitters for the children. Once again, the schools will be called upon to be Mr. Fixit for the nation.

The irony is that none of these new social obligations will be reflected in the SATs. We will impose on schools one set of social obligations and standards, and then use academic outcomes increasingly to measure the results. Therefore, as old-fashioned as it may be, the time is here to clarify the goals and redefine the content of the curriculum we teach.

A host of changes already have been made in response to the new demands. Our schools now serve more students from different racial, cultural, and social backgrounds than ever before. Counseling has increased. Experimental programs such as magnet schools have been introduced, and public schools are now educating vast numbers of handicapped students who previously were locked out.

There still remains, however, a large, even alarming, gap between school achievement and the task yet to be done. The best schools in the nation provide the best education in the world. Still we have 20 percent of our students dropping out, and the vast majority of our schools are neither good nor bad. They are somewhere between the outstanding institutions and the very bad, trouble-ridden schools that have few, if any, academic goals or rewards for students. The troubled schools, located most typically in inner cities, suffer problems of population dislocation and poverty. Unemployment and crime take priority over education. But even the good suburban schools reflect the social upheavals and the transitions of their communities. And educators, by their confusions, unwittingly have added to the problems.

There are no definitive answers to the pressing social dislocations that beset us. Problems cannot be solved overnight; there are no magic cures and no panaceas. But, as *Ethics* (a text in the *Mishna*) teaches, although it may not "be given unto us to finish the task, neither must we desist from starting it." And the starting point is to ask how we can, as John Gardner so aptly put it, have excellence and equity as well.

More money often is cited as the answer. Schools need more counselors and social support systems; teachers need to receive higher salaries and time to teach and study; students need flexible schedules that fit in with their personal needs and the demands of their homes; buildings need to be kept in good repair for a safe and healthy environment. All of this costs money, and budgets in many schools should be improved. But to talk about money before goals is to put a price tag on solutions before they are defined. It is to buy a ticket before the journey has been charted.

I conclude that the larger issue American public education now confronts has to do with goals. Will the schools focus on educational objectives, narrowly defined, or will they be called upon to serve as "youth service centers" for the culture?

A Shared Vision

A school, to be effective, must have a clear and vital mission. Students, teachers, administrators, and parents should have a shared vision of what, together, they are trying to accomplish. Unfortunately, the vision often is neither clear nor shared.

19

At most schools, the administrators—principals and superintendents—almost exclusively preoccupied with procedural matters, give little thought to educational goals. Nor do teachers have a clear sense of goals. When asked about objectives, principals respond with such platitudes as: "develop school spirit," "help students pass state-required exams," or "improve students' opportunities in life." Too few articulate as one principal did: "I'd like us to challenge our students to think." Teachers, when asked the same question, often think of goals in terms of preparing young people to get into a "good" college. Some teachers are honest in expressing the low aspirations they have for the students: "Our goal is to get our students (to) function in blue collar society." Is it any wonder that students' goals are circumscribed? Student responses to questions regarding goals and ambitions reflect both disenchantment and pragmatism. They want to "get out," "be with friends," "get into a good college," or "get a job." They view school as a place where one is kept off the street and out of trouble "until you're old enough to get out there and deal with it."

It may be that in the end all schools will be clinics, athletic centers, day care centers, and community club houses for our children. But the tragedy would come if we introduce the social functions and fail to reform the core, fail to define, with as much clarity as we can, just what it is *academically* the schools are seeking to accomplish.

Mastery of Language Skills

Language is the most essential tool for learning. Schools should help all students to develop the capacity to think critically and communicate effectively through the written and spoken word. American students must master English. People who do not become proficient in the language of the majority culture are enormously disadvantaged in and out of school.

Language is the centerpiece of learning; it is not just another subject. It's the process by which all other subjects are acquired. Language is the statement of who we are and how we relate to other human beings.

Language starts with the first cry of infants. Some say it begins in utero as the unborn infant monitors the mother's voice and then, after birth, turns almost instinctively to see the face behind the voice. Although we cannot, with certainty, talk of ultimate beginnings, we are in awe of the miraculous process. In the early weeks and months and years, words first are uttered, then syntax is imposed to shape an orderly arrangement of words, and finally subtle meanings are conveyed—all of this long before a child ever goes to school.

Children who can speak and listen are also capable of reading and writing once they learn how to translate their sound symbols into the visual squiggles we call letters. The child learns to listen and speak before any formal instruction is given, but the processes of writing and reading—which cannot be divorced from each other (after all, we read the written word)—require help. Writing is probably the most important skill, not only for the intrinsic value it has in communicating precise information (as in a crisp business letter or a recipe), but for forcing the thought processes into some coherent pattern. Writing is frozen thought, the means by which we discover what's rolling in our heads. It is through clear writing that clear thinking can be shaped. Our conviction is that writing should start early and continue through all of formal learning. And yet, most English teachers give limited writing opportunities to the students, while teachers of other subjects rarely demand more writing than single answers on quizzes.

One obvious reason for the failure to teach writing is the extraordinary demand it places on the teacher's time. Today, most English teachers meet five classes daily, with twenty-five to thirty students each. If the teacher gives one writing assignment every week to each student, he or she spends, at a minimum, more than twenty hours correcting papers. The arithmetic is simple: 125 papers times 10 minutes to correct, critique, and mark each one, equals at least 1,250 minutes—or 20.8 hours—for one assignment. Cut the teacher's time in half, let her spend five minutes with each paper, and she still has more than ten hours of work in correcting one written assignment. Is it any wonder that English teachers, who are given the mandate to teach writing, give few writing assignments? And science, history, or geography teachers, without the same mandate, give even less or none?

If clear and effective writing is to be a serious objective of the schools, then all teachers must consider themselves writing teachers also, while they deal with the discipline and language of their subject matter. Like the English teacher, they must give written assignments and critique carefully what students write, although the responsibility for teaching the skill rests with the English teacher. Those who teach basic English should have no more than twenty students in each class, and no more than two such classes should be included within the regular teacher's load.

The emphasis on language is one of the most important solutions to our problem. While most current reports on school renewal focus on secondary education, I am confident that elementary and perhaps preschool education is the key. Language skills are formed early, before formal education, and school programs must be developed to take advantage of that fact, especially for children who are disadvantaged. Experiments which have assessed children for many years make clear that early intervention has results that will endure.

A Core of Common Learning

Reading, writing, speaking, and listening—along with computation—are the basic tools of education. But the mastery of language is the beginning, not the end of education. Schools, as E. D. Hirsch (1983) suggests, must help all children achieve cultural literacy as well. We call for a core of common learning—a program of required courses in literature, the arts, foreign language, history, civics, science, mathematics, technology, health—to extend the knowledge and broaden the perspective of every student.

A serious study of literature and the arts, for example, gives students an understanding of the beauty and power of the written word. Further, literature addresses the emotional part of the human experience and provides another perspective on historical events. It also transmits, from generation to generation, enduring spiritual and ethical values. As an art form, literature can bring delight and recreation. As a vehicle for illustrating moral behavior by specific examples (Job, Ulysses, Oedipus, Lear, Ishmael, Holden Caulfield), it speaks to all and must be available to all students.

Students also should understand that we communicate not just with words but nonverbally as well. From the dawn of civilization, men and women have used music, dance, and the visual arts to transmit the heritage of a people and express human joys and sorrows. Written communication developed through the exotic extension of our various symbols, as some creative ancestor put on cave walls representations that could be seen by generations and generations yet unborn. Someone else began tapping on a hollow log, and another danced. It may be a simple view, but civilization is to be defined by the breadth of the symbol systems that we see and cherish.

Our various symbol systems, working together, communicate the full range of our visions, hopes, and ideas. When we speak the words, "Hallelujah! Hallelujah!" they fall like lumps of unformed clay on the floor below. However, if the Mormon Tabernacle Choir sings them, we get a clear, inspiring message.

Victor Weisskopf, the giant of modern physics, was quoted in *The New York Times* recently as having said: "The big bang theory of the universe is like a work of Haydn. . . . Music is at least as descriptive of the . . . theory as are the words of physicists" (Weisskopf, 1984). What is going on here? A physicist is saying if you want to understand the big bang theory, listen to the works of Haydn. There are feelings and ideas and insights that words cannot express and that can be captured only through the symbol systems: music, dance, and the visual arts.

Yet the arts at the elementary school level are given no more than 3 percent or 4 percent of school time per week. At the secondary school level, half of all the high schools in the United States offer no courses in the visual arts, and of the schools that do, only 15 percent of the students elect to take those courses in the four years they are in school. Students' intellectual abilities are measured by how well they do in solid subjects such as mathematics and sciences and not at all by how talented they may be in the arts. Few colleges

take into account grades in art, music, theatre, or dance when cal-
culating the students' grade point average or predicting their potential ability.

The arts amplify our understanding of history, not so much by
recording events as they happen but by telling us about an emotional climate that made those events possible. Art historians call
this *Zeitgeist*—the spirit of the times. To neglect the arts is to start
down the slippery slope toward noncivilization. It's no accident that
dictators, when they wish to control the hearts and minds of men
and women, not only silence speech, but silence art and dance and
music, too, because they know how powerfully these symbol systems can control and shape the opinions and ideas of people.

We also need to know the facts. As humans, we recall the past
and anticipate the future. An understanding of one's heritage and
the heritage of others implies a study of history as an essential part
of common learning.

In an age when family disruption, geographic mobility, technological change, and fast-paced electronic media so often seem to
make everything but the fleeting moment remote and irrelevant, the
study of history can strengthen awareness that there is a larger reality beyond the present. When the sources of fear and anxiety are
many and, indeed, when human survival itself has become problematic, a sense of continuity with the past can provide a kind of lifeline
across the scary chasm of our contemporary situation.

American history provides students with a deeper understanding of the central themes and dilemmas that continue to influence
American life. Beyond American history lies the long sweep of Western civilization, embodying a rich tradition of thought, culture, and
political experimentation upon which our own nation has drawn in
countless ways.

The history curriculum must extend beyond American history
and Western civilization to include non-Western studies. Specifically,
we recommend that all students discover the connectedness of the
human experience and the richness of other cultures through an in-
depth study of a non-Western nation.

We are being told that we are losing the high-tech race, and the

24

National Commission report says that we need to improve our education for competitive and economic advantage. Perhaps they are correct. But Thomas Jefferson had it right when he said, "In a democracy, education is for civic understanding." We have a pressing need for civic understanding, a knowledge of society's institutions and how they work.

"We do not make a world of our own," Ralph Waldo Emerson observed in his journal nearly 150 years ago, "but fall into institutions already made, and have to accommodate ourselves to them." Institutions are a fact of life. They touch almost every aspect of our being—economic, educational, familial, political, and religious. We are born into institutions, we pass much of our lives in institutions, and institutions are involved when we die.

Today, public trust in institutions is low, and alienation from them is high. Yet they cannot be abandoned. Institutions provide arrangements through which daily transactions are conducted, interpersonal relationships are nurtured, and social structure is maintained. Many institutions might profitably be studied—the family, volunteer organizations, social agencies, for example. However, we propose that knowing about government and how it functions is critically important.

When Thomas Jefferson was asked if mass opinion could be trusted, he replied in a letter, "I know of no safe depository of the ultimate powers of the society but the people themselves; and if we think them not enlightened enough to exercise their control with a wholesome discretion, the remedy is not to take it from them, but to inform their discretion by education."

The Jeffersonian vision of grassroots democracy that so captured the imagination of Alexis de Tocqueville when he visited America in the 1830s seems increasingly utopian today. As early as 1922, Walter Lippmann warned that public ignorance of increasingly complex problems was democracy's greatest challenge. Issues now facing the electorate have become enormously complex, and government seems increasingly remote.

Civics used to be a mainstay in the high school; recently it has declined. Civic illiteracy is spreading, and unless we find better ways to educate ourselves as citizens, we run the risk of drifting unwittingly into a new kind of Dark Age—a time when, increasingly, specialists will control knowledge and the decision-making process. In this confusion, citizens would make critical decisions, not on the basis of what they know, but on the basis of blind belief in one or another set of professed experts.

We need scientific and numeric literacy as well. The study of science introduces students to the processes of discovery—what we call the scientific method—and reveals how such procedures can be applied to many disciplines and to the practical ends of daily life. Through science, students learn to gather data, consider causal relationships, and discover how, through observation and testing, theories are found, refined, and sometimes discarded.

A study of science is an essential part of the core of common learning. It is through the study of science that students discover the elegant underlying patterns of the natural world and learn that, in some manner, all elements of nature are related. In 1980, Dr. Lewis Thomas of the Sloan-Kettering Cancer Center observed:

> There are no solitary, free-living creatures: Every form of life is dependent on other forms. . . . We should go warily into the future, looking for ways to be more useful, listening more carefully for the signals, watching our step, and having an eye out for partners.

Mathematics, often called the "handmaiden of science," can open a new realm of understanding and a whole new set of vocational and leisure-time options. Since mathematics is a sequential discipline in which previously gained insights and skills form the basis for continued learning, training in mathematics should begin early and progress steadily. A study of mathematics disciplines the mind to think in logical progressive steps and gives a student practical computational skills.

The Connectedness of Things

All worthy goals in education are best expressed in the one imperative called "connections"—helping students acquire information

26

and then helping them to see the relationship of that knowledge to their own lives, to their social responsibility, and eventually to their leading moral and ethical lives. Mark Van Doren said on one occasion that seeing the connectedness of things is the most important goal of education.

When students are required to take language or science or history, they give little thought as to how the separate subjects are connected or how collectively they relate to the larger world. We have to help students see the relationship between what they study and the issues and problems of our contemporary life. In our day-to-day affairs, politics and economics are often indistinguishable. There is a philosophy of art and an art to philosophy. The geography of nations often determines their history, just as history often determines their geography. Students, however, seldom develop a clear understanding of these connections.

Therefore, in addition to clarifying requirements, we must bring a new interdisciplinary vision into the classroom and the school. The content of the core curriculum must extend beyond the specialties to touch larger, more transcendent issues. It must help students see connections. Dr. Thomas wrote eloquently that if this century does not slip forever through our fingers, it will be because learning will have directed us away from our splintered dumbness and will have helped us focus on our common goals.

I am, quite frankly, deeply alarmed by the increased inclination toward parochialism in our nation and in the curriculum of the public schools. Several years ago, 40 percent of high school students surveyed thought that Golda Meir rather than Anwar Sadat was the president of Egypt. Some students in a California community college could not identify either Iran or El Salvador on a map. How do we hope to survive in an interdependent, complicated, and dangerous world if we have no notion about the geography, the history, and the traditions and cultures of those around us, on whom our destinies also will depend?

Since World War II, the world has changed irrevocably. No longer can any country consider itself an island, nor can the fortunes of any person be divorced from the fortunes of the community. What happens in New York affects Leningrad, and what happens in

27

Oslo affects Washington. The circumference of the world can be negotiated in twenty-four hours, and the world can be totally obliterated in twelve seconds. The world's 165 independent nations and 60-odd political units are interlocked. Our fates are joined, our futures are interdependent. We may not yet be a global village, but surely our sense of neighborhood must include more people and cultures than ever before.

Schools must educate our students to live with all our neighbors. They must help students not only to recognize and accept differences but to respect and cherish them as well. Refugees flow from country to country, but too many Americans—students, parents, and even teachers—can neither point to these great migrations on a map nor talk about the famines or wars or poverty that caused them. Artists, inventors, statesmen, and philosophers from around the world enrich our lives, but we barely recognize them. Both their contributions and names are largely unknown or unremembered.

April 18, 1984, was proclaimed World Heritage Day. On that day the International Council on Monuments and Sites designated 165 sites as of "universal value to mankind." These included the Pyramids of Egypt, the Palace of Versailles, the city of Cuzco in Peru, Persepalis in Iran, the Katmandu Valley in Nepal, the Old City of Jerusalem and its walls, to name a few.

It occurred to me that these priceless treasures may provide a marvelous curriculum for the core of common learning. Would it be possible for all students, throughout their twelve years of formal education, to learn about these magnificent monuments that are found on all continents of the globe? Would it be possible to study not just the places but the people, history, and traditions of which they are a part? Would it be possible for each student to become especially knowledgeable about one treasure? And would it be possible for every student to understand that we have a sacred obligation not to desecrate these priceless treasures that mark, so exquisitely, the human passage on this earth?

The world has become a more crowded, more interconnected, more volatile, and unstable place. If education cannot help students see beyond themselves and better understand the interdependent nature of the world, each new generation will remain more ignorant,

and its capacity to live responsible, confident lives will be danger-
ously diminished. Quality education in the 1980s and beyond means
preparing all students for the transformed world the coming generations will inherit.

Preparing for Work

The core of common learning should provide grounding in the basic
tools of education. But as we move toward the year 2000, it becomes
increasingly clear that twelve years of schooling will not suffice. New
skills to accommodate new technology will be required of all students. What, for example, will be the effect of the rapidly growing
population aged fifty-five and over? Of necessity, education must be
life-long. Schooling should help all students develop their own
unique aptitudes and interests so that they live with a sense of confidence and a capacity for independence as well.

A carefully selected cluster of electives should advance the
students' particular academic interests and provide opportunities
for students to explore career options. In order to do this, the
high school will have to make connections with the local resources
of the community. In this way, the school extends both its reach
and the perspective of its students. Work opportunities and the
search for careers can be successfully combined with service possibilities in the public good. Not only will students gain an appreciation of the needs of disadvantaged people in their own communities,
but they will also gain maturity and satisfaction from doing something that does in fact make a difference.

Commitment to Service

Finally, the school should help students understand that to be truly
human one must serve. The truth is that we have not just a school
problem, but a youth problem in this nation. Students are alienated
and adrift. There is an enormous gap in this culture between the old
and the young. We do not know of ways to have our young people
productively engaged. With all of the work that should be done in
our nation, many students feel useless.

Consider the remarks of a young student in a midwestern high
school: "Usually we don't do too much around here. I mean we just

hang around together, sit together when we can in class or at lunch. Sometimes after school, this year, I have been working at McDonald's. It's not all that exciting, but I do it because I want some new clothes, and a stereo set, and it makes me feel like I am an adult person. I'm doing something useful." It is unacceptable for students to define their usefulness by pushing Big Macs at McDonald's.

It's disturbing for teenagers to finish high school and never be asked to participate responsibly in life, never be encouraged to spend time with older people who are lonely, never help a child who hasn't learned to read, or even to help clean up the litter on the streets.

In our high school report, we propose a new Carnegie Unit, a service requirement for all students. We suggest that during their four high school years, students might do volunteer work in or out of school. They could tutor younger students, work in the library, in parks, hospitals, museums, or help in day care centers.

In a St. Louis high school, a six-foot junior had volunteered in the summer in the emergency ward of a hospital. He was there when a young child was brought in with meningitis and subsequently died. The experience matured the young man in a very profound way. "Do you know what it's like to see a kid die?" he asked.

There is a sad gap between the young and the work needed in the community. Schools, perhaps joining with parents and institutions, have an obligation to fill the gap. My convictions on this matter are well stated by Vachel Lindsay, that marvelous American poet, who wrote, "It is the world's one crime, its babes grow dull. Not that they starve, but starve so dreamlessly; not that they sow, but that they seldom reap, not that they serve, but that they have no God to serve; not that they die, but that they die like sheep." The tragedy of life is not death; the tragedy is to die having never served and having visions unfulfilled.

The Vitality of the School

Finally, in our push for excellence in education we dare not impose more rules and regulations on the local school and in the process ignore the people who meet with children everyday.

One year after the report of the National Commission, Secretary Terrel Bell presented *The Nation Responds*, a summary of school reform in all fifty states. The vast majority of these initiatives focused on more courses, more testing, more teacher preparation. Many of these initiatives were appropriate and overdue. But I am also deeply troubled that of the twenty school improvement categories cited in the secretary's report, only two are concerned primarily with the renewal of the teacher. It is ironic to me that while American business is beginning to recognize the importance of the worker, we still are trying to fix the system from the top.

In a recent interview Philip Caldwell, President of Ford Motor Company, said: "Why kick the man downstream who can't put the parts together because the parts really weren't designed properly?" Then he added, "Now, two years before production of the new vehicle, the prototype vehicles are taken to the plants where they are going to be made, and the people who are actually going to make them have a chance to go through the whole process and make suggestions."

The sad fact is that with all of our new mandates for school renewal, virtually none of the reforms has been taken to teachers for suggestions to see if the proposals will work in schools and classrooms.

In the Carnegie report we call for teacher excellence funds for every school—a discretionary grants program to help teachers quickly implement a good idea. We also call for teacher travel funds in every school to make it possible for teachers to stay in touch with new ideas. We are giving grants to local schools to provide teachers and principals a little discretionary money rather than just more mandates from above. Above all, I believe at this crucial time we need leadership at the federal level as well, leadership that will support the teachers rather than condemn them. It seems to me that a report entitled *A Nation at Risk* certainly calls for more than tuition tax credits or prayer in schools or a shootout over merit pay.

If the nation truly is at risk, then the nation should respond, and if the president is serious about helping the nation's schools, I suggest a national fellowship program for classroom teachers, similar to the National Defense Education Act enrichment program President Eisenhower launched nearly thirty years ago.

The time has come to recognize that excellence in education

will be accomplished not by experts on leave from Mount Olympus but by teachers in the classroom who urgently need more support, not more paperwork or more regulation. Teachers are the solution, not the problem. They must be given not only more responsibilities but more authority as well.

In the end, the quality of education will be shaped by the quality we assign to teaching, because it's the teacher who can shape life. In our processes of school improvement, we have legislatures to decide what we should do; we have state commissioners to present their leadership ideas. But teachers are being bypassed in the process.

The principal also has a pivotal role to play. The average high school principal is male, white, and in his midforties. He is appointed to his job in a random and often unreasonable way. Studies have found that more than a third had been high school athletic directors. Local customs establish evaluation criteria for candidates which are as murky as anything in the contemporary job market.

Professional training rarely prepares principals adequately for the job. Most eventually complete a graduate-degree program in educational administration, with courses in school management, school law, plant and personnel, finance, history and philosophy of education, and labor negotiations. But they, themselves, disparage the usefulness of their training and give low ranking to the usefulness of their college or university preparation. One principal we interviewed for *High School* gave a typical evaluation: "The university people I dealt with in my educational administration courses hadn't been in a classroom in years; they didn't know what kids were like, and, to my mind, they didn't care. . . . What they had to offer was really just Mickey Mouse courses that didn't reflect any of the realities in my high school. That's what you have to put up with to get your ticket."

The picture of the poor training, conflict, and frustration painted by many principals reveals more than individual irritation; it portrays a real crisis in leadership, which seriously undermines the effectiveness of the school. The principal is like an orchestra conductor directing the separate parts of the group into a harmonious whole. But whereas the conductor gets his strength and power from the willing participation of all members of the orchestra working together, the principal of a school gets heartburn from the frustration of bureaucratic management details, most of which probably could be handled by support staff. Principals typically have very little time to devote to their identified priorities of program development and personnel. Instead of evaluating the instruction and the curriculum, they are refereeing between contentious students and angry teachers.

Society's confusion about objectives sends mixed signals to the principal. Boards of education and superintendents of schools, to whom the principal must report, are often politicized and paralyzed by interest group pressures. Teachers cannot take over the leadership, nor can they find the leader in their principal.

The principal can make a difference. But first, there must be goals. A school without goals is a ship without a rudder. State and local leaders must stop talking about problems and start thinking about what they want schools to accomplish. In the meantime, teachers, powerful role models for their students, also must learn to be leaders themselves.

Conclusion

Here then is my conclusion. We do not need a school program for the winners and the losers. Rather, we need a clear vision—a social contract—of what is appropriate for all students. This means, I believe, discovering the importance of critical thinking through centrality of language and a core curriculum that is not only national, but global; it means giving recognition to teachers who are performing outstandingly in the classroom and giving more authority at the local level where the job genuinely must be done.

Today, the push for excellence in education is linked to the nation's economic recovery and to jobs. We are being told that tougher math and science standards are required to keep the nation strong. No one denies the obvious: education and the security of the nation are interlocked. Of course national interests must be served. But education is also to enrich the lives of individuals, to instill a love of learning, and to strengthen a commitment to achieve equality and opportunity for all.

We have the best opportunity of this century to improve the nation's schools. The work can begin as we clarify educational goals, as we give priority to language, as we agree upon a curriculum that helps to establish connections, as we give new status to the teacher and the principal, and as we help our students understand that, in the end, to be truly human one must serve.

The school is located in a community to which it is intimately connected. It is a common ground where all kids from the neighborhood can meet. In the end, the struggle for equity and excellence in the school will be won or lost in hundreds of thousands of classrooms and communities across the country and in the relationship between teachers and students, students and subjects, subjects and supervisors, supervisors and citizens.

Several months ago William Buckley had Mortimer Adler as his guest on the TV show "Firing Line." Mr. Adler discussed his marvelously provocative essay, *The Paideia Proposal*, and argued that education is for all of our children, not just the privileged ones. At the end, Mr. Buckley looked at Adler and said, "What makes you think that all children can learn?" Adler replied, "Well, Bill, I am not absolutely sure that all children can learn, but on the other hand, you're not absolutely sure that they can't. So, I'd rather live by my hope than by your doubt."

This is a time to reaffirm our commitment to our schools and also to reaffirm our commitment to the education of all students. James Agee wrote on one occasion that with every child's birth, under whatever circumstance, the potentiality of the human race is born again. In our rededication to education, we see the potential of each child. This is a brash experiment we pursue—an open system of education in which we seek, ultimately, excellence and equity. To achieve these ends, we must start building our public policies upon the basis of hope.

References

Adler, Mortimer. 1982. *The Paideia Proposal*. New York: Macmillan.
Agee, James, and Walker Evans. 1941. *Let Us Now Praise Famous Men*. Boston: Houghton Mifflin.

Bell, Terrel. 1984. *The Nation Responds: Recent Efforts to Improve Education*. Washington, D.C.: U.S. Government Printing Office.

Boyer, Ernest L. 1983. *High School*. New York: Harper and Row.

Emerson, E. W., and W. E. Forbes, eds. 1909. *Journals of Ralph Waldo Emerson*, 2:448. Boston: Houghton Mifflin.

Hirsch, E. D. 1983. Cultural literacy. *American Scholar* 52(5): 159–169.

Jefferson, Thomas. From *The Life and Selected Writings*, 1944, 604–605. New York: Modern Library.

Jefferson, Thomas. *Letters*, 1940, arranged by Wilson Whitman, 338–339. Eau Claire, Wisconsin: E. M. Hale.

Lindsay, Vachel. 1937. The Leaden-Eyed. *Collected Poems*. New York: Macmillan.

Lippman, Walter. 1922. *Public Opinion*. New York: Macmillan.

National Commission on Excellence in Education (David P. Gardner, Chair). 1983. *A Nation at Risk: The Imperative for Educational Reform*. Washington, D.C.: U.S. Government Printing Office.

Thomas, Lewis. 1980. On the uncertainty of science. *Harvard Magazine* 83(1): 21.

Weisskopf, Victor. 1984. Interview. *New York Times* (April 3), C-18.

The Elementary School

M. Carol Allen

What are the biggest problems of this school?" the new young principal asked. "The teachers and the pupils," said the veteran custodian. "If it wasn't for them, I could keep this place in fine order." And the irony of the conversation was that neither knew how right he was. Practically all the problems of an elementary school are *people* problems, and they won't be solved until they are approached that way.

After extensive research, Goodlad (1984) rank ordered the top three problems of elementary schools as student misbehavior, size of school/classes, and lack of parent interest. But when I asked a group of elementary principals to list the biggest problems in their schools, they mentioned proper student diagnosis and placement; scheduling pull-out programs; involving working parents, single parents, and apathetic parents; successfully implementing special education programs; and, sure enough, discipline.

It is this chapter's intent to interweave the practitioners' experiences with the researchers' findings to explore three types of problems: 1) student-related problems, 2) parent-related problems, and 3) programmatic problems.

37

Student-Related Problems

Study after study has listed discipline as the number one problem in schools. Perhaps the situation that undergirds discipline problems is the situation practitioners describe with growing concern—accurate diagnosis and placement of children. It is reasonable to believe that a lack of the latter contributes to student misbehavior. Both are serious student-related problems.

Discipline

A classroom is like a bag full of helium balloons. If there's one small opening, one balloon escapes. Try to catch that balloon and other balloons start to get away.

That's the way it is with one disruptive student in a classroom of twenty-five or thirty youngsters. Too often, as a teacher handles that one, other disturbances pop up. Unless the teacher has a routine, effective manner of preventing potential discipline problems or dealing with discipline problems as they occur (or scares the hell out of the kids), the classroom will quickly become bedlam.

Discipline problems are nothing new to the elementary classroom. In 1928, Wickman (1938) investigated the seriousness of behavior problems in elementary schools and learned that teachers most often reported problems that involved disruptions in the classroom or violations of the teacher's expectations regarding school work and standards of conduct. The most often cited problem behaviors were stubbornness, disorderliness, irresponsibility, untruthfulness, and disobedience.

Twenty-five years later, a similar investigation showed little change (Stouffer and Owen, 1955). Teachers were mostly concerned about infractions of rules and classroom routines or similar forms of classroom behavior.

In 1983, Baer, Goodall, and Brown took a slightly different approach. Teachers of grades four, five, and six were asked, "In your opinion what is the most serious type of misbehavior that a child can engage in within the classroom setting?" Teachers' responses were grouped into six categories: 1) violation of social standards,

2) illegal behaviors, 3) physically dangerous behavior, 4) violating the rights of others, 5) disruptions to learning, and 6) challenging the teacher's authority.

In first place was physically dangerous behavior: fighting, pushing, tripping, throwing, and other forms of physical abuse. This was followed by disruptions to learning: laughing, excessive talking, unnecessary walking around the room, showing off, note passing, whistling, and "other annoying behaviors of a non-physical nature which are directed at no one in particular." Passive resistance, daydreaming, noninvolvement, lack of concentration, and other nonparticipatory behaviors were included in this group as well.

Next most frequently mentioned was challenging the teacher's authority; this was followed by violations of social standards such as lying, cheating, stealing, and using foul language.

Fifth, the teachers reported misbehaviors in the category of violating the rights of others: teasing, verbal harassment, excluding certain individuals from activities, and picking on others. And, as might be expected in an elementary setting, "illegal" behaviors, such as vandalism, drug or alcohol abuse, and assault with a weapon, were reported least often.

Discipline problems have not changed drastically nor improved greatly over the past fifty years—a frustrating realization to any conscientious educator. One would not expect discipline problems to disappear, but certainly one might expect improvement. This does not seem to be the case.

Diagnosis and Placement of Students

The accurate diagnosis and placement of students is another problem. I have often thought of paraphrasing Emma Lazarus's words on the pedestal of the Statue of Liberty and placing the paraphrase over the doors of every elementary school in the country:

> Give me your gifted, your regular, your behaviorally disordered, your emotionally disturbed, your slow learners, your severely retarded, your orthopedically handicapped, your mild-moderates, your learning disabled, your gregarious,

your shy, your blind, your deaf, your speech impaired, your
beautiful, your ugly, your wealthy, your poor, your Asian, your
black, your white,
Send these, the seekers of knowledge to me,
I spread my arms and open up my doors of opportunity.

Such is the beauty and the dilemma of the elementary school. We
take them all, and we try our best to diagnose, place, and serve
every youngster, regardless of his needs, his differences, and his
strengths.

The problems associated with diagnosing students are not ex-
clusive problems of the elementary teacher or principal. Diagnosti-
cians themselves recognize and accept several considerations that affect the accurate assessment of a child's academic and emotional
levels: 1) special problems, such as short attention span, distrac-
tibility, novel situations, and strange people administering the assessment instrument; 2) the mode of administration, such as individual or group; 3) validity and reliability of the instrument; and
4) problems unique to assessing minority group children (Bloom,
Madaus, and Hastings, 1981, 118).

The problems confronting the teacher and principal are less
technical. They include:

1) difficulty communicating to parents and gaining their
   support, acceptance, and interest;
2) lack of resources: adequately trained assessment personnel, testing instruments, adequate space for testing, time;
3) turnaround time between referral, diagnosis, and recommended placement;
4) fear of lawsuits due to noncompliance with federal, state,
   or district requirements;
5) lack of materials and curriculum for instructing "different
   children";
6) fear of labeling a child;
7) inability to cope with and/or address the needs of a child
   who remains in a regular classroom while awaiting placement in a special program;

8) lack of planning time for the classroom teacher; and
9) lack of conference time for the teacher and principal.

Many educators still perceive the elementary teacher to be a mother hen, carefully taking care of her brood, tucking them all under her wings, knowing each one's frailties and strengths, and raising all to be strong and to survive on their own. This is probably an unfair expectation to place on a teacher.

To believe that the complexities of our society have not manifested themselves in the lives of our children would be naive. The effect of this complexity on the need for timely, thorough diagnosis of students' strengths and weaknesses is monumental. How else can teachers prescribe, teach, test, and know that each of their "brood" is achieving his maximum potential each day, each week, each month, and each year?

Parent-Related Problems

Most student-related problems multiply by two almost immediately and become parent problems. Educators have always experienced difficulties with apathetic parents. That problem, coupled with increasing numbers of single parents and parents working outside the home, has placed an imperative at the feet of elementary educators. We must cultivate positive relationships with *all* parents, and we must do so now.

Single Parents

The number of children under eighteen living with only one parent doubled between 1960 and 1978. In 1978, over 11.5 million children lived with one parent and more than 90 percent of those children lived with their mother only. In the eighties, the divorce rate climbed to one of every two marriages. What problems does this cause our schools? Robert Weiss (1981), head of Harvard Medical School's Laboratory of Community Psychiatry, says, "I can't think of anything worse for a child than losing a parent." Couple that belief with a statement by Ourth and Zakariya (1982) that "children who are troubled are children whose learning is at risk," and the problems confronting schools begin to take shape.

Consider these facts:

- Less than 7 percent of American families consist of a working father, stay-at-home mother, and two children, yet the books on our school shelves and the perceptions that leak through our comments and attitudes staunchly support the desired existence of this illusionary family.
- The average annual income of a three-member family with the mother as the only parent is $7000, yet schools continue to impose student fees for extra activities and materials, uniforms and so forth. A child not able to pay is too often excluded and separated from his peers.
- Problems at home do not become known in the classroom until the crisis is well under way. A teacher may watch a child gradually crumble before her eyes and have no idea of the reason unless she dares to probe. To do so is to risk treading on sacred family ground.
- Elementary schools are usually woefully understaffed with personnel skilled and hired to work with youngsters with problems. Counselors, nurses, social workers, and male role models are all too often not on the staff.

The problems associated with single-parent families are not new to schools; they are simply growing. Most important, however, is that the problems can be greatly reduced. Schools can offer solace to troubled children without putting a single new program in place. This requires awareness, commitment, planning, and hard work, but solutions are available.

Working Parents

An economic reality of today's society is that, single-parent family or not, parents work outside the home. The greatest problem this causes schools is poor communication between the school and the home. Parents find it hard to attend conferences or parent organization meetings. They are not home during the day to call should their child become ill, misbehave, or tear his pants. Parents do not drop in at the school, reinforcing the importance of school merely through their visibility. Parent volunteers are drastically reduced in number, forcing schools to be resourceful in locating other sets of helping hands. Children go home to parentless homes after school, often allowing extended school work to be ignored.

Perhaps most acute, parents are tired. They can divide their energy among just so many groups of people. Inadvertently, the school often finds itself at the bottom of the priority list. Frankly, this probably happens because working parents trust us educators to do our job unassisted and, for the most part, believe we are doing it successfully.

The problems of working parents and their elementary school children are clearly shared by the school. Parents are not going to stop working to solve the problems. Any solutions will have to come from the ranks of educators. Again, solutions are there; they simply must be grasped and implemented.

Apathetic Parents

They have always been there. They are not necessarily the parents who work, who are burdened with emotional problems, who have grave financial worries. They are simply the parents who do not care, the parents who cause teachers to cry. They are the parents who never show up for conferences, never attend a parent organization meeting, never return a note, phone call, or signed homework paper, and always answer, "He's *your* problem," if you happen to reach them by telephone to discuss a problem with a child. They are the parents of the child who is chronically sad or belligerent, the child who clams up when her classmates talk about their supportive parents or, on the other extreme, fabricates great tales about her parents' support because the truth is too painful to accept.

Again, the problems caused by apathetic parents are clearly shared by the schools. The indisputable fact is that they will always be with us. While schools may not change parent behaviors, they can certainly affect the results of those behaviors.

Whether parent-related problems concern apathetic, working, or single parents is not the issue. The issue is that such problems seriously impede the effectiveness of any elementary school. Problems with parents must be identified and addressed if schools are to be successful.

Program Problems

Two types of programmatic problems plague elementary administrators: what to teach, or curriculum, and how best to teach it, or instructional organization.

Curriculum

Goodlad's (1984) study revealed an unsurprising description of elementary school curricula. The greatest amount of instructional time is spent on the language arts, with mathematics following. Social studies and science receive almost equal amounts of time, and follow in third and fourth place respectively. Art, music, and physical education hover around the bottom, each receiving from one to two hours a week, and dance and drama receive only negligible attention. Despite strong arguments by Eisner and others that the arts are basic to a child's education, most people still consider "the basics" to be reading and math.

The problems associated with this are often indirect. As school administrators attempt to comply with parents' demands for additional time for the arts, they perform a juggling act of unbelievable intricacy. Scheduling becomes a green-eyed monster. If a school is tied to a six-hour instructional day, and accrediting agencies and board policies place time requirements for each discipline, how is a student talented in one or more of the arts to get his "basic" education? If the student goes to a drama class, he is likely going to miss either science or social studies in his regular class. Consequently, what courses to offer, how to offer them, and how much time to award to each course are decisions that give elementary school administrators serious problems.

This same problem occurs with various types of pull-out programs. I call it the "splintered" school day. Consider that children often leave the regular classroom for speech therapy, gifted instruc-

44

tion, Chapter I instruction, or some resource special education class. Classroom teachers must be master managers to insure that each child receives everything he is supposed to in every discipline in a given year. I fear this does not happen. In many cases it is simply impossible to schedule.

Instructional Organization

Another program-related problem is the learning environment used in the school. Generally, three types of learning environment are found in elementary schools: 1) self-contained classrooms, 2) open classrooms, and 3) departmentalized instruction. Each has its unique problems.

The self-contained classroom has traditionally represented a highly structured, teacher-oriented environment, with all children taught the same material at the same rate. Blocks of time for each discipline are rigidly followed. Research has shown that this type of environment does not promote adaptability and the growth of new or different ideas (Richmond, Phillips, and Blanton, 1972). The delivery of instruction in this traditional classroom may be construed as "mass production."

Open classrooms have their problems as well. They are supposed to be child-centered, rich in stimulus, and directed by a teacher who is more manager than lecturer. Generally, teachers perceive themselves to be more open than they are (Klass and Hodge, 1978). Unless teacher behavior is suited to the open classroom setting, student-directed learning does not occur.

Teachers are generally resistant to using individualized instructional approaches because they lack confidence in their ability to do so (Schubert and Baxter, 1982). Extensive inservice training is usually needed to persuade teachers to change their traditional methods. This, coupled with additional materials necessary to accommodate individual students' learning needs, forces additional costs on a school or system. Hence, a problem of funding may exist.

Probably the problem that bothers parents most with reference to open classrooms is related to rooms without walls. They say, and educators often concur, that open-space settings cause too much stimulation for too many students. Many an open-space school has seen the erection of walls due to pressure from disgruntled parents.

Open-space classrooms do not mean that open-classroom education is occurring. Traditional teachers construct barriers of bookshelves, ceiling hangings, file cabinets, and anything else that will "self-contain" their respective environments. Although open space connotes sharing, team teaching, interaction, and close working relationships, this, in fact, is not what actually occurs. According to Martin (1979), teachers in open-space schools are less cooperative with each other than their counterparts in traditional schools and are more argumentative.

In numerous stituations, the problems perceived with open classroom environments have forced school administrators to revert to more traditional instructional approaches. The self-contained classroom has been one recourse; departmentalization has been the other.

The problems with departmentalization equal and, in some ways, exceed those of the self-contained classroom. Most importantly, teachers are not able to learn much about their students in departmentalized settings. Departmentalization causes fragmentation of the curriculum, and interweaving among the disciplines is nearly impossible. Students are less inclined to conceptualize and apply their bank of knowledge across a variety of situations.

The assumption that departmentalization helps the child because teachers can concentrate on one discipline and therefore pupils will achieve more in that discipline is unsubstantiated (Ragan and Shepherd, 1977, 464). The fact of the matter is, the depth and breadth of content required in elementary curriculum is not such that subject matter specialists are necessary.

An argument generally promoted by teachers in favor of departmentalization is that it prepares students for the scheduling in junior high or middle school. My response to that is, "Why would we want to prepare students for something that is ineffective and exists only because it is a scheduling convenience for secondary schools?"

Self-contained classrooms, open classrooms, and departmentalization all present unique problems which affect student performance and teacher morale. They are difficult problems to address, but, as with all other problems, they offer challenging opportunities for all of us.

Every day in every elementary school, teachers and principals confront these problems with varying degrees of success. Discipline problems, student placement problems, parent problems, curricular problems, scheduling problems, organizational problems—individually they may merely be ripples in the stream. Collectively they may be disastrous. Combine their presence with an absence of effective schools indicators—strong, goal-oriented principal, high expectations, total staff involvement, wise use of instructional time (Mackenzie, 1983)—and a totally chaotic situation may erupt. If schools are to be effective, problems must be solved.

Practical Problem Solutions for Effective Schools

One should never believe that because a school has few visible problems, it is an effective school. Problems may not show because nothing is happening! On the other hand, a staff which recognizes the school's problems and seeks to solve them will be more effective, having done so.

Before we look at specific solutions to specific problems, we will consider a general, more conceptual solution to most problems that exist within an elementary school setting. First, we must "accept these truths to be self-evident": no effective school can operate in isolation from the community it serves, and no effective school can operate without adequate resources.

A school administrator can begin to eliminate isolationism and gain adequate resources by solving the people problems in and around the school. First, she must look at the various audiences: those affected by, involved in, served by, and serving the school itself. Then the administrator *must* roll those audiences into one, with one sole purpose: to make that school into the most effective school it can be.

47

Figure I

	VERBAL	WRITTEN

FORMAL	Faculty meetings
	Parent organization meetings
	  (general and board)
	Speeches to groups
		Letters to Parents
		  (variety of reasons)
		Memoranda to faculty
		Report cards
		School newsletters
		  (administrative)
		School newspapers (student)
		Information request forms
		Homework papers
		Flyers/brochures

INFORMAL	"Hall talks" Spontaneous conferences	Happy/sad notes (teacher generated)

The key to accomplishing this is nothing new; it is effective communication. What can schools do to improve their school-community and intraschool communication? First, they must look at what they are doing now.

Figure I represents typical modes of communication used by administrators and teachers. Generally, most communication between a teacher or administrator and groups of parents is formal and written. Numerous inadequacies exist with this. What the receiver believes about a message is usually from the message sender's nonverbal language. People believe and draw conclusions based not merely on the message but, more importantly, on the behaviors of its sender. They watch eyes and body motion, listen to voice tone and inflection, put that all together and make several decisions: Is this message important? Do I believe it? Will I do anything about it? When the sender is absent (i.e., the communication is written), the nonverbal element is lost from the communication process. Written communication is simply ineffective for getting support, yet it is what we in schools use most.

The absence of the message sender is not the only problem. Consider the amount of junk mail a person receives daily. A letter from a school, with its computer address label, is likely to be discarded with other junk mail. If it does not end up in the trash, its meaning may very well be misunderstood.

Educators are masters at writing letters filled with words they invented and no one else understands. We have become so adept at this that most times we do not realize what we are doing.

Formal written communication is not ineffective solely between schools and their external communities. Intraschool communication often borders on the absurd. If principals devoted the time they spend writing memos to visiting classes and conferring with staff and students, their esteem would undoubtedly escalate. They must stop "playing principal" and work at being humans. All of us can relate to other human beings. Many of us have difficulty relating to power figures.

What is the solution to this problem? The beginning is self-assessment. A school should identify every means of communication it uses. Following this identification process, each communication means should be evaluated for effectiveness. Changes should be decided upon, and commitment should be made to improving the school's communications.

The specific steps necessary to accomplish this task are:

1) Appoint a study committee of parent and faculty representatives, the school secretary, and the principal.
2) In a group meeting, using a model described in Figure I, brainstorm and list in the appropriate quadrants every means of communication used in and by the school.
3) If the results fall heavily in the formal/written quadrant, gather examples of the forms of communication listed and ask each person to assess their effectiveness using the following questions:
   - Do you feel the meaning of the communication is clear?
   - Do you feel the receiver knows why he/she received the communication?
   - Do you feel the receiver knows what is expected of him/her after having received the communication?
   - Do you feel the communication is consistent with other

information the receiver has received or knows of the subject?

• Do you feel this communication is relevant to the situation and responsibilities of the receiver?

• Do you feel this communication is useful to the receiver? Two studies (David, 1979; Williams, 1983) which described the effectiveness of written communication based on these five questions indicated that although the clarity of the message and its consistency with other information known by the receiver were acceptable, the action expected of the receiver and the relevancy or usefulness of the message to the receiver were problems.

4) In a group meeting, brainstorm alternative modes of communicating which can be placed in the informal or formal verbal quadrants.

5) Synthesize the findings of the study group and share with the entire school staff.

6) Obtain from every staff member a written commitment (there is a place for written communication!) to at least one means of verbal communication to be used consistently during the school year.

7) Periodically assess progress through input of affected audiences.

8) In May, review the effectiveness of the means of communication used during the year and establish a communication goal and plan for the following year.

I have no intention of simplifying the problems discussed in this chapter by saying good communication will solve them all. Nevertheless, every problem identified can be brought to solution more readily if communication among all parties involved is effective.

Solutions to Student-Related Problems

Discipline

No single teacher or administrator is likely to solve any child's discipline problem without involving the parent. Effective communication among the child, parents, teacher, and principal will lead to faster understanding of the child and also to successful measures for altering the child's unacceptable behavior. It will, in many cases, *prevent* disciplinary action from having to be taken.

The flagships of good discipline still prevail. A school should have a written discipline policy that is shared with parents. A teacher should have written class rules, defined with student suggestions. Measures for addressing misbehavior should be expedient, fair, and consistent. Students who habitually misbehave or who cause danger to others must be removed from the group. Schools without counselors must identify some means of supervising disruptive students who must be isolated from their peers. In summary, rules must exist, everyone must know the rules, and the rules must be enforced.

Probably one of the more renowned authorities on discipline is Lee Canter, who describes what he calls "assertive discipline." Canter's plan is simple to understand, relatively easy to implement, and credited by many users with producing great success. He describes four assertive discipline competencies teachers must have:

1) Teachers must know specific behaviors they want from students and must communicate those to students.
2) Teachers must know how to respond to disruptive behaviors and must provide a negative consequence every time students disrupt.
3) Teachers must know how to respond with appropriate praise or other meaningful reinforcement when students behave appropriately.
4) Teachers must work cooperatively with the principal and parents, sharing their discipline plan and explaining their expectations of the principal and parents (Canter, 1979).

One teacher alone cannot bring about effective discipline in a total school. Effective discipline must be an expectation and commitment of the principal. That expectation and commitment must be translated into a school-wide plan, enforced by *all* staff, including custodial, food services, and clerical staff as well as the teaching faculty. Finally, that expectation and commitment must be clearly communicated to parents with the explicit message that parents' support is crucial to an effective school-wide discipline plan. It can be done.

Diagnosis and Placement

All school systems must comply with Public Law 94–142 regulations in providing the least restrictive environment for children with handicapping conditions. Inherent in this is the establishment of acceptable procedures for identifying such youngsters and ultimately offering the appropriate educational settings. The personnel, materials, and other resources needed to accomplish both tasks must be provided by a school system; consequently it would serve little purpose to delve any further into those solutions at this time. Rather we shall explore school-based solutions to school-based problems caused by having to assign a child to a different setting or program for whatever reason. First, parents must be told of problems and their acceptance, support, and interest gained. Telling a parent his child needs special attention because something is "wrong" is very difficult. Again, the need for effective communication emerges.

I recall an incident where, with three other teachers, I sat across the table from a parent to discuss her son, who was giving all of us fits in the classroom. We had the parent outnumbered four to one, we were meeting in the principal's conference room, and we were telling her something was wrong with her son. That should have been bad enough, right? Wrong.

I was rocked on my heels when I heard one of my colleagues (bachelor's degree, four years' experience) blatantly tell the parent, "Your son has deep psychological problems." I was further flabbergasted to see the parent accept that indictment without question! She kept a stiff upper lip but left the conference visibly distraught. I think I would have cheered if she had looked the teacher in the eye and asked the clinical basis of the diagnosis.

How can schools resolve difficulties in telling parents about children's problems? First and foremost, they must know the child. Some schools use pupil personnel teams comprised of an administrator, social worker or counselor, nurse, classroom teacher, and any resource teachers who have contact with the child. Each member keeps anecdotal records of the child's behavior, performance, attendance, health condition, and any other information known about the child. Information from the parent is routinely gathered. The team meets and discusses the child. If information from specialists is needed, it is obtained. Basically, the team does its homework.

When it is time to present findings to the parent, the team member who has the best rapport with the child's family represents the team in a conference. Although as much information as possible has been collected about the child from as many sources as are available, an effort is made to minimize intimidation of the parent when presenting the information. Specific considerations for a school staff member to remember are:

1) Approach the conference with the facts and some suggestions but not with all the answers. Give the parent the dignity of knowing and expressing some possible solutions to the problem described. Consider the parent's suggestions in the final decision relative to the child's placement.

2) Refrain from overloading the parent with professional employees and educational jargon. If possible make the conference one-to-one. Prior to the conference, review all notes and highlight every educational term that may be confusing. When possible, substitute more common words. When that is not possible, make a note to explain to the parent what the term in question means.

3) Meet in a neutral setting. If a home visit is impossible and the school is the only alternative left, meet in the child's classroom.

4) Be direct and honest but sensitive. The subject of the discussion is not the outcome of last Friday night's football game; it is a human being, one who is growing, needs nurturing, and has unknown and unlimited potential. Treat the discussion with the respect it is due.

5) Regardless of the nature of the problem (discipline, achievement, hygiene, etc.) and regardless of the solution

chosen, involve the parent. Give the parent some specific responsibility in the child's attaining success.

6) Write an action plan which will be used with the child. Include strategies, time lines, persons responsible for specific actions and evaluative measures. Keep track of progress and be ready to revamp when necessary.

Following these suggestions will not remove the feeling that a parent experiences when he realizes his child is "different." It will likely get the parent positively involved and will establish trust, which is what the school must strive to attain.

Another very real school-based problem related to student diagnosis and placement is the question of what to do with a child in the interim. While data are being gathered, parents are being consulted, results are being interpreted, and placement options are being considered, the child is still in a regular classroom with twenty-five or thirty students and a concerned but frustrated teacher. This condition may exist for weeks!

The nature of the child's problem, academic or behavioral, has much to do with the teacher's alternatives. If the problem is a behavioral one, the teacher should consider the following:

1) To the extent possible, keep a daily log of the child's behavior and keep the building administrator, counselor (if available), and parent informed.

2) Establish some type of time-out procedure with the administrator, another classroom teacher, or counselor so that the child can be isolated from his peers when circumstances become too disruptive.

If a child is not awaiting placement for behavioral problems, but rather, is experiencing academic problems, the teacher may consider other options:

1) Get another person to work with the child during part of his instructional day. Consider every possible source: par-

ent volunteer, grandparent volunteer, student volunteer, or community volunteer.

2) Set up a tutoring program where an older student in the school comes to the child's classroom and tutors him one-on-one in a subject especially difficult for the child.

3) Seek placement for the child on a temporary basis in any resource program operating in the school which has no legal restrictions or criteria for placement.

4) Consult with computer-assisted instruction experts for recommendations on self-directed learning packets and place the child in a program at his instructional level.

It is important to remember that this child is no less frustrated than the teacher. Everyone needs to experience some success, some praise, daily. School personnel must work diligently to see that this occurs.

Another problem associated with properly diagnosing and placing students pertains to a lack of adequate materials for the child. A child not able to function on grade level, usually in reading, must be provided high-interest materials to motivate him to achieve. A first step for the teacher is to use the basal texts judiciously. To put a third grader who is reading on a primer level in a primer basal text is seldom the best decision. A number of relatively inexpensive supplementary materials are available to classroom teachers.

Book fairs, book clubs, libraries (both school and public), and RIF (Reading Is Fundamental) are excellent sources of books. Students can see, feel, and peruse the available books and hopefully get "hooked" on reading more. Garage sales and flea markets are excellent places to find paperbacks, comic books, joke books, and "outgrown" children's books. The child should be involved in making selections from several possible materials.

Books accompanied by audio recordings which allow children to hear and follow along visually are another motivating tool. Some excellent high-interest computer software has been developed which can be used in the early elementary grades.

One school took its old discarded basals and gave them to the students in the gifted program, who in turn disassembled the books and created new stories for children in the early grades. This grew into a publication center in the school which involved students who were reading at all levels in all ability groups. Imagine the satisfaction a child must feel when he sees the story which he wrote published and shared! This is particularly poignant for the so-called poor reader.

Materials in content areas other than reading are likewise available but seldom necessary. Reading tends to be the predominant subject in which students experience difficulties in the elementary schools.

Another problem related but not confined to diagnosis and placement of students is a lack of noninstructional time for elementary teachers. They need time to plan for their students' instructional needs and to confer with the people who influence their instructional decisions. A study done at the University of South Carolina revealed that elementary teachers in that state reported having anywhere from no planning time at all in the regular instructional day to five hours per week (Burleson, 1982). As a result, elementary teachers are forced to spend time before or after school or use a portion of their lunch periods in order to put together data, to confer with staff members or parents, and to develop plans for their students.

This poses many problems. Teachers should not have to squeeze planning time out of their personal time. This belief has been championed by teachers' organizations all across the country. Given that many teachers do give up their personal time for planning, they are often confronted with other obstacles. They may not be able to retrieve needed records from another teacher or the office because the person needed to release the records is not available. They may need to see the student but be unable to force the student to come early or stay late. They may need simple things like copies made or something typed but not have access to machines.

If a school system has adequate fiscal resources, the most expedient way to solve this problem is to build in an extra hour each day and pay for it. Generally, however, this is not the case.

Some school principals have partially solved this problem through the use of resource personnel. By using music specialists, physical education specialists, art specialists, and librarians to deliver instruction in their specialized areas, principals are able to free-up the classroom teacher. With adequate personnel and careful planning, a principal can schedule every teacher with a planning period each day.

One principal got approval from her superintendent to implement an innovative solution to the problem. It met with such success that several other schools adopted it as well. She met with her teachers and parents and got support for having students report to school daily fifteen minutes earlier than the system required. Each Thursday, she dismisses her students at 1:30, and all staff remain until at least 3:00 for joint planning, conferences with parents, and inservice. Although it still means a longer day for teachers, they have accepted the idea with enthusiasm and support. In fact, the teachers usually remain at school long after 3:00. The plan would not be palatable in every setting, but it certainly is worth a try.

The last problem to be addressed relative to student diagnosis and placement is the fear and reluctance on the part of many to label a child. Indeed we have placed so many labels on so many children that we have even identified a category called "regular." Labeling begins as a semantic problem, but all too often it becomes a box tied with cord from which a student never escapes.

School personnel have few options to avoid placing a label on a child. In essence, federal programs dictate that a label must be verified before the child in question can receive services. What educators can do is be more sensitive, more aware, and less hurried. Many times we use a label because it is the shortest distance between two points. Saying "He is a BD child" takes less time and effort (and sensitivity) than saying, "He is a child who is having serious behavior problems."

Consider these alternatives:

Say: He is taking advantage of one of our special programs.
Not: He is a Special Ed child.

Say: He is having some difficulty in math.
Not: He is deficient in math.

Say: He cannot speak or hear.
Not: He is deaf and dumb.
    or
    He is hearing- or speech-impaired.

Say: Learning is difficult for Mark.
Not: Mark is learning disabled . . . or mild moderate . . . or
    a slow learner . . . or mentally retarded . . . etc.

The key is to say what the child is or is not *doing*, not simply what he *is*.

If we reflect, we can remember that fifteen or twenty years ago many of the labels that roll off our tongues today did not even exist! We simply must monitor our speech habits constantly and not get trapped into expeditiously labeling children.

Student-related problems consume more time and attention of school personnel than any other. While other student problems certainly exist, most are related to behavior or learning. Water pipes don't burst every day, parents don't complain every day, but students are there, every day, and by their very existence cause problems to arise. Experience has taught us that the qualities we need to solve these problems are compassion, attentiveness, patience, and, most importantly, a sense of humor. As we develop these qualities to our fullest, we become more successful problem solvers and children become winners.

Practical Solutions to Parent Problems

As stated earlier, whether a parent problem involves a single, working, or apathetic parent, at its base is usually a communication problem. Basically, many parents are not available when they are needed.

What does this mean to school personnel? For principals, it means getting out—not only from the office but from the school. Meet parents on their own turf. Schedule an after-school conference at the parent's kitchen table. Reduce the number of organized parent meetings and have parents plan neighborhood coffees (day or evening) where the principal attends and everyone shares in discussions about the school. Use the merchants in the school's attendance area. Buy gas from the neighborhood service station and some grocery items from the local market.

I know one principal who spends thirty minutes every day walking a different street in his attendance area. Some might say he is "sloughing off" on the job. The results of such "sloughing off" should exist in all schools! He knows his community and it knows him. The whole community provides a voluntary neighborhood watch for the school. And woe to any child who decides to skip school for the day. Some other community member will march him straight to school as soon as he is seen.

Visibility, openness, handshakes, eye-contact, a listening ear, and a few well-asked, well-placed questions will open up communication lines for a school principal quicker than anything.

For teachers, the general message is the same. Forget the union contract momentarily and make a few home visits. Patronize some of the community merchants. Linger after parent organization meetings instead of bolting out the door as soon as the gavel drops. Attend a few community events such as hockey or softball games, piano recitals, and so forth. Such familiarity will not breed contempt; it will build trust, respect, and cohesiveness.

I can hear the prophets of gloom and doom. "What about bussed districts?" "They don't want us in their homes." "They don't pay me enough to do that." I would simply respond that for every obstacle there is a logical solution. Surely someone with a bachelor's or master's or, heaven forbid, doctoral degree can find it if he tries hard enough.

Communication is not the panacea for all parent problems. The problems unique to specific types of parents must also be addressed.

Single Parents

Problems related to single parents usually pertain to one or more of the following: 1) emotional adjustment of the child due to the separation or divorce of the parents, 2) financial status of a single-parent family, 3) inaccessibility of the custodial parent due to the work schedule, 4) absence of any communication with the noncustodial parent, and 5) blatant and subtle messages within the school itself that say the single-parent family is not OK.

The emotional welfare of the child must be a number one priority of the staff. First, school staff must recognize that just because one parent leaves the home, the child is not automatically headed down a one-way course toward emotional self-destruction. All of us know well-adjusted, self-confident, independent children who are products of single-parent homes. What we must quickly recognize, however, is that when a child suddenly begins to change behavior and it is known that one parent in the home is no longer present, we can assume a cause and effect relationship exists.

The first fear the school staff must dispel in a child who has recently lost a parent is that he is suddenly different, in a negative sense, from everyone else. As common as divorce is in our society, most people affected by a divorce still behave as though divorce is no less deadly than drinking arsenic.

One third grade teacher, upon learning that one of her students had recently become a single-parent child, immediately paired her with another child who had the same experience two months earlier. The teacher's opening statement was beautiful: "Margie, Jill is sort of like you. Her daddy had to leave home, and she is going to have to help her mom a little more around the house. Maybe you can tell her what some of the things are you do to help your mom." In no time at all, the two children were jabbering about their chores which, incidentally, grew and grew as the conversation progressed. Jill was free to express her problem with "someone like her."

Another teacher, who happens to be a single parent herself, starts every school year and every after-winter holiday with this question: "OK, who went to visit his or her dad lately? What did you do? Where did you go?" It works every time. The children, *many* of them, open up and talk freely about their visits with their dads.

This same teacher provides for any youngster who did not get to see his absent parent. She says, "Now I know some of you have not had a chance to see your dad yet. What are some of the things you plan to do when you see him?" It works!

Some schools have organized group counseling sessions for

children of recently separated households. Since this is not usually possible without additional money, it is not common. In most schools, the teacher is the primary person to get a child over the emotional hump. Her sensitivity will go a long way toward keeping a child in the mainstream.

Another problem single-parent children usually face is a reduction in money coming into the home. When a school imposes gym suit costs, field trip costs, supplementary materials costs, and the all-time-worst, exchanged gifts costs on such a youngster, it may create financial havoc in the home.

Specifically, a school should confidentially identify youngsters who may be in financial need and look for sponsors for such youngsters. School business partners, church groups, and parent organizations are usually more than willing to lend a helping hand to a youngster in need. The key again is sensitivity. Such dealings *must* be kept confidential.

One principal implemented a school work program whereby a list of tasks in and around the school was advertised monthly and student applications for doing the work were solicited. Tasks included watering plants, emptying waste baskets and pencil sharpeners, cleaning erasers, etc. A committee of teachers and the principal selected the students. Students were given a number of points for each task which could be "cashed in" for items which would otherwise cost the student money (e.g., one free book at the book fair).

Of course, this principal was immediately confronted by his colleagues with doubtful pronouncements: "Your custodians will grieve to the union." "You're going to get slapped with a law suit." The principal simply replied, "I'll try it until I am convinced it cannot work." It has been working for six years with tremendous success. Naturally the first thing the principal did was sell everyone on the idea. And he keeps selling.

Schools and businesses must both tackle the problem of inaccessibility of the custodial parent. Usually this parent is the mother, and typically she works outside the home at a job that pays less than $10,000 a year. Such a job is not one that will allow the parent to drop everything and run to the school. A school can offer parent-teacher conferences in the evenings by giving teachers compensatory time off during the day. Another avenue a school can pursue is to have coffee and rolls one morning a month so those parents can stop on their way to work and bring their children, who would be supervised in another part of the building. More radically, schools can attempt to hold conferences on the work sites in communities where the majority of the community members are employed at one site (i.e., paper mill, oil refinery, steel mill). Logistical details could be worked out between school and company officials.

Although I have spoken against the effectiveness of formal written communication, I believe some positive things result when a school sends its newsletter to businesses in town, asking that it be posted on the company bulletin board. This could become a routine procedure for a school.

A final approach a school can take is to establish a relationship with Parents Without Partners organizations. One way is to offer the school as a meeting place for the organization. Another is to get on the organization's agenda and discuss problems the school has in keeping communication open between the school and the single parent. Solicit suggestions from the members of the organization. Some may even volunteer to help!

Related to the inaccessibility of the custodial parent is the total absence of the noncustodial parent, usually the father. While studies indicate that more and more fathers are gaining custody of their children (Pichitino, 1983), they are still clearly in the minority. Generally, attorneys have given legal interpretations to school personnel which support the rights of the noncustodial parent to attend parent conferences and receive copies of the child's report cards and other records.

As soon as school administrators realize that one parent is absent from the home, they should attempt to make contact with the parent and send him or her a form similar to the following, which should be completed and kept on file in the school:

Parent's Name _____ Child's Name _____
Address _____

Phone Number _____

Do you wish to receive information from your child's school?

Yes _____ No _____

If you answered yes, please check those items you wish to receive:

_____ notification of parent organization meetings

_____ notification of parent/teacher conferences

Do you wish to have one scheduled for you?

Yes _____ No _____

_____ notification of school and/or classroom programs

_____ copy of report card

_____ school newsletter

_____ routine communications the school sends to the home

_____ other (please list)

The noncustodial parent must be made to feel welcome at the school. When he visits or telephones, he must be given the same courtesy and respect as the custodial parent. The school staff should never put themselves in the judgment seat attempting to determine which parent was "right" and which was "wrong." They should instead remember the noncustodial parent, usually the father, wishes to be involved and is already fighting his own emotional battles associated with guilt or loneliness. Manning (1983) has outlined several specific suggestions schools can effectively implement for making fathers feel comfortable at school.

The final problem related to single-parent children is that, through materials and attitudes, schools convey a message that single-parent families are strange. My first suggestion is that a school count heads among its own to see how many are or ever have been single parents. Then the "strangeness" may disappear, at least in attitude.

Schools need to stop such practices as holding Dad's Day or Mom's Day, acquiring room mothers, using art class for Mother's Day or Father's Day cards; instead, such activities should be neuter. Using terms like "parent" or "special person" works just as well.

In addition to these blatant mistakes, school staff members, being human, make subtle mistakes which can, over time and with attention, be corrected. Recall classroom situations where these questions and statements were heard:

"If you don't behave, I'll call your mother."

"Maybe your father can help you build your science project."

"Where does your father work?"

"Go home and ask your mother and father where they were born."

In countless ways, day in and day out we imply that families should be two-headed. A browse through any bookstore would offer any educator several choices of excellent books that offer practical suggestions to adults who are around children of single-parent families.

Materials are another means schools use to imply that all families have a father and mother in the home. Although publishers have greatly improved their books and films over the past several years, schools have not bothered to purge the old stuff. The single-parent family issue is the same as the minority issue that confronted us in the early sixties. We had simply ignored that population.

Although instructional materials more appropriately represent the American family of today, educators still need to review materials before using them in their classrooms. Such review, coupled with an awareness that one of three children in a class is living with only one parent, will allow a teacher to adapt the material, if necessary.

Single parents are providing ever-increasing challenges to schools. Probably no other agency in society can have a greater impact on easing the difficulties for single-parent families than schools, and schools can help without incurring any additional costs.

Working Parents / Apathetic Parents

Most of what has been said applies equally to working and apathetic parents. The general need is better communication, and the general direction is toward understanding the parents' situation and altering school practices to accommodate the parent.

One additional caution must be mentioned about a frequent means of "trapping" apathetic parents. Have you ever heard this statement? "Put the kids in the program. If the kids are on stage, the parents will always come to see the kids." The fact of the matter is the parents will *not* always come to see their kids perform.

Using student performances to entice parents to come to school, setting quotas (the class who has the most parents present gets free pizza), demanding that every parent be responsible for some task or donation in the classroom will accomplish little more than using a child as a pawn to anger his parents. These parents, in turn, will thrust their anger upon the child *and* the school and will continue to be alienated from the school. The additional accomplishment is that now the child feels guilty because he was unable to get his parent to do what the school wanted.

Of the parent community in general, Losen and Diament (1978, 13) wrote: "Parent participation will continue to increase, not decrease, and school systems which do not make efforts to respect parents' roles will face increasing hostile pressure from frustrated parents and parent lobby groups. The choice, then, is not between whether to include parents or to exclude them, but between whether to include them grudgingly or to develop new strategies for working with parents to achieve important mutual goals."

The effective elementary school must take on characteristics of the true community school. It must reach out and serve. Rather than being the big building that stands out on the hill, it must be like the cat that snuggles down into the corner of the sofa. It must "fit."

Practical Solutions to Program Problems

Problems related to curriculum, scheduling, and organizational patterns may be the simplest to identify but the most difficult to solve. This is because they exist under tight controls. A school administrator's hands are generally tied by federal, state, and local mandates, board policies, union contracts, and so forth when it comes to these issues. Nevertheless, some alternatives do exist.

Curriculum

The first step a principal should take regarding curriculum problems is to assume an offensive position. Before the first hint of parental discontent with the program offerings, the principal should survey the parents to get their opinions. The survey should be brief. For instance, the parents should be asked:

1) What percentage of time in a week should a student spend in the following subjects:
Language Arts (reading, English,
  spelling, handwriting)?   _____
Mathematics?   _____
Social Studies?   _____
Science?   _____
Music?   _____
Physical Education?   _____
Art?   _____
Other?   _____
2) Are you satisfied with your child's program at _____ School?
3) If no, please give us your suggestions for improvement.

If the parents' recommendations closely match the current state at the school and the majority of parents express satisfaction, the school administrator should take no overt action. He should, however, stay attuned for trendy topics and pressure groups.

Generally, curriculum decisions in a school are policy decisions and must comply with school district policies. Before making any curriculum changes, a school administrator should communicate with central office personnel to be sure his ideas are in compliance with board policy.

Scheduling problems exist in elementary schools because classrooms are usually heterogeneous groupings but programs operating in the school serve homogeneous groups. For example, in a class of twenty-seven third graders, three may go to speech therapy two hours a week, five may go to a gifted class ten hours a week, one may go to physical therapy three hours a week, two may go to a resource learning disability class five hours a week, and so on. What is a school administrator to do?

First, protect the first two-hour block in the morning at all costs. To the extent possible, schedule all pull-outs after 10:30 in the morning so that teachers do not have to manipulate their language arts blocks. After all, this is the discipline our public has told us is most important.

Secondly, schedule *anything* that can be classified as extra-curricular outside the regular instructional day. Usually, instrumental music and choral groups can fit into this category. This is inconvenient to some parents, but as long as schools must operate within existing time constraints, the needs of the majority of the youngsters must prevail.

Another approach to pull-outs is controversial but worthy of consideration: that is to substitute in-class models where possible. For instance, Chapter I services do not have to be delivered in a separate class; tutors can provide the services in the regular class-room, right beside the regular teacher. While this requires acceptance and adjustment by the classroom teacher, it provides for better opportunities to supplement, and not supplant, the regular curriculum, which is what it is supposed to do.

The last consideration for scheduling is to have the specialists meet with the regular classroom teacher and jointly develop a schedule that will cause the least disruption in the regular classroom yet provide all of the content to which a child is entitled.

I cannot overemphasize the frustration this problem causes, and I have yet to find any viable solutions. Perhaps the best a school can do is find a means of easing the frustration.

Instructional Organization

The problems described with self-contained classrooms, open classrooms, and departmentalization can be solved for the most part with one merger. Schools can maintain self-contained classrooms but operate with open classroom methods. The ultimate outcome, a child-centered, exploratory instructional environment operating within one enclosed classroom with one teacher, can only be achieved after much groundwork is completed.

Schubert and Baxter (1982) have stated that the newer strategies of open education are the best methods for developing the mental, social, and emotional aspects of a child. If this is so, schools should initiate movement in that direction now.

Faculty must be led to understand what open classroom methods are and must philosophically embrace those methods. This may require extensive self-analysis and in-depth inservice with a great deal of follow-up. Schools can look to local universities and regional service units to provide assistance.

Generally speaking, as school personnel face program-related problems of curriculum, scheduling, or instructional organization, they should turn to the current research on the topic. Although the people on the firing line have little time to read what researchers are espousing about the day-to-day operations of schools, such research exists in abundance, especially on program-related topics.

Program problems are no less difficult to solve than people problems, but they are different. They are generally more technical, more distinct, and more quickly identifiable. Usually the school administrator is faced with less flexibility in solving them. Regardless, their existence has a negative impact on the effectiveness of a school.

Summary

An effective elementary school is one that accurately identifies and successfully addresses its problems. For the most part, those problems are people-related problems, and in most cases, effective communication is essential to solving them.

Educators must stop talking to themselves and reach out. When a problem exists with a child, we have to be able to say to the parent, "Tell us what *you* think." When a problem exists with a parent, we have to ask, "How can we work better together?" And when a problem is identified as a program problem, teachers, administrators, and parents must come to the table, erase the chalkboard clean, and be willing to start over. Then maybe, just maybe, some of the rigid guidelines will be replaced by more flexibility.

What is an effective elementary school? Ask a researcher and you will likely get a quantitative analysis based on effective schools research. Ask a citizen and you will probably hear about the school that serves a middle-upper income bracket community and gets a lot of positive press. Ask a principal and you will likely learn about that school whose staff works together with the community to identify and solve its problems. Ask Tony, who is nine, and he will tell you, "It's my home when I'm not home; it's where I like to be."

Bibliography and References

Baer, Thomas G., Robert Goodall, and Lester Brown. 1983. Discipline in the classroom: Perceptions of middle grade teachers. *Clearing House* 57 (November): 139–142.

Bloom, Benjamin, George Madaus, and J. Thomas Hastings. 1981. *Evaluation to Improve Learning.* New York: McGraw-Hill.

Burleson, Calvin R. 1982. A study of the relationship between in-school planning time of fourth-grade teachers in South Carolina public schools and student achievement. Ph.D. diss., University of South Carolina.

Canter, Lee. 1979. Competency-based approach to discipline—It's assertive. *Thrust for Educational Leadership* (January): 11–13.

David, Patricia M. 1979. An analysis of perceived effectiveness of written communication from central office administrators to building level administrators in a metropolitan school district. Ph.D. diss., University of Nebraska.

Goodlad, John I. 1984. *A Place Called School.* New York: McGraw-Hill.

Klass, Wendi H., and Stephen E. Hodge. 1978. Self-esteem in open and traditional classrooms. *Journal of Educational Psychology* 70 (May): 701–705.

Losen, Stuart M., and Bert Diament. 1978. *Parent Conferences in the Schools.* Boston: Allyn and Bacon.

MacKenzie, Donald E. 1977. Research for school improvement: An appraisal of some recent trends. *Educational Researcher* 12 (April): 5–17.

Manning, M. Lee. 1983. The involved father: A new challenge in parent conferences. *Clearing House* 57 (September): 17–19.

Martin, Wilfred B. W. 1979. Teachers' perceptions of their interaction tactics. *Education* 99 (Spring): 236–239.

Ourth, John, and Sally Banks Zakariya. 1982. The schools and the single-parent student: What schools can do to help. *Principal* 62 (September): 22–28.

Pichitino, John P. 1983. Profile of the single father: A thematic integration of the literature. *The Personnel and Guidance Journal* 37 (January): 295–299.

Ragan, William B., and Gene D. Shepherd. 1977. *Modern Elementary Curriculum*. New York: Holt, Rinehart and Winston.

Richmond, Bert O., Victor K. Phillips, and William Blanton. 1972. Creative growth and cognitively structured stimulation in education. *Journal of Psychology* 81 (November): 321–328.

Schubert, Nancy A., and Milton B. Baxter. 1982. The self-contained open classroom as a viable learning environment. *Education* 102 (Summer): 411–415.

Stouffer, George A. W. Jr., and Jennie Owen. 1955. Behavior problems of children as identified by today's teachers and compared with those reported by E. Wickman. *Journal of Educational Research* 48 (January): 321–331.

Weiss, Robert. 1981. The school life and social situation of the single-parent child. Paper Presented at the I/D/E/A/Special Institute on Critical Issues in Education, Washington, D.C.

Wickman, E. 1938. *Teachers and Behavior Problems*. New York: The Commonwealth Fund.

Williams, Alphonso. 1984. An analysis of perceived effectiveness of written communication from central office administrators to elementary level administrators in a metropolitan school district. Ph.D. diss., University of New Orleans.

Early Childhood Education

Kevin J. Swick

Toward Excellence in Early Childhood Education

The beginning of every child's life is a time when development and learning occur rapidly or at least have the potential to do so. From conception to age eight is a time of tremendous growth in all facets of the child's life: physical, cognitive, social, and emotional. Research in the fields of biology, psychology, child development, and early childhood education substantiates the powerful influence of events during this part of a child's life. Summarizing the findings regarding the influence of the home environment on the child, Bloom (1981) suggests that each family has an established "curriculum" which can advance the child's learning capacities or delimit and even damage such potential. Children who are malnourished, abused, or neglected suffer from a "press of events and ultimately find school difficult if not impossible" (Green, 1982). In marked contrast, the child who benefits from a "positive press" of home-school-community influences during the early years internalizes the needed skills for school functioning (Breedlove and Schweinhart, 1982).

The use of early learning programs to support the development of children and their families has proven successful. Recent research findings indicate that exemplary early childhood education programs can reduce the number of children needing special education courses, increase children's potential for succeeding in school, decrease the likelihood of juvenile behavior problems, and increase the possibilities that children will complete their high school program (Lazar et al., 1977; Breedlove and Schweinhart, 1982).

While the research data supports the value of early childhood education as the first link in the nation's track to educational excellence, the reality is that there are far too few quality efforts under way. Further, society's support of children and their families is in question. The potential to provide children with effective learning environments is great, but the challenges in bringing about such arrangements are even greater.

Critical Issues in Early Childhood Education

Early childhood educators are confronting many issues: the professional identity and function of the field itself; societal malaise toward the quality of life young children experience; the support, education, and involvement of parents as key partners in the education of children; the development and continuing education of various professionals who contribute to early childhood programs; the development of public policy favorable to supporting quality programs for children and families; the disparity of views within the profession regarding what is best for children; and the protection of children and families from neglect or abuse.

Three major categories provide a framework for examining these issues: 1) professional identity and training, 2) child development and learning, and 3) program and curriculum. There are, of course, macrosystem issues such as public policy and societal trends that influence many facets of early childhood education. For example, recent budget cuts in family support programs have influenced parent-child situations in negative ways (Green, 1982). Likewise, inappropriate television programming has been linked to children's aggressive and passive behavior in school (Elkind, 1981). On the other hand, recent positive events in the public domain, such as state-adopted child development programs for four year olds and federal initiatives in child abuse prevention, are likely to influence children and families in productive ways.

Professional Identity and Training Issues

The quality of children's educational experiences is dependent upon the professionals who design and implement early childhood programs. The performance of professionals who work with young children is shaped by two factors: their educational and training background, and the perceptions they have developed of themselves in relationship to their societal value and their importance to young children and their families. This self-image of early childhood educators is often categorized as their professional identity. Caldwell (1984) suggests that the issues of training and identity of early childhood professionals are related to other issues in the field: What is the function of the early childhood education professional? What should a quality program for children include? What are the procedures for bringing about desirable programs? Professional associations such as the National Association for the Education of Young Children and the Southern Association on Children Under Six are now beginning to address these issues (Caldwell, 1984; Swick, Brown, and Graves, 1984).

Part of the identity issue in early childhood education is rooted in the nomenclature that permeates both theoretical and practical aspects of the field. Terms like "day care," "child development," "child care," "extended-day programs," and "infant intervention strategies" mean different things to different people. For example, "day care" implies simply taking care of children, while "child development" implies a more comprehensive program of services to children and families. While this may appear to be an issue of semantics, it raises critical questions regarding what quality early childhood programs should include, and it raises concerns about the level of training of professionals and paraprofessionals who operate the programs.

The training and certification issue is related to the staffing of preschool programs (Swick and Hanley, 1980). While all states have certification standards for kindergarten-primary teachers, the requirements for preschool teachers are negligible and further complicated because of the deregulation of child care efforts now under way in many states (Dickerson, 1984). This lack of standards and certification laws accounts for the large disparity of instructional quality in early childhood/preschool programs. While one center may be staffed by master teacher professionals, another may lack capable, trained teachers (Swick and Kierce, 1981). Steps which have been taken to alleviate this problem include the use of a career development training model as designed for the Head Start program (Davis, 1982) and the development of the Child Development Associate credential program (Caldwell, 1984). Both designs use a competence-based approach to training teachers and aides in basic skills for teaching young children.

The low self-image of many early childhood professionals is linked to the conditions in which they work. For example, in many states the licensing requirements for child care programs are minimal and totally inadequate (Dickerson, 1984). Even publicly sponsored programs often suffer from inadequate funding, a lack of qualified personnel, and less than desirable facilities. The situation in kindergarten-primary programs is somewhat better, and yet these programs too have felt the impact of various financial and resource shortages. Recent emphasis on the crisis in American education has focused new concern on child care standards and the need for quality in early childhood programs.

Attempts to improve the status of early childhood education professionals need to focus on increasing the quality of training and improving conditions where these professionals work. A current effort that includes these components in its design is the National Academy of Early Childhood Programs. Sponsored by the National Association for the Education of Young Children, the academy attempts to define "benchmarks of excellence" for early childhood professionals to use in assessing their program effectiveness (CAPS, 1983). Additional efforts by professional associations and state and local early childhood leaders are needed to improve the identity and self-image of teachers of young children.

Issues Related to Development and Learning

Knowledgeable professionals in early childhood education note that a lack of training has influenced the development of many misconceptions regarding children's learning and development. In turn, Elkind (1981) explains that societal ignorance of how children develop is creating an unhealthy situation in which children are pushed beyond their developmental limitations. For example, the emergence of "academic preparatory preschools" is one indicator of the misconceptions of what children actually need during this state of life. Selecting preschool programs, buying toys, and determining how to spend time with children are issues about which parents often make decisions without adequate knowledge (White, 1980). For example, the recent computer craze has led many parents to buy their child an instant education in the form of a home computer—not a critical or even high priority need for young children. Teachers of young children are not immune to this problem. Depending upon their training and understanding of child development, teacher decisions regarding instructional design will range from outstanding to totally inadequate.

Although incomplete, a body of knowledge has been developed that can be used in making decisions related to children's development and learning. It is known, for example, that from birth the child interacts with the environment rather than passively receiving information (Piaget and Inhelder, 1969). Unfortunately, many educators continue to make decisions using a receptor model of learning (Hart, 1983). Children are natural explorers, examining all facets of their situation and utilizing the results of this exploration to develop schema or patterns of the world as an initial basis for functioning. Given a supportive environment, children gradually develop understandings of the people, events, and things that combine to make up their curriculum in a sequential manner (Osborn and Osborn, 1983).

A recent statement summarizing the ways in which children learn and develop (Swick, Brown, and Graves, 1984) identifies the following insights:

- Children use all of their senses and capacities in learning about the world.
- Children learn in a holistic sense, grasping patterns of

75

events and ideas from the environment through their specific involvements.

- Children use their natural surroundings as an initial curriculum and extract meaningful events as a basis for language development, social functioning, thinking skills, and self-development.
- Children develop in a sequential pattern, from concrete to abstract and from simple to complex.
- Children follow similar developmental sequences, but in unique ways and at different rates.
- Children learn by actively participating in things, manipulating objects, and expressing their ideas through many dimensions such as music, art, sociodramatic play, puppetry, science experiences, and other modes.

In order to develop and learn in these modes, children must have relationships with significant adults; be able to function in a safe, secure, nurturing, and stimulating environment; and have many opportunities to use that environment as a setting for learning. Children who never develop lasting relationships with significant adults have little chance of success in any endeavor. Parents and teachers provide children with the essentials for developing a sense of importance, the foundation upon which all learning is based. Research in early childhood education indicates that within minutes after birth, the infant seeks out the mother for protection and interaction (Honig, 1983; Stern, 1977). Throughout their lives, children utilize adults as role models by which they can secure their footing as they learn about various things (Swick and Duff, 1982).

Maslow's (1959) work in the psychology of learning indicates *children and adults need security, love, and other basic needs met before they can extend themselves to more sophisticated involvements.* Work in the field of early childhood education supports Maslow's proposal: malnourished children, for example, have difficulty in school and usually are developmentally delayed or damaged in one or more dimensions (Green, 1982). Children's security is linked to the total family's well-being. Green (1982) notes that any disruptive force influencing the family will eventually affect the child's development and learning. The transactional nature of socioeconomic forces and family dynamics is clearest in the case of the chronically unemployed, where all family members suffer denigration and possible pathologies in social and educational functions (Bronfenbrenner, 1979). A more productive picture emerges when family effectiveness is in place: generally children internalize constructive images of their surroundings and acquire the self-confidence to transfer this sense of control to other environments like the school (Stinnett, 1980).

Beyond safety and security is the need for stimulating yet balanced learning environments. Children need experiences of many kinds to develop their ideas of how things work. For example, White and Kaban (1979) found that home environments where children were encouraged to participate and take an active role in family decisions were more advanced in language skills and social competencies. Environments devoid of materials, objects, interesting people, and opportunities produce passive, boring children. Efforts to develop environments of excellence for children at home and in school must be centered on the way children learn and develop as well as what children need in order to reach personal excellence in their own functioning. Instead of expanding existing educational practices (which are often ineffective), early childhood professionals should place more emphasis on the development of meaningful adult-child relationships and on the formation of learning situations that support children's natural inquiry and encourage children to experience many different learning procedures and events.

Issues Influencing Program Decisions

While no absolute answers have evolved from early childhood curriculum research, much discussion and extensive analysis of program components have provided a context for articulating some of the major issues. The most critical curriculum and program issues facing early childhood educators include:

1) What age group should receive priority attention in terms of the limited resources available?
2) Of the various delivery systems (center-based, home-

based, combination efforts) used in early childhood programs, which systems are most effective?

3) What content should be given priority in early childhood
programs?

4) Which instructional strategies and assessment procedures
are most effective with young children?

5) What are the most successful modes of involving parents
in the education of young children?

Answers to these curriculum and program issues are not readily apparent. There is, however, a foundation of knowledge in child development and learning that can be used in making effective early
childhood curriculum and program decisions. In addition to the issues already examined, current studies by Elkind (1981) support
the idea of designing programs based on the developmental needs of
children.

In spite of a knowledge base that supports a developmental approach to early childhood curriculum, current social efforts are in
the opposite direction: condensing, distorting, and in some cases,
abolishing childhood as a distinct stage of development (Postman,
1981; Bain, 1981; Manning and Manning, 1981). Beginning with
the societal curriculum that ignores children's distinctiveness by ex-
posing them to content that is mostly adult, and moving to the preschool classroom which emphasizes abstract and isolated learning
at the expense of more productive experiential learning, the message
is clear: what are known to be effective learning approaches for children are largely ignored.

Toward Excellence in Early Childhood Education

Any thrust to achieve excellence in early childhood education must
have a framework inclusive of competent adults who can design
learning environments that are based on the needs of children. We
must educate parents and teachers about children's developmental
stages and inform these adults of learning designs consistent with
these stages. Then it will be possible for quality programs to emerge
and for children to begin realizing their potential. Four items related

to achieving improved programs for children include: 1) involvement and education of parents, 2) development of appropriate educational programs for children, 3) development of a professional training/continuing education process which greatly enhances the status and skill of early childhood educators, and 4) deployment of an advocacy plan to influence public policy toward supporting excellence in programs for children.

Involving and Educating Parents

The key to children's learning and development is having access to significant and competent adults. Parents, as Gordon (1975) noted, are the child's most influential and long-term teachers. Gordon's notion has been confirmed by all of the major studies in early childhood education over the past decade. For example, White and Kaban (1979) found effective parents influenced the child more than any other factor during the first three years of life. Schaefer (1983), in his research on parental locus of control, found consistent correlations among parents with a high internal locus of control and children who were highly successful in school. Parents who felt a sense of powerlessness seemingly infected their children, who then found school tasks difficult. Schools and other early childhood centers that have utilized parent involvement strategies have had more success in helping children develop and learn than programs that lacked this critical program component (Lazar et al., 1977).

Initial efforts to achieve successful parenting should focus on the important function of parents and family in children's development. While the importance of effective parenting may initially appear to be obvious, the lack of quality parenting has stimulated professionals and citizens to develop media awareness programs.

The emergence of information substantiating the positive influence of parent and family actions on children provides a foundation for awareness programs. For example, Stinnett (1980) identifies six characteristics of families that are highly influential in promoting positive behavior in children: 1) sense of family identity, 2) clear family purpose, 3) balance between family and individual development, 4) good family communications, 5) family planning times, and 6) sense of family spiritual beliefs. When these characteristics were absent in families, children tended to lack direction and experienced many problems in social settings such as day care centers and schools. The core of future early childhood program designs must include a parent and family education component.

Additional study on roles that effective parents use in creating environments conducive to children's development is available for both awareness and instructional efforts (White and Kaban, 1979; Swick, 1984). Roles that have consistently emerged as influential include: parent as model, parent as guide, parent as problem solver, and parent as designer of learning environments (Swick and Duff, 1982). Researchers such as White and Kaban (1979), Stern (1977), Gordon (1975), and Bronfenbrenner (1979) report that the performance of these roles by parents contributes to a balanced development of the child's skills in language, behavior, self-concept, intellectual functioning, and social competence.

The use of parent effectiveness information in awareness programs has influenced the development of extensive parent education efforts in schools, churches, and community agencies. Educational efforts directed toward reaching potential parents, expectant parents, parents of preschoolers, parents of school-age children, teenage parents, and parents of exceptional children each have distinct functions of improving parent skills in dealing with various parent-child situations. Contact of early childhood educators with parents through these programs has had an impact on enhancing family functioning. While parent education is essential in order to equip parents with needed skills for carrying out their roles, it is not a solution to all family problems. Parent educators, for example, must recognize the need for understanding the situation parents face in trying to support children in reaching their potential.

Bronfenbrenner (1979) warns that traditional approaches to working with children and families are failing to meet the needs of most people because they are no longer in traditional social contexts. Today's family is quite different from the family of twenty years ago in many ways: smaller in size, highly mobile, and functioning within a high-stress environment. In addition, today's family is confronted with a situation where expectations are high but resources in short supply (Masnick and Bane, 1980).

Early childhood educators and community leaders need to account for family situations in planning programs for children. Parent surveys, examining the demography of the school-community context and maintaining informal but directed contacts with parents, can produce information which is helpful in program development (Swick, 1982). Family support efforts such as extended day care, industry-sponsored child development centers, community support programs for parents of handicapped children, and interagency-sponsored family counseling centers have proven valuable in strengthening the parent-child bond and influencing improved performance of family members in community roles.

Self-reliant parents are the core of any plan for educational excellence. Family support projects should attempt to aid parents and children in developing autonomous and constructive modes of functioning. Components of successful programs include: 1) developing networking skills in family members, 2) providing critical services in areas of health, child care, and nutrition, 3) involving parents in acquiring needed job skills, 4) educating parents about available services for use in strengthening the family, and 5) supporting families during crisis and helping them cope with long-term special needs (Swick, 1984).

When supported by appropriate societal efforts, parents can assume their leadership role in educating young children. Early childhood educators should utilize parent education projects to assist parents in strengthening their skills as family leaders. These programs should focus on the following components, allowing for individual parent differences and needs (Swick, 1984):

1) Provide programs that teach parents during their early stages of parenting.
2) Include content which prompts parents to examine their personal development as well as their development as parents.
3) Involve parents in refining their understanding of how

children learn and develop, and in acquiring skills they can use in supporting this development.

4) Organize activities that stress family management and marital development skills. Time management, communication skills, and problem-solving strategies are three specific competencies in which all parents need assistance.

5) Inform and educate parents about available community support services for use in strengthening family development.

The education and support of parents is a continuous process. As parents and children grow and enter new stages of life, their need for assistance is evident in several areas: discipline; selecting quality child care services; dealing with children's transitions to school, development shifts, and their own transitions (such as entering the work world); and handling special situations such as death, divorce, and illness (Swick, 1984).

Parents who have established a productive family arrangement can make extended contributions to school and community groups. Meaningful parent involvement influences children in ways that increase their ability to function successfully in school (Irvine, 1979). Through service as tutors, resource faculty or aides, and in other dimensions, parent support of school activities serves at least two functions that are central to educational excellence: enrichment of the school program and strengthening of parent-child relationships (Swick, Brown, and Robinson, 1983). Emerging from productive family-school interactions are many possibilities for parents to develop a community support system, including resources to expand their skills and experiences to enrich the lives of their children (Hetherington, 1979).

Competent parents can make the child's early years stable, secure, interesting, and challenging. To accomplish their many roles, parents need access to educational programs that provide ideas for handling child development and family issues, and a support system which enables them to implement family skills in a productive manner. Therefore, the involvement of parents in early childhood programs can expand the power of families and schools to create learning environments of excellence.

Toward Quality Programs for Children and Families

The early experiences of children establish, in many ways, their approach to learning, physical growth, intellectual orientation, and moral development. These experiences occur as the child goes through concrete involvements with parents, teachers, and the environment. We are probing for an agenda for excellence in early childhood education when we ask questions like the following: How does the child develop his self-image? How can the child's health and physical well-being be advanced? What are the most appropriate learning and development modes for young children? Answers to these questions are important because they influence the curriculum children experience.

An agenda for excellence in early childhood programs includes both the global criteria and specific elements that comprise the child's environment. Five criteria of excellence that should permeate all aspects of the child's early life are as follows:

1) Comprehensive health services for all family members, beginning with the mother's first pregnancy and continuing throughout the life cycle. Early detection and correction of health problems is not only economically sound but also establishes a foundation for achieving the maximum potential of all family members (Klaus and Robertson, 1982; Sasserath, 1983; Green, 1982).
2) Quality child development centers that include a strong parent involvement and family support component. Provision for quality care outside the home, related to family needs, will increase children's educational and social functioning in school as well as strengthen parent-child bonds (Watson, Brown, and Swick, 1983; White and Kaban, 1979).

3) Prevention of child abuse and neglect and use of rehabilitation centers. Large increases in sexual abuse, psychological abuse, and severe neglect of children cost society a tremendous resource. While prevention should be the focus, rehabilitation efforts can restore family relationships in many situations. Family counseling programs are useful in supporting families during times of high stress which often lead to the abuse of children or other family members (Kempe and Kempe, 1978).

4) High quality preschool programs for every child and family in need of such care. Exemplary projects such as the High/Scope program provide an initial basis upon which future program experimentation can be conducted (Breedlove and Schweinhart, 1982). These centers should be comprehensive to meet the diverse physical, social, educational, and health-safety needs of children and families. Educational experiences that are developmentally appropriate should be selected to stimulate the learning interests of children and parents (Caldwell, 1984).

5) Kindergarten-primary school programs that extend the preschool learning environment, attend to the individual needs of children, and strengthen the parent-child relationship. By utilizing such an approach and combining it with a focus on what is developmentally appropriate for the child, kindergarten-primary school programs can strengthen the child's learning capacities (Goodlad, 1983).

Most of these global criteria for excellence can be realized through the development of quality teachers who have the resources and learning conditions required for effective instruction.

Specific early childhood curriculum components are needed to create effective learning situations in classrooms, child development centers, and other school arrangements. These components should be based on the following guidelines: 1) curriculum philosophy should be shaped by the needs of children, 2) progam design should support children's development and learning, and 3) assessment procedures should focus on promoting children's talent and skill development (Swick, Brown, and Graves, 1984).

A clear understanding of the learning needs of children is, or should be, the core of any early childhood curriculum. The curriculum should recognize that children constantly strive to make sense of their environment, that they need adult guidance in learning about their world, that they learn more when they are encouraged to participate in activities such as play and drama, and that their social, emotional, intellectual, and physical needs are interrelated.

In order to achieve excellence, early childhood programs should include the following:

- Quality teachers who are knowledgeable in child growth and development, committed to children, and capable of designing programs which meet children's developmental needs.
- Adult-child ratios that promote meaningful interaction in the classroom and allow for the development of close home-school relationships.
- Learning situations which encourage children to use all of their senses and which use the children's real and fantasy worlds for problem-solving and creative thinking processes.
- Encouragment of children's creativity through dramatic play experiences, participation in artistic and musical expression, and hands-on activities.
- Varied opportunities for children to use language and to base language activities on their experiences.
- A participatory curriculum to foster a sense of autonomy in children, encourage children's decision making, and give the child's needs, interests, and discoveries paramount consideration.
- A variety of instructional approaches that promote interaction of children with each other and the teachers; individualized instruction and small group projects, for example, allow for the personal attention children need in order to develop fully and to learn.

- Assessment as an on-going analytic process, providing each child with the kind of planning that will enable him to use his potential to the fullest.
- A variety of assessment techniques used in a continuous, caring, and flexible manner to plan for children's individual needs.
- Consideration of the children's real world in assessing their development and learning. Home life, cultural setting, and learning style must be integrated into assessment plans to develop a comprehensive and valid picture of the child.

Designing programs for children according to these guidelines will provide a basis for achieving excellence in many ways: enhancing the child's potential for using the learning environment effectively, broadening teacher perceptions of what can be accomplished in the learning program, and increasing parental support of the early childhood program both in school and at home. (A more comprehensive view of essential early childhood program criteria is available in Swick, Brown, and Graves, 1984).

Educating Teachers for Achieving Excellence

The key to improving education is in the development and continuing education of quality teachers (Kohl, 1984). Recent national reports on educational issues have concluded with a call for critical reforms in teacher education (Goodlad, 1983). While early childhood education has benefited from dedicated, quality teachers, it has also suffered from a shortage of quality personnel. A lack of uniform professional certification standards for teachers of preschool children has created a confusing situation where teacher quality ranges from inadequate to excellent, depending upon the particular situation. In too many cases, kindergarten-primary certification requirements are minimal or are a hybrid arrangement between early childhood and elementary school teacher training.

Any agenda to create excellence in the early childhood teaching ranks must include the following:

1) Professional standards and certification requirements should focus on educating an early childhood teaching force for the birth-to-ten-year age range. This proposal requires a complete revamping of current certification patterns (early childhood, elementary, middle school) to a more developmental-functional design (early childhood, middle childhood, and adolescence). These standards can be drawn from the best thinking of professional organizations such as the National Association for the Education of Young Children (Caldwell, 1984).

2) Professional standards and certification designs must include career development patterns which promote constructive initial training and functional continuing education for early childhood professionals. One possibility is the use of an initial two-year child development credential, with extended professional training leading toward a baccalaureate degree and, through a career ladder, to a master teacher certificate (Swick, Rawls, and Kuhs, 1984).

3) Standards that promote excellence in teaching young children must come in three areas: a) increased admission requirements for those entering early childhood education, b) rigorous professional training and continuing education of teachers, and c) increased financial reward as well as more diverse incentive plans for professional growth (Hanley and Swick, 1983).

A reconceptualization of the development and education of teachers must focus on a life-span curriculum in which a teacher's initial training, early development, and continuing education are organized into a career spiral system (Hanley and Swick, 1983). For example, the "Charlotte plan" allows for differentiated roles in teaching as well as career incentives that attract capable early childhood teachers to new levels of professional skill, involvement, and development. The plan provides teachers with initial intern experiences under master teachers and also offers individual choice regarding an individual's career pattern (Charlotte Mecklenberg Teacher Career Development Plan, 1983).

Three critical components of quality early childhood teacher education are: 1) an expanded knowledge base of content relating to children's development and learning needs and curriculum experiences appropriate to these needs; 2) effective instructional design strategies relating to home-school dynamics and home- and school-based programs; and 3) a broadened arena and expanded agenda for educating and continually refining the development of early childhood educators (Katz, 1977).

The initial training of teachers of young children should center on core attitudes, knowledge, and skills drawn from the areas of child development, parent education, instructional design, and teaching effectiveness (Swick, 1984). A combination of theory and practicum arrangements is the basis of this proposal. Entrance into the early childhood profession would be linked to university experiences through university-school mentor teachers. As teachers acquire competence in these core teaching skills, they would have increased opportunities to refine their skills and broaden their development to include leadership and mentoring (Gideonse, 1982).

Beyond the entry level, professional development would include two major career stages: the master's degree or certificate in advanced studies of early childhood education, and a specialist degree in teaching with an emphasis on acquiring mentor or master-teaching skills. These two advanced levels of professional development support the acquisition of advanced teaching skills, extended knowledge of early childhood, and development of leadership, research, advocacy, and mentoring skills. Such a design for professional leadership in early childhood education will substantially improve the quality of education for young children.

Inherent in the career development plan for educating teachers of young children is the need for articulating major teacher roles which research finds critical to quality instruction. Three teacher roles which produce positive outcomes in children are: continuous assessment of professional behavior, use of proactive planning and instructional design strategies, and reliance upon a variety of teaching resources. Goodlad (1984) identified "teacher renewal" as one indicator of effective teaching. Schools where teachers were continuously involved in meaningful professional development experiences rated higher in effectiveness than schools where teacher development was lacking.

Teacher control of the learning environment has long been recognized as a factor in the instructional arrangement. Proactive teachers plan their interactions with children and utilize thoughtful approaches in responding to immediate problems that arise in the classroom. Teachers who have a high locus of control provide children with a structure in which they can explore many ideas and benefit from various learning experiences (Osborn and Osborn, 1981). The utilization of many resources to produce an organized and stimulating instructional setting is a hallmark of excellence in early childhood education. Emphasis on continued teacher growth along with the development of proactive instructional skills and the purposeful use of many human and material resources must become a part of every teacher's "skill kit" (Swick, 1984).

Promoting Excellence Through Advocacy and Research

Essential to the development of support systems for children and families, improved teacher education and professional development, and the creation of quality early childhood programs is the use of both advocacy strategies and research and development designs.

Professional organizations provide a natural arrangement for stimulating advocacy activity at all levels of the society. For example, the National Association on Children Under Six has developed plans for influencing public policy as it affects children and families and has created mechanisms which professionals can use in educating the public to the value of early childhood education. In addition, research and development groups such as the High/Scope Research Foundation and the Bush Center on Public Policy and Child Development function in support capacities for agencies and individuals working toward improved early childhood education programs. These initial public policy efforts on behalf of children and families have proven successful and need to be expanded to include the development of training programs for potential teacher-advocates.

Research designs which focus on longitudinal and ecological assessment of early childhood program efforts will provide a system for assuring continual refinement of teacher functioning, curriculum designs, and family support practices. Examples of recent research that have utilized this approach include the efforts of Bronfenbrenner (1979), White and Kaban (1979), Lazar (1976), and Goodlad (1984). Empirical studies of children's development and learning, parent-child interactions, instructional designs, and program assessments should provide substance to new early childhood projects over an extended period of development and refinement. A renewed commitment on the part of every citizen to strengthening families, improving the education and continuing development of teachers, and creating programs that are based on children's developmental needs are the primary tools for reaching excellence in early childhood education.

References

Bain, W. 1981. With life so long, why shorten childhood. *Childhood Education* 58:81–83.

Bloom, B. 1981. *All Our Children: A Primer for Parents, Teachers, and other Educators*. New York: McGraw-Hill.

Breedlove, C., and L. Schweinhart. 1982. *The Cost Effectiveness of High Quality Early Childhood Programs*. Ypsilanti, Mich.: High/Scope Educational Research Foundation.

Bronfenbrenner, U. 1979. *The Ecology of Human Development*. Cambridge, Mass.: Harvard University Press.

Brown, M., and K. Swick. 1979. The neighborhood as a support system for children and families. *The Clearing House* 54:350–354.

Caldwell, B. 1984. What is quality child care? *Young Children* 39:3–8.

CAP 5. 1983. Progress report on the center accreditation project. *Young Children* 38:35–46.

Charlotte Career Development Center. 1983. *Teacher Career Development Plan Fact Sheet.* Charlotte, N.C.: Charlotte-Mecklenburg School District.

Davis, M. 1982. The preparation of administrators, teachers, and caregivers. In M. Dickerson, M. Davis, and G. Rose, eds., *Young Children: Issues for the 80s.* Little Rock, Ark.: Southern Association on Children Under Six.

Dickerson, M. 1984. The status of church-related day care licensing exemption in the southern states—What can advocates do? *Dimensions* 12:12–26.

Elkind, D. 1981. *The Hurried Child: Growing Up Too Fast, Too Soon.* Reading, Mass.: Addison-Wesley.

Elkind, D. 1984. *All Grown Up and No Place to Go: Teenagers in Crisis.* Reading, Mass.: Addison-Wesley.

Erikson, E. 1982. *The Life Cycle Completed: A Review.* New York: W. W. Norton.

Gideonse, H. 1982. The necessary revolution in teacher education. *Phi Delta Kappan* 64:15–18.

Goodlad, J. 1983. A study of schooling: Some findings and hypotheses. *Phi Delta Kappan* 64:465–476.

Goodlad, J. 1984. *A Place Called School: Prospects for the Future.* New York: McGraw-Hill.

Gordon, I. 1975. *Research Report of Parent Oriented Home-Based Early Childhood Education Programs.* Gainesville, Fla.: Institute for Human Development, University of Florida.

Green, F. 1982. Child development: Young children in the 80s. In M. Dickerson, M. Davis, and G. Rose, eds., *Young Children: Issues for the 80s.* Little Rock, Ark.: Southern Association on Children Under Six.

Hanley, P., and K. Swick. 1983. *Teacher Renewal: Revitalization of Classroom Teachers.* Washington, D.C.: National Education Association.

Hart, L. 1983. *Human Brain and Human Learning.* New York: Longman.

Hetherington, M. 1979. Divorce: A child's perspective. *American Psychologist* 34:851–858.

Honig, A. 1983. Meeting the needs of infants. *Dimensions* 11:4–7.

Hymes, J. 1981. *Teaching the Child Under Six.* Columbus, Ohio: Charles E. Merrill.

Hymes, J. 1982. Young children: Past accomplishments, future priorities. In M. Dickerson, M. Davis, and G. Rose, eds., *Young Children: Issues for the 80s*. Little Rock, Ark.: Southern Association on Children Under Six.

Irvine, D. 1979. *Parent Involvement Affects Children's Cognitive Growth*. Albany, N.Y.: State Department of Education, Division of Research.

Kamii, C. 1984. Autonomy: The aim of education envisioned by Piaget. *Phi Delta Kappan* 65:410–415.

Katz, L. 1977. *Talks with Teachers*. Washington, D.C.: National Association for the Education of Young Children.

Klaus, M., and M. Robertson. 1982. *Birth, Interaction, and Attachment*. Skillman, N.J.: Johnson and Johnson Roundtable Books.

Kempe, C., and R. Kempe. 1978. *Child Abuse*. Cambridge, Mass.: Harvard University Press.

Keniston, K. 1978. *All Our Children: The American Family Under Pressure*. New York: Harcourt, Brace, Jovanovich.

Lazar, I. 1976. *The Persistence of Preschool Effects: A Summary Report*. Washington, D.C.: U. S. Government Printing Office.

Lazar, I., V. Hubbell, H. Murray, M. Rosche, and J. Royce. 1977. *The Persistence of Preschool Effects*. Washington, D.C.: Department of Health and Human Services.

Manning, M., and G. Manning. 1981. The school's assault on childhood. *Childhood Education* 58:84–87.

Maslow, A. 1959. *New Knowledge in Human Values*. New York: Harper & Brothers.

Masnick, G., and M. Bane. 1980. *The Nation's Families: 1960–1990*. Cambridge, Mass.: Joint Center for Urban Studies of MIT and Harvard.

Nevius, J., and A. Filgo. 1980. Effective parenting: What can it teach the teachers? *Dimensions* 8:110–115.

Osborn, K. 1980. *Early Childhood Education in Historical Perspective*. Athens, Ga.: Education Associates.

Osborn, K., and J. Osborn. 1981. *Discipline and Classroom Management*. Athens, Ga.: Education Associates.

Osborn, K., and J. Osborn. 1983. *Cognition in Early Childhood*. Athens, Ga.: Education Associates.

Piaget, J., and B. Inhelder. 1969. *The Psychology of the Child*. New York: Basic Books.

Perrone, V. 1981. Testing, testing, and more testing. *Childhood Education* 58:76–80.

Postman, N. 1981. Disappearing childhood. *Childhood Education* 58:66–68.

Sasserath, V. 1983. *Minimizing High Risk Parenting*. Skillman, N.J.: Johnson and Johnson Roundtable Books.

Schaefer, E. 1983. Parent-professional interaction: Research, parental, professional, and policy perspectives. Chapel Hill, N.C.: University of North Carolina. Mimeographed paper.

Stern, D. 1977. *The First Relationship: Infant and Mother*. Cambridge, Mass.: Harvard University Press.

Stinnett, N. 1980. *Family Strengths: Positive Models for Family Life*. Lincoln, Nebr.: University of Nebraska Press.

Swick, K. 1982. Parent education: Focus on parents' needs and responsibilities. *Dimensions* 10:9–12.

Swick, K. 1984. *Inviting Parents into the Young Child's World*. Champaign, Ill.: Stipes Publishing.

Swick, K., M. Brown, and S. Graves. 1984. *Appropriate Educational Experiences for Kindergarten*. Little Rock, Ark.: Southern Association on Children Under Six.

Swick, K., M. Brown, and S. Robinson. 1983. *Toward Quality Environments for Young Children*. Champaign, Ill.: Stipes Publishing.

Swick, K., and E. Duff. 1979. *Parenting: What Research Says to the Teacher*. Washington, D.C.: National Education Association.

Swick, K., and E. Duff. 1982. *Involving Children in Parenting/Caring Experiences*. Dubuque, Iowa: Kendall-Hunt.

Swick, K., and P. Hanley. 1980. State leadership in early childhood education: A 1980 status report. *The University of South Carolina Education Report* 23:1–4.

Swick, K., and P. Kierce. 1981. Early childhood education in the 1980s. *The University of South Carolina Education Report* 24:1–3.

Swick, K., M. Rowls, and T. Kuhs. 1984. Educating teachers for today and tomorrow. *The Palmetto Principal* 1:28–30.

Thornburg, K. 1982. Services for strengthening families. In M. Dickerson, M. Davis, and G. Rose, eds., *Young Children: Issues for the 80s*. Little Rock, Ark.: Southern Association on Children Under Six.

Watson, T., M. Brown, and K. Swick. 1983. The relationship of parents' support to children's school achievement. *Child Welfare* 62:175–180.

Weber, L. 1982. Education: Issues for the 80s. In M. Dickerson, M. Davis, and G. Rose, eds., *Young Children: Issues for the 80s*. Little Rock, Ark.: Southern Association on Children Under Six.

White, B. 1980. *A Parent's Guide to the First Three Years*. Englewood Cliffs, N.J.: Prentice-Hall.

White, B. 1981. The education of preschool children. Paper presented at the Infant Education Institute, Atlanta, Ga., February 16.

White, B., and B. Kaban. 1979. *The Origins of Human Competence*. Lexington, Mass.: Lexington Books.

The Teacher

C. Emily Feistritzer

Attracting and retaining quality people into the field of teaching is one of the most serious problems facing American education today. For the past couple of decades we, as a nation, have not paid very much attention to what was happening with the teaching occupation. There seemed to be no particular need to examine the status of the profession or the quality of those going into it. In large measure, we had been lulled into a feeling of security about the people, mostly women, who were staffing our children's classrooms. Because women had for so many decades headed for the classroom as naturally as a duck seeking water, no one paid very much attention when changes began to occur. Yet abruptly women, who historically have constituted 70 percent of the teaching force, began choosing to do other things. Now more women than men are going to college, and the best and the brightest of them are getting degrees in fields other than teaching. For example, in 1982 women received one-third of all law degrees conferred, compared with only 3 percent in 1965. They were awarded one-fourth of the medical degrees in that year, as compared with 6 percent in the mid-sixties, and 15 percent of new dental degrees went to women in 1982, compared with 1 percent in the earlier period (Feistritzer, 1984).

While there has been a lot of publicity, largely positive, about the changed and broadened career aspirations of America's most academically able young women, until recently little thought or publicity was given to what was happening in those fields that these same women might otherwise have been entering. And teaching without question headed the list of occupational areas losing out on a talented and committed pool of bright, dedicated workers.

That the situation was ignored, however, is not surprising. We were not facing a shortage of classroom teachers. In fact, as the birth rate and subsequently school enrollments declined, college students and recent graduates heard the news that teaching jobs were hard to find. Not only was there no teacher shortage, but there was actually a teacher surplus. And even those who had successfully completed teacher training programs were often hard-pressed to find full-time employment.

But in the 1980s, all that is beginning to change. For a number of reasons, the demand for teachers is expected to far exceed supply in the immediate future. The Department of Education's National Center for Education Statistics (NCES, 1984) projects that the demand for additional teachers in the fall of 1985 will be 157,000, while the supply of new teacher graduates will be 146,000—93 percent of demand.

In addition, NCES data reveal that the gap between demand for additional teachers and the supply of new teacher graduates will continue to widen throughout the decade unless current trends are reversed. By 1992, the center estimates, the supply of new teacher graduates will meet only two-thirds of demand, with 137,000 new teacher graduates available to fill an anticipated 209,000 classroom positions. And these are optimistic predictions!

An analysis of survey data collected from institutions of higher education in the spring of 1984 shows that supply could be as low as one-half of demand as early as 1986. The National Center for Education Information (NCEI) surveyed every college in this nation purported to have a teacher education program (Feistritzer, 1984). Eighty-two percent (179 out of 217) of the institutions enrolling more than ten thousand students responded to the survey. While these colleges and universities constitute only 17 percent of the total number of schools now training teachers, they produce over one-half (53 percent) of this nation's classroom teachers.

The NCEI survey found that in the last decade the number of persons newly admitted into teacher preparation programs plummeted by 44 percent—from 195,000 in the fall of 1973 to 110,000 in the fall of 1983. At the same time, these data also show that an average 80 percent of the students who begin a teacher education program complete it. Thus, using this 80 percent completion rate as a guideline, the class of students who entered teacher education programs last fall will graduate only 88,000 teachers. To darken the picture even further, NCES (1984) data reveal that only 80 percent of those who actually graduate go on to teach. Simultaneously, NCES projects that we will need 170,000 new teachers in 1986. This demand projection is based on three assumptions: total school enrollment will rise, teacher-pupil ratios will improve only slightly, and the turnover of teachers will remain constant at an estimated 6 percent annually.

The first two assumptions seem to be valid. However, some experts believe that the turnover rate for teachers will be greater than 6 percent in the coming years because of an increase in the retirement rate and stepped-up pressures to terminate incompetent teachers.

The National Education Association (1983) reports that retirements have produced a 2 to 3 percent annual attrition rate from teaching for the past fifteen years. However, the current teaching force is aging; the average age of a classroom teacher today is forty-one. Further, the 1983 NEA Teacher Opinion Poll revealed some startling statistics about the current teaching force: 26 percent of teachers today have been teaching for twenty years or more; those who entered teaching in the last five years represent only 8 percent of the profession; in the decade between 1963 and 1973 the proportion of all teachers having ten years or more teaching experience declined from 51 to 44 percent, while in 1983 the percentage of teachers who had been in a classroom for longer than ten years was up to 69 percent. Clearly, the time is long past due for the American public, and particularly the education establishment, to take a good hard look at how we will go about recruiting new teachers and who we will be recruiting.

Unfortunately, the problem facing the nation today is not merely one of finding more bodies to fill present and projected job vacancies. It is essentially a question of who will be selected to train and educate the millions of young people we can expect to be born in this country during the next two decades. To whom shall we entrust the responsibility of teaching the coming generations of Americans?

If the current data are meaningful, we shall quickly have to do something drastic to upgrade the quality of people currently being drawn into teaching. Even though teaching has never attracted *the* best and brightest, the gap between the academic caliber (using college entrance aptitude test scores) of those choosing teaching today and those entering almost every other field is widening dramatically. This is true both nationally and in individual states. The average Scholastic Aptitude Test (SAT) score for students indicating education as a major field fell from 59 points below the national average in 1973 to 81 points below the national average in 1983, while the average SAT score itself fell from 926 in 1973 to 849 in 1983.

Even 1984 SAT data, which reversed an eight-year decline in the scores of prospective education majors, do not provide us with much about which to be heartened. The group's average score of 823 still lagged a dismal 74 points behind the national average score achieved by all other college-bound students, and education majors outperformed only those who intended to major in vocational education, home economics, and ethnic studies. Former Education Secretary Terrel H. Bell has termed the group's performance "tragic."

In addition to providing such SAT data, NCES's National Longitudinal Study of 1972 (1974) and its High School and Beyond Study (1981) showed that college aspirants who intended to major in education scored lower on standardized vocabulary, reading, and mathematics achievement tests than other college-bound seniors. The prospective education majors also averaged lower high school grades and had fewer courses in science and mathematics than students intending other majors. None of this seems to matter, however, to those institutions currently involved in the training of teachers.

Nowhere in American teacher education is there greater diversity than in admissions requirements and procedures for entering a teacher preparation program. Data gathered by NCEI (Feistritzer, 1984) during the summer of 1984 indicate that some institutions require a minimum SAT or American College Test (ACT) score; others do not even look at these scores. Some colleges and universities require passing one or more tests measuring basic skills, content, or proficiency; others do not. Some require prior work experience with students; some want recommendations, and others use interviews to decide who gets into a teacher preparation program in their institutions. And many colleges and universities preparing elementary and secondary classroom teachers only require that the student be accepted by the admissions office of the college or university.

In short, not many institutions of higher education have well-defined, much less rigorous, standards for admission into their teacher education programs. And while over three-fourths of the in-

Table 1. PERCENTAGE OF INSTITUTIONS THAT USE
THE FOLLOWING CRITERIA FOR ADMISSION
INTO TEACHER EDUCATION: 1984

Type IHE	High School Class Rank	H.S. GPA	SAT Score	ACT Score	College GPA	Recommendations	Interviews	Experience with Children
Total	9	10	18	17	78	65	52	39
Public	9	7	19	21	81	57	46	40
Private	9	12	17	14	76	71	57	38
<1K	9	5	9	13	77	77	67	45
1–5K	7	9	16	15	76	70	54	41
5–10K	11	9	19	21	79	58	46	32
10K+	18	16	27	22	81	50	42	36

SOURCE: Feistritzer, C. Emily, *The Making of a Teacher*, August 1984

stitutions responding to the NCEI survey did say they considered college grade point averages (GPAs) to determine who gets into their program, the average college GPA required among the 543 institutions providing these data was 2.29 on a 4.0 scale—about a "C" average.

It should come as little surprise that rarely does anyone who seeks admission into a teacher education program get rejected. Private institutions and those with smaller enrollments have higher acceptance rates than public colleges and universities and those with enrollments over five thousand students. Of those institutions which responded to an NCEI survey question asking, "What percent of those who apply are accepted in your teacher preparation program?" 78 percent said between 75 and 100 percent, and an additional 17 percent reported between 50 and 75 percent.

Not only is it relatively difficult to be rejected by a teacher education program, but the prospective candidate does not have to be too far along in college before he or she is admitted. The largest proportion of colleges and universities accept students into teacher education programs during the sophomore year—48 percent for prospective elementary teachers, compared with 44 percent for students aspiring to teach at the secondary level and 40 percent training to teach in areas of special education.

Only twenty universities responding to the NCEI survey (3 percent) reported that they admit students into both elementary and secondary teacher preparation after they have completed undergraduate work. Interestingly, seventy-seven institutions (16 percent) said they formally admit students training to be special education teachers at the graduate level, while 22 percent of the NCEI respondents in the over-ten-thousand category reported accepting prospective special education teachers after they have received an undergraduate degree. Accepting students into a professional teacher education school or program only after they have completed undergraduate work has not seemed to hurt the special education field, since the number of new graduates in special education increased in the last decade while the total number of new teacher graduates dramatically decreased. This is particularly noteworthy in light of cur-

Table 2. PERCENTAGES OF INSTITUTIONS THAT ADMIT
TEACHER EDUCATION STUDENTS IN GIVEN YEAR
OF COLLEGE, BY CONTROL OF INSTITUTION AND
ENROLLMENT SIZE: 1983

ELEMENTARY

Type IHE	Freshman	Sophomore	Junior	Senior	Graduate
Total	15	48	33	2	3
Public	11	40	43	3	3
Private	18	54	24	<1	3
<1K	17	59	24	0	2
1–5K	10	54	33	2	2
5–10K	20	42	35	0	2
10K+	19	32	39	3	6

SECONDARY

Type IHE	Freshman	Sophomore	Junior	Senior	Graduate
Total	12	44	39	1	3
Public	8	40	45	3	3
Private	16	47	34	1	2
<1K	14	54	32	0	<1
1–5K	10	49	39	2	2
5–10K	16	41	40	1	2
10K+	15	29	46	3	6

SPECIAL EDUCATION

Type IHE	Freshman	Sophomore	Junior	Senior	Graduate
Total	12	40	30	2	16
Public	9	35	37	2	17
Private	16	46	22	1	15
<1K	5	62	22	2	10
1–5K	10	45	30	1	14
5–10K	14	40	30	0	16
10K+	16	26	34	3	22

SOURCE: The National Center for Education Information, Washington, D.C.,
Teacher Education Survey, 1984.

rent discussions about steps that need to be taken to make teaching more of a profession.

If it is easy to get into a teacher education program in this country—and it appears that anyone determined to enter teaching need only find one of many colleges that will accept evidence of a high school diploma and a check for tuition as entry requirements— it is not very difficult to exit the program either. NCEI found that fewer than half of the institutions surveyed—47 percent—administer any kind of test upon completion of their programs, and only 5 percent demand that graduates pass a test in the content area they will teach.

In forty-nine of the fifty states and in the District of Columbia, the primary criterion for certification is completion of an approved teacher education program—one standard that can be met by virtually anyone whose mind is set to it. That these "approved programs" fail to attract the quality people Americans would like to see in the classroom is becoming increasingly clear since some states have begun requiring minimum competency tests for their prospective teachers.

The data concerning these tests are grim, to say the least. For example, only 68 percent of those seeking credentials to teach in California (1984) passed the state's competency test last May; in fact, on all seven administrations of the test only about 68 percent passed. Stated another way, over 30 percent of all students who completed a teacher preparation program in California have been found wanting in at least one of the basic competencies measured by the examination.

Other states' rates for their own basic skills tests are: Florida, 85 percent (blacks, 38 percent; whites, 92 percent); Alabama, 81 percent; and Georgia, 86 percent. Arkansas, pilot testing its recently enacted examination program, found that 47 percent of its black teachers and 3 percent of the whites would have failed to meet the cutoff point. And in Louisiana, where there are currently acute shortages of math and science teachers, the State Superintendent of Education, Thomas G. Calusen, has come out in favor of lowering the passing scores on several of the state's teacher certification tests.

His plan, which has encountered some stiff opposition, calls for lowering the passing grade in mathematics from the 68th percentile to the 39th percentile—clearly not a move to attract more competent and talented individuals into teaching (Feistritzer, 1983).

A host of other indicators point to a crisis in teaching that centers largely on the caliber of the people that this calling can hope to attract in the near future:

- A poll by the NEA (1983) in which 46 percent of the teachers questioned said they either certainly or probably would not become teachers if they had it to do over again. This compares with 11 percent twenty years earlier and 12 percent a decade ago.
- The finding in the 1983 Gallup Poll of the Public's Attitude Toward the Public Schools that only 45 percent of the respondents would like to have a child of theirs take up teaching as a career—down from 75 percent in 1968. In 1983, one-third of the respondents said a definitive "no" to the question, compared to 15 percent in 1968.
- The finding that salaries of teachers are generally low and have dropped significantly in purchasing power in the last decade. While per-pupil expenditures increased 22.5 percent in real dollars since 1972, per capita income by 6.5 percent, and total personal income by 17.8 percent, the average salary of a classroom teacher dropped by 12.2 percent (Feistritzer, 1983).

What does all of this mean? In short, the teaching profession needs to attract—and to keep—competent and dedicated professionals to meet an anticipated significant shortage of classroom teachers. It needs to do this at a time when available data clearly show that the calling is not attracting the most qualified people into institutions that do little and sometimes no screening and which in over 50 percent of the cases administer no exit examination of any type.

It is little wonder that the states—at least some of them—are looking for new and innovative ways to attract talented, academically capable teachers. Two leading examples of these efforts are New Jersey and Florida, both of which are side-stepping the traditional route to teacher certification in an effort to attract college graduates who for whatever reasons do not want to have take "all those education courses." The programs require that prospective teachers receive classroom training, but that they receive it essentially outside of the system. The rationale is that the persons drawn to the alternative program will be those who have spent years in other careers, who know their subject matter thoroughly and would really like to teach, but who do not want to have to complete many requirements to do so. Advocates of certifying such persons argue that they can learn pedagogical skills and the essentials of teaching methodology without having to go back to college for education courses. The question, however, when examining alternative routes to certification, should not be what can we do "instead of" offering traditional education courses, but rather, "What should every classroom teacher know and be able to do, and how can they best be taught?"

Circumventing college education courses entirely is not the answer to attracting the best people into teaching. There is a body of knowledge which every classroom teacher should have and which is probably best learned in an academic setting. Indeed, most state-approved teacher education programs require that prospective elementary teachers take anywhere from 20 to 50 percent of their college bachelor's degree work in general education, and persons aspiring to teach in secondary schools are required to have 25 to 45 percent of their coursework in education. Colleges and universities are insisting their teacher candidates have, on the average, five more semester hours of clinical experience (student teaching/practicum, classroom observation) than were required in 1973, and they are demanding students take an additional four semester hours of education courses.

Even when competent students choose and complete teacher training, they can become discouraged—sometimes enough to leave the profession. A recent study (Darling-Hammond, 1984) focusing

Table 3. AVERAGE NUMBER COLLEGE SEMESTER HOURS
REQUIRED TO COMPLETE THE TEACHER
EDUCATION PROGRAM BY FIELD OF STUDY

Field of Study	AY 1983			AY 1973		
	Elem.	Sec.	Sp. Ed.	Elem.	Sec.	Sp. Ed.
General Studies	62	64	55	62	59	51
Professional Studies	36	25	38	32	22	34
Clinical Experience	17	15	19	12	10	14
TOTAL	115	104	112	106	91	99

Definitions: *Elementary* includes general elementary, early
childhood, preschool, and/or kindergarten.
Secondary includes all subject specialties in
junior or senior high or middle school.
Exclude—physical, fine arts, occupational/
vocational education and support personnel.

General Studies—include liberal arts courses;
exclude SCDE courses.
Professional Studies—include SCDE courses;
exclude student teaching/practicum.
Clinical Experience—include student teach-
ing/practicum, classroom observation.

on how teachers view their work environment revealed that those
considered the most highly qualified (i.e., teachers holding a bachelor's or master's degree in their academic discipline in addition to a
teaching certificate) are most dissatisfied with their work. They generally cite lack of administrative support, bureaucratic interference,
too little autonomy, and salaries and other working conditions as
the leading causes of dissatisfaction. And, with the exception of the
area of "too little autonomy," academic majors cite these difficulties
more often than do their education major counterparts.

Of course, it is precisely these well-educated—and at present
thoroughly dissatisfied—individuals that educators and the public
wish to keep in the classroom, and it is these same people who are
most likely to flee to other, more rewarding professions. A study of
attrition (Schlecty and Vance, 1981) among white females entering

teaching in North Carolina in 1973 found that over a seven-year period those women who had scored near the top of the National Teachers Examination were more likely to leave the classroom than those who had scored near the bottom. By 1980, only one-third of the women in the bottom tenth had left, while nearly two-thirds of those in the top had given up teaching as a career.

There is little disagreement, even among teacher educators and organizations representing classroom teachers, that there is a crisis in the classroom and that public concern is increasingly focused upon the quality of those people who are teaching future generations of Americans. However, there seems to be substantial disagreement on how to remedy the situation. What should be done to attract and retain high-caliber, competent individuals to an occupation that has been viewed for too long and by too many as a thankless, low-status job that drains one both emotionally and intellectually while returning little in the way of monetary compensation and, in many cases, much less in the way of personal fulfillment?

Before almost any other step can be taken, those involved in making and shaping the policies that govern how teachers are educated, certified, and ultimately rewarded must make a determined and unified effort to raise teaching to the ranks of a true profession. Teachers like to refer to themselves as professionals, and at one time that designation may have been apt. For some time now, however, teaching has been more an occupation than a profession, and it has never taken to itself those trappings which we have come to identify with such professions as medicine, law, accounting, and the like.

For teaching to become a true profession, it must adopt standards of excellence and set up uniform, effective criteria for selecting, training, certifying, and ultimately placing those who are genuinely qualified to teach. We already know how to do this—existing research has uncovered clear guidelines for effective teaching—but we must recognize that we have reached the point where firm action is necessary. What teaching needs and presently lacks are rites of passage, clearly defined criteria that must be met and steps that must be taken before an individual can embark upon a career in the classroom.

When NCEI conducted its 1984 survey, it not only contacted institutions of higher education that train teachers and state departments of education that certify them, but it also checked with associations that represent other professions—law, medicine, accounting, and nursing—to see how those fields compared with teaching. All of these professions, except teaching, require the passage of a proficiency examination before one can be licensed to practice. Save for nursing, all of them are considerably more selective than teaching about who actually gets into the profession. With regard to salaries, the other occupations have a wide range from starting to peak salary. They also have ranges in each salary category determined not only by education and experience but also by competence. The other occupations, including nursing, have entry grades or levels tied to the salary structure. For example, a lawyer can start out as a clerk or higher, depending on proficiency. A nurse can begin as a licensed practical nurse (LPN) or a registered nurse (RN) with or without a bachelor's degree. Functions and pay are determined by level of education and experience. Career ladders are based not only on education and experience but also on professional competence.

To illustrate more specifically the gap separating teaching from other professions, one need only examine what occurs within the medical profession when an individual seeks the right to care for the physical well-being of other human beings. A fall 1984 study, *Physicians for the Twenty-First Century*, prepared by the Association of American Medical Colleges (AAMC) Panel on the General Professional Education of the Physician and College Preparation for Medicine, reveals many highly significant differences in the ways we go about recruiting and training doctors and the ways we recruit and train our teachers.

For one thing, 127 medical schools in the U.S. produce about 66,000 doctors a year. That is 126 graduates per school, compared with 105 graduates per institution preparing teachers (1,287 schools turned out 135,000 teacher education graduates in 1984).

The 127 medical schools are highly selective about entering students. In 1983, of the 35,200 people who tried to get into medical school only 47 percent were accepted. Almost all medical schools, moreover, require that students planning to apply take the Medical College Admission Test (MCAT), a nationally recognized standardized examination. According the AAMC, "all medical schools maintain high standards necessary for accreditation by the Liaison Committee. Most have essentially the same basic undergraduate course requirements, and all seek to admit students with strong intellectual abilities and personal and social maturity." Medical schools consider not only grades and test scores but also such factors as personality, character, letters of evaluation, stringency of course work, and interview impressions.

Compare this now with the criteria needed to enter the teaching profession. As already noted, many of the institutions which train our teachers are less than selective about those they admit. They require no special test on par with the MCAT for admission, and they rarely look at SAT scores which, in any event, fall far below those of other college-oriented young people. In fact, NCEI found that the single most-often-used criterion for admission to a teacher education program was the college GPA, and that average was acceptable at the "C" level. Thus, one can conclude with a great degree of safety that few if any prospective teachers will ever be denied admission *everywhere* to a teacher education program, while there are a large number of prospective doctors—53 percent in 1983 alone—who fail to be accepted by this nation's medical schools.

In responding to these data, one might counter that doctors hold literal life and death authority over the people for whom they care, while teachers of course do not. But conversely, teachers are the individuals to whom we entrust our children from the time they are six years or younger, and we expect them to prepare future generations of literate, articulate individuals who will be capable of filling every role in our society, from president to physician to electrician and, yes, even to the next generation of teachers.

To sharply upgrade the status of teaching and attempt to bring it on a par with other professions, we should begin by defining what teaching is, or ought to be, in the United States. From that will flow the accoutrements of a genuine profession, which certainly will include assessments before, during, and after academic training. If teaching were to meet the criteria of other high-paying, prestigious professions, it would be far easier to lobby for higher salaries for its membership.

A number of steps in this direction can and must be taken. Uniform and rigorous standards for entry into teaching need to be established, standards similar to those required for entry into medicine, law, and the like. We cannot and will not achieve this end as long as there are teacher training institutions which will admit virtually anyone and everyone. These institutions, which are in every instance under the control of the states in which they are located, should be identified and summarily shut down. There must be no institutions deserving of the label "teacher mill." Neither this nation nor any state would continue to accredit, fund, or otherwise support a school of law or medicine that consistently turned out grossly incompetent doctors or lawyers who, upon graduation, could not pass a basic skills test designed to measure the most elementary competencies that they needed for their careers. Why should we, and do we, continue to close our eyes to teacher training institutions who graduate such individuals? And even worse—as is being considered in Louisiana—why do we consider lowering passing grades on basic skills tests to allow even less competent individuals into the classroom?

Along with moving to eliminate the "teacher mills," these same states should set about identifying those institutions which are doing the best jobs of training teachers. These are the schools whose teacher preparation programs have standards of excellence for screening teacher candidates. They have programs based on the most current research of effective teaching and learning and provide valuable clinical experiences. They also have well-defined exit criteria.

Identifying the best teacher education programs would allow prospective teachers to know where to find the highest quality program. Only these institutions should be qualified to participate in the federal government's scholarship program for academically able students who wish to become teachers.

Having identified the best institutions and having insured as well as possible that these schools are recruiting the most talented candidates and offering them the best available education, the next step is to put an end to the drastic proliferation of teaching certificates which are offered within and among the fifty states. At a time when we are in desperate need of a streamlined certification process and national standards for certifying teachers, we are confronted with certification processes and criteria that are so convoluted they virtually defy description.

Each state currently makes its own rules concerning who can be certified and what they can be certified to teach, and the requirements from state to state make virtually no sense (Feistritzer, 1984). A person certified to teach U.S. government in one state would not be certified to teach American history in that state, but the same teacher could not only teach American history in another state but political science as well.

A person could meet all the requirements to teach every elementary grade in one state and only certain grades in another state. Some states hand out broad certificates that allow an individual to teach several different grades and subjects, while other states give certificates that are specific about what subjects and grades may be taught. In addition, most states give emergency credentials that permit people to teach who do not meet the requirements. Only two states, Vermont and Virginia, fail to issue some type of emergency or substandard credential to people who have less than a bachelor's degree. At this writing, only eighteen states require passage of any type standard credential to people who have less than a bachelor's degree. At this writing, only eighteen states require passage of any type of paper-pencil test for certification, and while thirty are currently planning to introduce such a test sometime within the next three years, it took an almost unprecedented wave of educational reform to move states in this direction. Finally, only seven states currently require an on-the-job post-college internship of any kind before fully certifying a prospective teacher.

Compare this with the road still faced by prospective doctors, lawyers, accountants, and other "true professionals" for whom completion of their formal schooling is followed by internships, formidable state and/or national tests, and entry into their field at a relatively low level. We would not think of naming a newly minted doctor as chief of surgery at a major medical center, but we think little or nothing of sending a newly minted teacher to preside over a classroom of twenty-five or thirty students—and then bark at him or her for failure to complete a variety of bureaucratic forms on time or in the proper manner.

Given this long-established road to becoming a full-fledged classroom teacher, it is not surprising that we hear reports of teacher incompetence and that we are greeted with studies on how to deal with it among tenured teachers. Just how overdue these studies are is reflected in surveys (Bridges and Groves, 1984) conducted by the American Association of School Administrators, which indicate that as far back as 1974, teacher incompetence ranked as the school administrator's "third most serious administrative problem." And the numbers of incompetent teachers may well be expected to grow, if changes are not implemented which will not only upgrade the quality of our teaching force but sharply improve the conditions within the profession.

In teaching, as in all other areas of endeavor, performance should be a primary criterion of evaluation, and when performance is good, it should be rewarded. The opposite side of that coin is when performance is poor, the teacher should be removed from the job if he or she is unable to make the needed improvements. Unfortunately, this is not the case.

The dismissal of a tenured teacher for incompetence appears to be one of the rarest events that can occur within a school system, although it is beginning to occur with greater frequency. Recently, an "exhaustive study of court cases" centering on the firings of incompetent teachers came up with only eighty-six court cases in the forty-three-year period from 1939 to 1982 for all the United States. It was found, however, that there were more such cases in the three-year period from 1980 to 1982 than in the thirty-year period from 1940 to 1969 (Bridges and Gumport, 1984).

These figures are staggering enough simply for what they say about the significant percentage of incompetent teachers remaining

Table 4. CREDENTIALS OF TEACHERS IN CLASSROOMS: 1983–84

States	Total Cert. In '83	No. Teachers In 1983–1984	No. Teachers On Emerg. Credential	% Teachers With No Credential	Estimated % Teachers Given Cert. In 1983–1984	Estimated % Teachers On Emerg. Credential
Alabama	5,862	39,200	141	0	15%	0.40
Alaska	NA	6,387	7	0	NA	0.10
Arizona	9,520	25,662	NA	0	37	NA
Arkansas	2,383	23,897	6	.0004	10	0.03
California	7,500	170,435	5,738	0	4	3.40
Colorado	8,000	29,447	1,631	0	27	5.50
Connecticut	3,974	32,715	59	0	12	0.20
Delaware	NA	5,436	294	0	NA	5.40
D.C.	2,075	5,648	<1%	0	37	<1.00
Florida	5,777	83,074	10,000	.0001	7	12.00
Georgia	4,976	56,270	9,900	.0001	9	17.60
Hawaii	286	8,073	65	0	4	0.80
Idaho	NA	9,900	21	0	NA	0.20
Illinois	10,192	101,056	NA	0	10	NA
Indiana		49,456	612	NA		1.20
Iowa	NA	30,686	400	0	NA	1.30
Kansas	4,187	25,802	NA	1	16	NA
Kentucky		32,000	15	0		0.05
Louisiana	2,195	41,620	421	16	5	1.00
Maine	1,000	12,273	300	0	8	2.40
Maryland	NA	37,437	250	0	NA	0.70
Massachusetts	NA	48,267	125	2	NA	0.30
Michigan	6,000	72,955	100	0	8	0.10
Minnesota	NA	38,554	92	0	NA	0.20
Mississippi	2,250	24,864	1,031	0	9	4.10

Table 4 (*continued*)

States	Total Cert. In '83	No. Teachers In 1983–1984	No. Teachers On Emerg. Credential	% Teachers With No Credential	Estimated % Teachers Given Cert. In 1983–1984	Estimated % Teachers On Emerg. Credential
Missouri	6,500	46,714	2,200	0	14	4.70
Montana	NA	9,350	1,500	10	NA	16.00
Nebraska	2,412	16,785	728	0	14	4.30
Nevada	3,000	7,293	5%	0	41	5.00
New Hampshire	1,687	9,718	130	<1	17	1.30
New Jersey	10,500	73,262	2,000	1	14	2.70
New Mexico	NA	15,530	800	0	NA	5.20
New York	NA	164,000	5,000	1	NA	3.00
No. Carolina	6,400	54,709	10	0	12	0.02
No. Dakota	700	7,385	8	0	10	0.10
Ohio	9,800	92,765	3,733	0	11	4.00
Oklahoma	1,982	35,693	600	0	6	1.70
Oregon	2,700	23,990	200	0	11	0.80
Pennsylvania	9,800	102,150	1,900	0	10	1.90
Rhode Island	NA	7,441	17	0	NA	0.20
So. Carolina	3,172	32,070	1,252	0	10	3.90
So. Dakota	1,328	7,989	100	0	17	1.30
Tennessee	5,500	39,136	NA	0	14	NA
Texas	9,830	171,096	4,330	0	6	2.50
Utah	2,423	15,433	152	0	16	1.00
Vermont	675	6,235	11	NA	11	0.20
Virginia	NA	56,154	0	0	NA	0.00
Washington	3,552	33,979	48	0	11	0.10
W. Virginia	4,102	22,417	3,000	0	18	13.40
Wisconsin	NA	47,600	1,100	0	NA	2.30
Wyoming	300	7,059	0	0	4	0.00

SOURCE: The National Center for Education Information, Washington, D.C., *Teacher Certification Survey*, 1984.

in our schools. They assume an even greater significance when one considers that thousands of incompetent teachers are working side by side with the hard-working, dedicated classroom professionals who receive the same salaries and suffer the same daily frustrations as their less able counterparts. Is it any wonder that so many of our best teachers are leaving the classroom for other professions? That so few academically able students are choosing teaching as a career? That parents no longer take pride in a child's announcement that he or she wants to be a teacher? Perhaps the greatest puzzle of all is why so many able teachers opt to stay in the classroom when the promise of reward is so small.

Former Education Secretary Terrel H. Bell declared repeatedly that the single most important step we must take to attract more talented individuals into the classroom (and to retain those already there) is to raise salaries for classroom teachers. He has termed the current "single salary schedule" that rewards the teacher-of-the-year candidate and the most incompetent instructor in identical ways as archaic and "antediluvian." While I do not view salary restructuring as the lone answer to the current problems plaguing teachers, I do agree with Bell's concern over the current system of "equal pay for nonequal performance."

Unless school systems get serious and do so quickly about introducing pay plans tied to job performance, the hope of retaining highly qualified teachers will grow even dimmer. Both the National Education Association and the American Federation of Teachers have recently spoken in favor of evaluation procedures that would remove incompetent teachers from the classroom. One way to weed them out is by leaving them far behind their better-performing peers on payday.

There are a number of ways in which pay plans can achieve the desired effect. The Merit Pay Task Force Report of the House of Representatives' Committee on Education and Labor (1984) stated: "The performance gauged may be by the individual teacher, as individual classroom, or for meeting schoolwide or district-wide goals. For example, an individual teacher may meet the performance standard of increased reading ability in the classroom and receive merit pay. A school building of grades K–6 may see a multi-class increase in standardized scores for students, and all teachers in that building may be rewarded. A school district may set system-wide goals such as general levels of increased competency in reading and writing. Teachers fulfilling . . . goals would receive merit pay."

The Task Force Report also examined the question of career ladders, which might begin with a Provisional Teacher position earning an entry-level salary of $15,000 and peak with a Master Teacher ultimately earning $35,000 and receiving periodic inservice bonuses for continued performance. While the report goes on to note that these formulas will not always work in every school system and are not the total answer to problems within teaching, nevertheless they are ideas which seem essential to drawing in and retaining talented teachers who would ultimately feel pride in being members of a true profession. Higher salaries and a revised salary schedule are one link in a chain of reforms that must begin with the establishment of uniform and rigorous standards for entry into the profession. Until teaching improves its image—and improves it in a real rather than a cosmetic way—it will continue to be an occupational haven for our least accomplished college graduates, and it will encounter stiff public opposition to efforts to improve salaries substantially.

Teaching *is* a noble occupation. It is among the most important work in a society. Teachers directly influence the lives of nearly every individual in the community. It is imperative that they be held in esteem—legitimately. By raising its standards and raising them now, the teaching profession will make it easier to get taxpayers to pay higher salaries, and it will attract more people from among the best and brightest of our college graduates.

The time for reform is now.

References and Bibliography

Association of American Medical Colleges' Panel on the General Professional Education of the Physician and College Preparation for Medicine. 1984. *Physicians for the Twenty-First Century*.

Bridges, Edwin M., and Patricia Gumport. 1984. *The Dismissal of* the Tenured Teacher for Incompetence. Palo Alto: Stanford University School of Education.

Bridges, Edwin M., with Barry Graves. 1984. Managing the Incompetent Teacher. ERIC Clearinghouse on Educational Management and Institute for Research on Educational Finance and Governance.

California Commission on Teacher Credentialing. 1984. Memorandum on results of the March 1984 administration of the California Basic Educational Skills Test.

Darling-Hammond, Linda. 1984. Beyond the Commission Reports: The Coming Crisis in Teaching. Santa Monica: The Rand Corporation.

Feistritzer, C. Emily. 1983. The Condition of Teaching: A State-By-State Analysis. Princeton: The Carnegie Foundation for the Advancement of Teaching.

Feistritzer, C. Emily. 1984. The Making of a Teacher: A Report on Teacher Education and Certification. Washington, D.C.: National Center for Education Information.

National Center for Education Statistics. 1974. National Longitudinal Study of the High School Class of 1972.

National Center for Education Statistics. 1981. High School and Beyond: A National Longitudinal Study for the 1980s.

National Center for Education Statistics. 1984. The Condition of Education, 1984 Edition. Washington, D.C.: Government Printing Office.

National Education Association. 1983. Nationwide Teacher Opinion Poll, 1983.

Schlecty, Phillip C., and Victor S. Vance. 1981. Do academically talented teachers leave education? The North Carolina case. Phi Delta Kappan 63 (October): 106–112.

U.S. House of Representatives. 1984. Merit Pay Task Force Report, 1984.

Teacher Education

David G. Imig

American teacher education is in transformation. Its remaking is occurring as a result of the initiatives and interventions of academics and policymakers, of politicians and the public. Current school reform efforts add impetus to this movement, as do demographic changes, new funding commitments, research findings, societal expectations for schools, and new incentives to attract and retain quality teachers. The transformation of teacher education is likely to result in decidedly different structures, students, faculty, and curricula within a decade. Whatever the result, much energy and effort will be expended in achieving this transformation. It is difficult to set our sights on the eventual outcome when today we are locked in debate about teacher education. Contrasting perceptions predominate as policymakers and professional educators debate alternatives and consequences.

Gordon Allport, the noted social psychologist, describes perception as what a person experiences in contrast to what the physical world contains (Allport, 1954). Perception is an important concept because people often assign different meanings to common experiences. For teacher education, contrasting perceptions make it difficult to agree on either what we have or where we should be headed. The contrasting and often conflicting descriptions, analyses, studies, and research findings make it difficult to lay even a basis for the necessary transformation of teacher education.

There appear to be two different views. One perception is held by many public policymakers, representatives of the media, state officials, many academics, and some parents. The other is held by professional teacher educators, administrators of schools of education, some state certification officers, and a significant number of teachers and educational organization leaders. The former perception may be described as that held by the public at-large, while the latter is what may be described as the professional view of teacher education. The apparent inability of the public to perceive teacher education as professionals do, or conversely, for the professional community to fully understand the experiences that give meaning to the public's perception, creates tensions and can lead to bitterly contested public policymaking, often with unintended consequences.

The public perception of teacher education is of a relatively small, monolithic system, standardized in function and form, inadequately regulated, and uniformly low in quality. It views teacher education as largely separated from the real world of teachers and schools, dominated by certification procedures, based on the lore of pedagogy, and largely resistant to change. On the other hand, the professional perception is of a highly complex and expansive system of teacher education with little consensus on function, form, or purpose, dominated by experience and by professional interactions with cooperating teachers, uneven in quality and overregulated by the state and the university. Most of the professional community sees teacher education as based on a promising and rapidly expanding knowledge base of demonstrated practice, with both faculty and leaders committed to significant change and to the institutionalization of reforms to improve the quality of teacher education.

Why these separate views of the same phenomena? What causes the different perceptions? It is possible, I believe, to trace these perceptions to different concepts of teaching. For the public, teaching is the telling of a subject, whereas for professionals it has come to mean the interaction of learners and content in a social setting through the influence of a teacher. The significance of these different concepts and the influence they have on the way we view the need for reforms in education is important to understand.

For some time there has been an unceasing examination of education in America. Public interest groups have issued numerous studies, task force reports, and commission documents. These have ranged from the National Commission on Excellence in Education (NCEE, 1983) to the analyses by Adler (1982), Goodlad (1984), Boyer (1983), and Sizer (1984). These reports once again challenged many of the basic assumptions upon which schooling and teaching are based. They share a common theme: a) that time is a critical element and must be used more efficiently; b) that the school curriculum must be more tough-minded or rigorous, stressing the basic skills; c) that materials used in schooling must be more challenging; d) that adults, community leaders, and school boards must reassert their primacy in the schooling process; e) that the responsibility of various levels of government needs more careful attention; and f) that schools need to be more rule-directed places with the principal assuming greater responsibility for curriculum, discipline, instruction, and parental involvement.

The majority of the current two hundred reform reports emphasize the teacher as the critical element in achieving quality schools and raise fundamental questions about attracting more and better candidates into teaching, building adequate support systems for practicing teachers, differentiating among various members of the school staff, teaming teachers, restructuring school staffing, basing salaries on merit incentives, and certifying and recertifying teachers. In short, the reform reports have caused many to look seriously at the role and quality of teaching in America. In doing so, the public and the profession often view the need for reform and the ways to promote reform in contrasting ways.

As the public has focused attention on teacher education, five common reform strategies have been posited: a) increase the quality of the applicant pool, b) reduce the number of methods courses, c) increase subject matter content, d) increase the time prospective teachers spend in classrooms with real teachers, and e) add a series of exit or certification examinations. The gap between these reform measures and those proposed by the schools attests to the limited perceptions many in the public hold of teacher education, inspired by long-standing prejudices and "commonsense" notions.

As the public has formulated its recommendations, professionals have been vigorous in their own efforts to address quality issues by asking themselves key questions:

1) Should the practical or the theoretical, the technical or the reflective, thinking skills or learning styles be emphasized in preparation programs?
2) Can the discontinuities between the arts and sciences and teacher education be overcome?
3) How can convergent and divergent behavior be promoted in a classroom at one and the same time, and how can it be taught in preparation programs?
4) How can cognitive developmental theory be better incorporated into teacher training programs?
5) How can the existing knowledge base regarding effective teaching be used, and how can emphasis be given to the expansion of that knowledge base?

The enormous number of reform reports, commission and task force analyses, association resolutions, foundation programs, and governmental initiatives that have grown from the school reform efforts have buttressed one or the other of the contrasting views of teaching and teacher education. In marked contrast, while professionals have advocated far-reaching changes in structure and form— e.g., extended programs (deans) and field-based programs (teachers)—the public has supported a significant increase in subject matter content or the development of alternative routes to certification and the dispersal or abolishment of selected programs. Finding ways to reconcile these contrasting views becomes important for policymakers as they seek to ameliorate the philosophical differences advocated by various groups.

Often the locus of the debate is the very institution that serves as the focus of much criticism. Many critics and advocates are housed within the nation's schools, colleges, and departments of education. Goodlad (1984), Sizer (1984), Clark (1984), Ravitch (1983), Finn (1984), Cremin (1977), Gideonse (1982), Scannell (1983), Smith (1980), and Kluender and Egbert (1983) speak from positions within colleges of education and speak of either disestablishment or enhancement.

Change and Innovation in Teacher Education

The contrasting perceptions of teacher education are perhaps best highlighted when considering the concept of change. The public perception seems to emphasize inertia and inactivity, while the professional perception is of pervasive and significant change underway within schools, colleges, and departments of education. Fullan (1982) begins his text on educational change by noting that "schools are being bombarded by change and yet nothing is new under the sun." While Jordan (1984) documents a decade and a half of unprecedented interventions in teacher education, Sykes (1983) concludes that "over this period teacher education has remained unchanged in important respects."

Many within the profession view teacher education as having undergone far-reaching changes within the recent decade—a decade of intervention, in which forty-three federal programs expended nearly six billion dollars in personnel preparation monies, and the foundations and institutional initiatives better than doubled that amount. The decade brought enormous changes to programs, efforts, and activities in the nation's schools of education. The sense of accomplishment is best highlighted in a report from the National Center for Education Statistics that reported "almost all (94%) of the nation's schools, colleges and departments of education have implemented one or more measures to improve the quality of teacher candidates during the past five years . . . over four-fifths (85%) of the schools, colleges and departments of education reported making the curriculum more rigorous" (Wright, 1983). As if to reinforce this view, Daly (1983) cited evidence of profound changes: a) testing candidates for admission and for certification, b) changing course content and program evaluation strategies, c) expanding the array and efforts of faculty development through coordination with both academic disciplines and school settings, and d) structurally reorganizing institutions.

Given the magnitude of the investments, the initiatives, and other efforts, why weren't the changes recognized by the public? Why didn't the changes lead to genuine reform? Why has the public maintained its disestablishment orientation? Why have public policymakers continued to seek structural and organizational changes in teacher education? These questions lead back to the contrasting perceptions of the enterprise known as teacher education. If, as some conclude, the change in teacher education has been haphazard, short-term, and merely responsive to external mandates rather than emerging from planned and comprehensive change by those responsible for teacher education, then it is not surprising that both the public and the profession share a common frustration. Both sides expect and want it to be different than it is. In such a climate, many see change as reform and equate change with excellence (Clark, 1984).

To accomplish genuine reform, reconciliation of the two contrasting views of teacher education is essential. Analyzing various characteristics of teacher education can partially resolve the contrasting views and perhaps lead to common efforts in setting goals to transform professional education.

Teacher Education: An Expansive and Dynamic System

At the present time, the training system consists of more than 1200 colleges and universities which offer preservice and continuing education, largely through university-wide programs; local education agencies that provide inservice education ranging from workshops to full-scale staff development efforts; state education agencies that provide academies for administrator training and inservice courses for teachers; an expanding array of private sector businesses that do training; and teacher organizations. It is a system that has grown enormously in both size and complexity in the last decade in order to meet the demands of a mass profession. One curiosity is that the expansion of the system is often overlooked and the noncollegiate-based training aspects of the system are ignored by those who call for change.

Today, the initial or basic preservice preparation of teachers takes place in an expanding array of institutions of higher education, with the largest share of prospective teachers trained in state colleges and universities that were at one time normal schools. All of these institutions offer at least a bachelor's degree. Two-thirds operate master's level programs. More than one-third offer sixth-year programs and 20 percent offer doctoral programs (Heald, 1983). Despite severe economic pressures confronting institutions of higher education during the 1970s, and a surplus of education graduates, the number of institutions training teachers actually increased by more than a hundred as institutions responded to market realities and added inservice programs. While the few institutions that closed or reduced their education programs during the 1970s captured the attention of the public, it is the expansive character of the system that is most noteworthy (Feistritzer, 1984).

The fact that three-quarters of all colleges and universities operate programs raises significant concerns. While this proliferation of training does provide geographic access and proximity for students, it also offers a wide variation in size of program and in environment (Clark, 1984). One of the most persistent themes in recent years has been the low status of teacher education programs in the academic hierarchy, as measured by low rewards to faculty devoting time to it. In many cases, teacher education is an income-producing program, often funded using formulas for other didactic or lecture-oriented programs. The allocation of resources to promote clinical or laboratory programs occurs in few institutions (Feistritzer, 1984; Peseau, 1982).

Virtually all commentaries on teacher education (Gideonse, 1982; Clark, 1984; Kerr, 1983; Joyce, 1984; Sykes, 1983; Feistritzer, 1984) suggest that this proliferation of institutions undermines the quality of teacher education. Clark (1984) believes that the size of the enterprise diffuses resources, impedes reform, and often divorces training from knowledge production and utilization. Intuitively, one believes this is true. But unfortunately, it is not possible to identify research-based criteria for distinguishing between effective and ineffective programs (Evertson, 1984).

Efforts to show the relationships between teacher preparation and performance have attracted the attention of policymakers for a generation. Some see this as a necessary condition in determining program quality. How one both defines and assesses quality in teacher education is a current "hot issue." Yet there is absence of agreement on the criteria. In a recent study, the use of various admission and exit criteria to assess candidates was deemed essential in making judgments regarding quality (Feistritzer, 1984). Others have suggested that follow-up studies of teacher performance and effectiveness are the basis for making such judgments (Andrews, 1984; Wilson, 1984). Highly successful teachers are prepared in quality programs, or so the argument goes. At the present time, teacher educators are developing criteria to judge program quality based on educational experience—i.e., hours of experience in "real" schools, doctorates, books in library, etc. These are based on assumptions regarding necessary conditions. Perhaps the best-known of these initiatives is the current NCATE Redesign, which is looking at ways of identifying performance standards, making judgments about student quality and the productivity of faculty as well as the environment or resource base. Other forms of output or product evaluation include state efforts to assess institutional quality by measuring passage rates on standardized achievement tests. Given the flaws in both measures, it is not surprising that there is little consensus regarding ways to curtail the numbers of institutions engaged in teacher education or to make judgments about quality among those that offer such programs.

In such a system, there is much redundancy and overlap. Increasingly there is a multiplicity of actors. Leadership academies provide staff development to school administrators, private sector initiatives serve teacher inservice needs, and collegiate preparation programs provide both preservice and continuing education for teachers, counselors, and administrators, yet there is often little coherence among these efforts. While Feinman-Nemser (1983) reminds us that the education of teachers is a multi-staged and phased process—from pretraining through preservice to induction and on-the-job learning—the greatest focus by reformers and the public has been on the education of prospective teachers and the role that colleges and universities play in that education. Subsequent sections of this paper will focus exclusively on the function and form of teacher education as a university-based program.

It is perhaps instructive to recognize that the contrasting perceptions of teacher education are not new; since the creation of the normal school in New England in the first quarter of the nineteenth century, such institutions have been at "the epicenter of hostility" (Haberman, 1984). Teacher education developed later in universities and colleges drawing heavily on the German traditions of inquiry and scholarship. While the former stressed the experiential and technical, the latter focused on experimental, scientific-based programs drawing from the analytic psychology and assessment work of scholars in the great American universities. These two traditions persist a century later (Powell, 1976) but have been gradually blended. A significant commonality in program has resulted from reliance on experiential programs and common learning during the past thirty-five years. Perhaps the most notable characteristic of teacher education today, in terms of its form, is its reliance on a four-year undergraduate degree model which is housed within the undergraduate academic environment of a campus and is the responsibility of a number of campus interests and disciplines (Tucker and Mautz, 1984).

Preservice Teacher Education

Cruickshank (1984) describes preservice education as that part of a collegiate program in which one learns how to teach, by acquiring presentation, discussion, management, and supportive skills that assist subsequent teacher performance. He also defines it as the engagement of teacher educators and teacher candidates in instructional interactions with each other and with the curriculum in both tertiary institutions and elementary or secondary school settings, the intention being to provide opportunity for aspiring teachers to acquire abilities sufficient to enter the profession. Denmark complements this definition by seeing preservice programs as directed toward preparing teachers to work effectively in a wide range of educational settings and to utilize a broad array of instructional skills in responding to the different learning styles of many children (Denemark and Nutter, 1980).

Missions, Goals, and Objectives

The contrasting perceptions of teacher education are also evident in the public's and professionals' views of the mission, goals, and organizing themes of schools of education. The public defines the educational task as simply preparing teachers. Rarely is the mission or program expectation defined more broadly or explicitly. This is undoubtedly due to the absence of a broader view of "educator" and a perception that teacher education only prepares prospective teachers. The growing trend to broaden the role and mission of selected institutions, with an increasing emphasis on preparing large numbers of nonschool professionals, is ignored. The fact that nearly a third of the institutions responding to a survey questionnaire regarding program indicated they prepare professionals for other human service institutions (AACTE, 1984) indicates how widespread is this phenomenon. While some of this reflects strategic goal setting from an era of teacher surplus, it also is a response to new opportunities and an enormous expansion of educational settings in the society. Helping the public understand this broadened mission of a substantial majority of all schools of education could facilitate broader understanding of other facets of the program.

The Education Professoriate

One of the most widely held public perceptions about teacher education is of low productivity and quality among the education faculty. Tucker and Mautz (1984) address this theme by faulting the education faculty's productivity, questioning the applied nature of its work, and criticizing its "pretentiousness and unimportance." Since the exhaustive study of Clark and Guba (1976), the profession has been aware of the reluctance of faculty to do research or theory building. Others have noted faculty disinterest in contributing to or even using the knowledge base that comprises teacher education.

In contrast to this perception, at all institutions faculty are more heavily involved with teaching and supervising activities than with other assignments. Ducharme and Agne (1982) have also found education faculty sometimes criticized for not publishing at a rate comparable to faculty members in other disciplines. These same studies have also found that the faculty in education is largely white, male, and campus-bound, not engaging in off-campus consultation (AACTE, 1984). Some 30,000 persons hold rank in programs collectively known as schools, colleges, and departments of education. The size of faculty varies according to type of institution, with the median number of full-time faculty members in large, predominantly land-grant institutions at fifty; for public non-land grants, it is approximately forty-three, and the average number in small liberal arts colleges is about five. These numbers correspond to patterns of student enrollment (Imig, 1982). A recent AAUP study reported that full professors in education, on the average, earn $5,000 less than the mean salary of colleagues in other disciplines and that they rank below all other disciplines, excluding library science and fine arts, in salary levels (Imig, 1982).

One of the most important and glaring characteristics of the education professoriate is their significant number of years of elementary and secondary school experience prior to entry into the university community. Ducharme and Agne (1982) found a mean of eight years of experience in elementary or secondary education prior to completion of advanced degrees and entry into the higher education setting. They assert that this influences both orientation and subsequent scholarly interests and suggest that this group is among those K–12 teachers who have left teaching because of conditions of practice. Almost 84 percent of those in the professorial ranks hold a doctorate, with a larger percentage of Ph.D.s than Ed.D.s in the higher ranks, and more than two-thirds of the professoriate is tenured (AACTE, 1984). One of the most important dimensions of the teacher education program is the significant increase in the connections between higher education and the elementary and secondary schools; one of the least studied or understood dimensions of this, the qualities and characteristics of supervising or cooperating teachers in K–12 education, needs examination. The increasing role these persons play, largely independent of the collegiate-based program, has generated numerous proposals for closer connections, adjunct professorial status, and other forms of linkage. Dependence on these professionals becomes even more important in the move to initiate probationary experiences for beginning teachers.

Student Profile

Perhaps there is no issue more hotly contested between the public and professionals than the quality of teacher education students. While the public has focused on the problem of quality, the most pervasive problem for leaders of schools of education over the past decade has been the decline in enrollment. The National Center for Education Statistics has documented the fact that enrollments in education fell from 1.118 million in 1966 to 781,000 in 1978, and the National Education Association has reported that productivity decreased from an all-time high of 317,254 in 1952 to 159,485 in 1980, a decrease of 49.7 percent (Imig, 1982). While some modest upturns in enrollments are reported, a major concern is to find ways to attract additional students into teacher education. Understanding the characteristics and motives of the existing teacher work force and formulating realistic but far-reaching incentives must be a common endeavor for policymakers and professionals.

Today, the education student profile exhibits characteristics long associated with the public school teacher (Harris, 1984). More than half of the students are first generation college attendees, more than two-thirds are female, almost 90 percent are white, parental income is lower than for other students, 50 percent attend universities and colleges no more than fifty miles from home, and one quarter transfer into their present progams from a community or junior college (Imig, 1982). For recruitment strategies, these characteristics are important, as is understanding the incentives that attract such students to teaching.

Lee (1984) found that prospective teachers see teaching as "interesting" and education as a place where they earned good grades. Students who are not teacher candidates place emphasis on the interest, availability, and financial prospects of other jobs. This contrasting emphasis on incentives is also important in fashioning recruitment strategies.

Of greatest concern to both public policymakers and professionals in education is the issue of student quality. A host of policymakers have asserted that individuals who become teachers are less qualified academically than those who enter other fields. There have been numerous references to "bottom of the barrel" students and to prospective teachers coming from the lowest quarter of the college population. The basis for these assertions, as reported by Schlechty and Vance, is that "since 1973 college bound juniors and seniors taking the Scholastic Aptitude Test have been asked to choose from a list *the* field that would be your first choice for your college curriculum. Data show that the SAT scores in 1973 of intended education majors were lower than those of all other college-bound seniors, and by 1981 the gap in test performance had widened further" (NCES, 1983). In contrast, Lee (1984) found that college grades of a national sample of prospective teachers are slightly higher than non-teacher candidates, while Feistritzer (1984) reports SAT scores for a small sample of admitted education candidates to be higher than the national average for all college students.

The absence of comprehensive and detailed data regarding the quality of the actual candidate pool in teacher education raises a variety of conflicting signals. In California, administration of the state's Basic Education Skills Test (CBEST) to prospective teachers indicates a high incidence of failure among a large proportion of candidates. At the same time, a study conducted by the California state college system concludes that students recommended for teacher certification at eighteen of nineteen state colleges had slightly higher grade point averages than those who did not enter a teacher preparation program (Cohen, 1984). The University of Missouri-Columbia has reported that there are no statistically significant differences between the averages of education students and other campus majors in twenty-four common courses on that campus, while institutional studies at places as diverse as the University of North Dakota, the University of Wisconsin-Milwaukee, and the University of Kentucky suggest that education students are the equal of if not slightly better than their peers enrolled in liberal arts and sciences, as measured by grade point averages in common courses and academic majors.

Whether valid or invalid, this issue of candidate quality has prompted efforts to raise admission criteria for teacher education on the assumption that the quality of teaching will improve (Sandefur, 1984a). A wide range of criteria are being used to make judgments about students for admission, including high school and college grade point averages, candidate performance in the introductory courses in education, scores on standardized aptitude tests, requirements to observe and participate in school experiences, faculty recommendations, written language proficiencies, autobiographies, and basic skill examinations. As many as thirty-three separate admission criteria are used by institutions to make quality judgments, with increasing use of nationally standardized or normed screening tests.

Whether these screens guarantee quality candidates remains uncertain. Evertson and her colleagues (1984) have reviewed the extensive research which looks at principal and supervisor ratings of teacher performance and scores on academic aptitude tests. These suggest that increased admission criteria and quality of teaching are not significantly related, although there is modest evidence that teachers' or teacher candidates' verbal ability is correlated with student performance. The major conclusion is that there is little evidence available to support conventional ways of screening teachers. Nevertheless, the profession has committed itself to the use of screens and hurdles as a way of satisfying public expectations.

The commitment to the use of screens raises a whole other set of questions: What are we measuring? What instruments are we using? What should we be using as admission criteria? What is the relationship between candidate quality and teacher effectiveness? What judgments ought the profession render? What is the "gatekeeping" role? What obligations does the profession have when disproportionate numbers of selected ethnic and racial groups "fail" such measures? Trying to live down an image of low quality has prompted strenuous efforts at raising selectivity in some institutions at the same time that efforts are being made to make programs less readily accessible. While some are hopeful that there will be a successful turnaround in the public perception as a result of tougher screening measures, Kerr (1983) suggests that the efforts of education schools to raise admission standards can be rejected by other university faculty because of the low cost per student in education and the need for a university dumping ground. If, as Ishler (1984) reports, the average grade point requirement for admission into programs is 2.25 on forty-three semester hours of university work, further moves to adjust this requirement upward will affect the flow of students through the university and particularly into teacher education programs. This holds serious implications for the provision of adequate numbers of new teachers to replenish the work force in a time of shortage.

Program Profile—The Elusive Black Box
The public perception of the content of teacher education is four long years of "Mickey Mouse" courses that dwell on "tiny tools," "kiddy lit," and "paint-by-numbers." The perception is often reinforced by professional educators who complain that programs are dominated by fact and method, taught by faculty who focus on the practical and the immediate (Kerr, 1983; Clark, 1984; Sykes, 1983; Kluender and Egbert, 1983). Both the public and professionals agree that there is a remarkable sameness to programs, with frequent complaints about their inadequacy. There is also a lack of consensus about how to make them adequate.

Today, teacher education remains caught in the impasse that has preoccupied us since the 1920s. Advocates on the one hand stress the *technical*—rules, prescriptions, practical solutions for carrying on specific tasks in the classroom, an almost "atomistic" concept of teaching and teacher education. On the other hand, there are those who stress the analytic (or what Borrowman (1956) called the *liberal* three decades ago)—preparing educators who are reflective, autonomous problem solvers, who understand the importance of value questions and emphasize thinking skills, critical thinking and reasoning, and logic. Unfortunately, there is *no shared view* of the curriculum for teacher education. Too often we forget that these divergent points of view reflect different traditions and accomplishments and have a history at least as old as the first great school reforms of this century (Powell, 1976). We *have* viewed them as irreconcilable opposites rather than as compatible and potentially convergent philosophies.

Despite this, teacher candidates in virtually all institutions complete a program that draws upon subject specialization and faculty from the humanities, arts, letters, sciences, and education. Once students are admitted into the college (having met university requirements for admission), they pursue a four-year program that Sykes (1984) has described as the familiar "professional quadrivium" of general studies, academic specialization, professional studies, and a practicum or student teaching experience. Sykes observes that, despite persistent criticism of the existing program for preparing teachers, virtually all the reform proposals retain this same model. Some would give greater emphasis to professional studies (Scannell, 1983), even adding a preprofessional program stressing the social and behavioral sciences (Denemark and Nutter, 1980); others would expand the practical or experiential components (Boyer, 1983; Sizer, 1984) or postpone the pedagogical components to a postbaccalaureate program (Gideonse, 1982; Clark, 1984). Virtually all observers of teacher education would increase the amount of time spent in the academic specialties, general studies (NCEE, 1983), or student teaching. Even those who propose a radical restructuring of the entire program (Pickle, 1984) retain the same basic elements in the professional preparation program but rearrange their sequence. Only those who advocate disestablishment (e.g., the leaders of the New Jersey alternative certification effort) would delete pedagogical or professional studies and have students circumvent such training, although even they include a ten-day workshop to orient prospective teachers to schools and their responsibilities.

Many have proposed using liberal arts graduates as teachers, particularly in these times when excellence is stressed. Those who do so hold different conceptions of teaching and learning which need to be considered for their logical, theoretical, and research bases. In recent months, a number of studies have examined this disestablishment sentiment and concluded that, in contrast to what many in the public believe, teacher education does make a difference. Evertson (1984), Haberman (1984), Clark (1984), and Joyce (1984), after reviewing available research, concluded that teachers who have been professionally prepared perform in ways which principals, supervisors, lay persons, and students rate higher than do those without such training. A much smaller data base makes similar conclusions regarding teacher training and student achievement. The current reform climate offers teacher educators an opportunity to examine these findings, premises, and assumptions and to work to strengthen teacher education. It also offers teacher educators a basis for helping policymakers understand the nature and impact of teacher education programs.

The Program

Once admitted to the college or university, prospective education students engage in a two-year program of liberal or general studies. Few in the public appreciate the fact that this is the same program in which all undergraduate students participate or that education students do as well if not slightly better in these courses in communications, mathematics and natural sciences, social sciences, humanities, fine arts, and physical education than do their college classmates (Lee, 1984). While there is increasing concern about the purposes of these courses, few would argue that they are unnecessary or unimportant in the preparation of teachers. Many see as the problem that they have too little impact on teacher training (Smith and Traver, 1983).

General studies programs are intended to provide students with an understanding of the "range and depth of the human experience" but, according to Smith and Traver (1983), they often become "a convenient and expeditious means" for faculty to assess the calibre and quality of students. For the prospective teacher, general studies are intended to act as a foundation for subsequent specialization. Unfortunately, for many students, they are forty-five to sixty credit hours with little coherence or interrelationship and too little connection to teacher training. Currently efforts are underway to improve general studies. Assuring that the public recognizes the importance of such studies and assisting liberal studies faculties to see the necessary connections to teacher education are important.

The second part of the program of the prospective teacher consists of study in an academic specialty. For virtually all prospective secondary teachers, this means the candidate enrolls in an arts and science program and declares a major in mathematics or history or English. Because many in the public have chosen to ignore this reality, policymakers often attempt to legislate remedies to the perceived inadequacies of the teaching force by requiring more subject matter content. While virtually all prospective secondary teachers complete the same academic major as a person preparing in the field but not planning to teach, a consistent theme in the reform literature is that prospective teachers need more subject matter content. Part of this assertion rests on the claim by some of the public that prospective American history teachers need to major in American history (not social studies or social sciences) and biology teachers in biology (not life sciences) despite the structure and integrated curriculum of the American high school (Lanier, 1984). An outgrowth of the school reform movement has been the promotion of a more integrated high school curriculum, with emphasis on concepts drawn from a variety of disciplines rather than a series of segmented and stratified courses (Miller, 1984). Whether the traditional academic major can prepare prospective teachers to teach a general high school curriculum emphasizing integrated courses and experiences is one of the issues to be dealt with in the coming years. What adds meaning to this debate is the lack of connection between high school sciences and mathematics and those subjects at the college level. Many suggest that there is little in the college mathematics curriculum that will help prospective high school mathematics teachers teach basic mathematics, beginning algebra, or plane geometry. Issues of remediation and focus become important when schools of education must provide such content. Yet if education faculties fail to offer such experiences, prospective teachers often forego such learning (Miller, 1984).

A related issue is whether more content in an academic discipline will affect the success of the teacher. After reviewing a number of research studies correlating teacher mastery of content and pupil achievement, Evertson and her colleagues (1984) concluded that knowing one's subject matter did not necessarily make an individual a good teacher of that subject. Extensive knowledge of the subject matter is a necessary but not sufficient condition for quality teacher preparation (Smith, 1980). With few exceptions, all agree that prospective teachers should study the subjects they intend to teach at the elementary or secondary level so as to understand the nature of knowledge, the structure of the discipline, the relationship between them, and the process of inquiry and research methodology as it pertains to that subject (Scannell, 1983). Unfortunately, however, many have concluded that much of what a teacher candidate learns in the subject matter specialization is not related to teaching that subject to children and youth. It seems important that teacher educators, subject matter faculty, high school principals, subject supervisors, and teachers engage in a discussion of what content is needed. Whether more integrated college preparation (Goodlad, 1984) is possible should be one aspect of this discussion. The potential clash of those who advocate the integrity of separate disciplines with those who call for their greater integration is real and needs to be examined by policymakers and professionals in the coming years.

The issues surrounding the academic disciplines and the program for preparing elementary school teachers are no less real. In most programs, because of the nature of their future assignment, prospective elementary school teachers major in elementary education and specialize in a number of academic areas. Although in some institutions and in some states persons preparing to be elementary teachers must have an academic major, this is not a common pattern. Whether specialization (as distinct from an academic major) provides sufficient depth of understanding in any field to permit a teacher candidate to understand the nature of knowledge and the structure of the discipline is unlikely. Some now advocate an academic major for all prospective teachers (Scannell, 1983). The concern this effort presents is whether such specialization strengthens the capability of the elementary school teacher to deal with an assignment and the nature of the elementary school curriculum. There is agreement that the prospective elementary teacher does need familiarity with a broad range of elementary school subjects including reading, writing, arithmetic, life and physical science, social science, art and music, health and physical education. There is also increasing agreement that these candidates need to study one of these subjects in sufficient depth at an advanced level and that employers need to take these strengths into consideration in building a faculty to teach all elementary school subjects.

The third program element, professional studies, is the most controversial. Upon admission to the program at the end of the sophomore or beginning of the junior year, a pattern common for 85 percent of all prospective teachers (Feistritzer, 1984), students participate in a professional studies program that constitutes only 16 percent of a prospective secondary teacher's program and 26 percent of a prospective elementary teacher's program (Wright, 1983). This is far less time in professional study than is generally acknowledged and is caused by the inability of this program to compete successfully for time and resources in the undergraduate curriculum. The proportion of time actually devoted to professional studies has decreased in the past thirty years (Stoddart, 1984). Recently more and more attention has been directed to the nature, content, and necessity of the professional studies component. There is increasing acceptance of dividing this component into foundation studies in education, generic teaching knowledge and skills, specialized or subject-specific pedagogical knowledge and skills, and field or clinical experiences (Scannell, 1983). One of the most important issues confronting teacher education is to gain legitimacy for this division of professional studies and for each component of its curriculum. Gaining acceptance of this division, given time constraints, faculty expertise, and the available knowledge base for each component, will be particularly difficult.

Foundation studies in education apply the knowledge base of

the undergirding disciplines (sociology, philosophy, anthropology, and psychology) to education settings. Typically they focus on orienting prospective teachers to teaching, on learning and human development, and on social, philosophical, historical, and economic policy studies in education. In general, all students begin their professional program with an introductory course that carries a title such as "The American Elementary School," "Introduction to Education," or "Careers in Education" (Kluender and Egbert, 1983). This course may be followed by a foundations of learning or human development course as part of an educational psychology requirement. Only a third of all programs require a foundations course which includes either history or philosophy of education.

Concerns about foundation studies have emerged from both public and profession: the public sees courses in the philosophy or sociology of education as redundant to those offered by the subject department, without applicability to classroom teaching, and it calls for their elimination or merger. Many within the profession point to the theoretical nature of foundation studies and caution those who seek application to classroom situations (Smith, 1980). At the same time many professional educators see such courses evolving into full-fledged disciplines with highly specialized conceptual frameworks, investigative procedures, and their own research methodologies (Howsam et al., 1976) and call for their refocusing. A major issue confronting teacher education is how to retain foundation studies while gaining consensus on their purpose. Should they provide interdisciplinary and conceptual illumination of issues, problems, and procedures so that teachers can understand and act upon them (Howsam et al., 1976)? Or should the emphasis be on content that develops diagnostic and analytic skills to help prospective teachers understand and interpret learning conditions, human development, and the relations among social variables (Smith, 1980)? The continuing ambiguity regarding foundation studies warrants the attention of both the public and the profession.

Specialized pedagogical knowledge and skills are the focus of courses that prepare teachers to teach specific subjects or to work with special populations of students. For prospective secondary school teachers, these courses are intended to teach methods applicable to a specific portion of the high school curriculum—e.g., methods of teaching English, life sciences, social studies, etc. (Kluender and Egbert, 1983)—and in many institutions, they are taught by arts and science faculty. Specialized methods courses for prospective elementary school teachers are most often offered by education faculty. Virtually all institutions offering elementary programs include as many as a dozen of these courses (reading, language arts, mathematics, science, social studies, etc.) and require students to enroll in four to six methods courses. Typically, all methods courses have been subject-specific and have focused on a distinct array of concepts or methods pertaining to teaching a particular school subject. This emphasis on methodologies for particular subjects has dominated teacher preparation for the past thirty years and has grown as the school curriculum has expanded. Each course relies upon techniques specific to that subject with different ways of sequencing content, dealing with concepts, and explaining difficult elements. A knowledge base for teaching each of these courses has emerged and has served as the basis for most methods courses.

In contrast to content or subject-specific methods, teacher performances common to teaching all subjects have been identified (Berliner, 1984). These are called generic teaching methods and are largely derived from the recent research on effective teachers and schools. Smith (1984), Kluender and Egbert (1983), Vaughn (1984), and others have described this research as an effort to examine effective teaching performance and to apply it to program content. An imposing array of teacher educators have concluded that the effective schools research offers teaching behaviors, knowledge, and skills that are sufficiently generic to be understood by all teachers, regardless of subject field, grade level, school size, or student population, and which should be included in all programs (Scannell, 1983; Denmark and Nutter, 1980).

Identifying such a set of generic teaching skills has preoccupied teacher educators for nearly twenty years (Nelli, 1981). First through the competency-based movement and later through the "effectiveness" movement, professional educators have attempted to identify the behaviors of teaching. A significant breakthrough occurred when researchers were able to identify, describe, and test the effectiveness of these generic teaching elements. Smith (1984) and Goodlad (1984) compiled sets of papers which give validity to this approach, while others have sought to compile these findings into performance lists (Wilson, 1984) for use in program development. While there is danger that some will see in the school effectiveness literature a unitary approach to teacher education (Garrison and Macmillan, 1984), there does seem to be a sufficient research base to warrant adding the following generic teaching behaviors and instructional skills to programs: analysis and interpretation of student abilities, cultural backgrounds, achievements, and needs; design of instruction that will meet learner needs through appropriate instructional materials, content, activities, format, and goals; conduct of instruction to best facilitate learning; management of the classroom to promote productive learning; management of student conduct to create a positive climate for student learning; promotion of classroom communication; evaluation and assessment to determine the extent to which students meet instructional objectives; and the arrangement of conference and referral opportunities with parents and other professionals (Scannell, 1983).

At least two other bodies of knowledge are found (or should be) in the generic teaching component of the program: concept teaching and developmental psychology. Both derive in large part from the work of Jerome Bruner and offer theoretical constructs that are broadly applicable to all subjects. The former, with its emphasis on building understanding of subjects through rules, laws, principles, etc., relates to an understanding of the methods children use to learn about the world (Smith, 1984; Stoddart, 1984). Cognitive psychology, with its emphasis on how children learn, will become the next major source of content in developing a science of pedagogy.

Methods courses have tended traditionally to focus on the technical or the mechanical and to rely on extensive experience in schools and simulated situations (Zeichner, 1983) as "the way" to do teacher education. While the technical emphasis has long been important, it seems likely that with a validated research base regarding both generic and subject-specific teaching performances, it will become even more important (Evertson, 1984). Some predict that recent findings will give renewed emphasis to competency-based teacher education and will enable policymakers to build new accountability measures based on competencies (Sanders, 1983). This behavioristic model will be reinforced by those who advocate increased reliance on a diagnostic-prescriptive model of administering "treatments" in classroom settings. The increase in school-based experiences, with supervising, clinical, or mentor teachers doing much of teacher training, has tended to reinforce such "technical" orientations. Others argue that such behavioristic and often mechanistic efforts are wrong, given the demands for thoughtful, skilled, humane, and well-educated teachers in the coming decade.

Whether or not teacher educators can arrive at a consensus regarding program goals and emphases is an important consideration. The eclectic nature of most programs promotes discontinuities within programs and a lack of coherence between courses, sequences, and experiences. Greater reliance on the teacher effectiveness research is essential but cannot foreclose efforts to develop humanistic educational values and attitudes. At the present time, when process and product research is relied upon so heavily in designing new curricula, it is important that teacher education provide a philosophy of education to help teachers think seriously and continuously about what and why they do what they do (Howsam et al., 1976; Boyer, 1983).

Finally, the fourth part of the professional studies program consists of student teaching. While there is need to differentiate between clinical experiences and field experiences, with the former just as likely to take place on campus as off, the enormous growth in field experiences has been a condition of teacher education in recent years. As a part of this trend, pre-student teaching experiences in the schools have increased significantly while the time allocated for student teaching commonly has been expanded from part to all of an academic semester. In spite of the enthusiasm of prospective teachers for school experiences, a number of studies question the efficacy of such experiences in terms of influencing successful teaching (Zeichner, 1980). Student teaching is usually identified by new teachers as the best, most useful aspect of teacher education (Griffin, 1983), but existing research suggests that it is not a very effective way to educate teachers (Evertson, 1984): little change occurs in student teachers (Griffin, 1983), exposure is to situation-specific teaching strategies rather than to options and a variety of modes of instruction, and actual negative changes in attitude and teaching behavior often occur (Peck and Tucker, 1973). Glassberg and Sprinthall (1980) found that student teachers became more authoritarian, rigid, impersonal, restrictive, arbitrary, bureaucratic, and custodial by the end of their student teaching experience. Arriving at models for improving the quality of clinical and student teaching experiences is a problem confronting both the public and professionals. Many have written of the stages and responsibility to be assumed by prospective candidates and the variety of experiences (microteaching, reflective teaching, observation) that can substitute for in-school experiences (Scannell, 1983). The care that is exhibited in creating these experiences and monitoring and assessing the candidate's progress seems to be the critical element in providing a quality program.

Increasingly, the candidate who completes this series of professional experiences is confronted by a series of additional hurdles before being certified to teach. Among these are standardized tests for graduation and certification and periods of probationary certification. Nearly a third of all institutions use some form of exit examination (AACTE, 1984), a return to procedures that were common in the 1950s before being gradually replaced by graduation requirements from the normal school or college and by program approval procedures (Gardner and Palmer, 1982). The use of the National Teacher Examination (NTE) or state-initiated and -driven examinations has proliferated since the introduction of the NTE in Louisiana in 1976 (Kauchak, 1984). Questions abound regarding the efficacy of competency examinations; the debate focuses on whether paper and pencil tests can measure effective teaching, whether such tests should include performance evaluations and demonstrations, and how assessments of subject matter content should be made (Andrews, 1984). Yet public policymakers seem determined to add these measures. The impact that such examinations have on different ethnic and racial groups is a problem of significant importance (Dilworth, 1984; G. P. Smith, 1984) that should command much attention from both professionals and the public and thus far has escaped the attention it deserves.

Given the existence of this design for teacher education, a design that many perceive as being resistant to change, one would have to conclude that the internal workings of the curriculum merit major overhaul. Unfortunately, we know very little regarding what happens in any course beyond the loose descriptions contained in the college catalogue or the most recent accreditation self-study. There is enormous variability—with differing philosophies, values and emphases, and experiences—even between sections of the same course offered during the same semester on virtually all campuses. As we seek to provide quality experiences for prospective teachers, there is need to test these differing perspectives against an ultimate criterion, i.e., what a beginning teacher needs to know and be able to do. While this has served as a goal for thirty years (Nelli, 1981), we often lose sight of its importance. Indeed, one of the major issues emerging within the profession has to do with how a beginning teacher acquires such competencies, understandings, skills, and attitudes. For some the argument centers on the concept of "deficit entry," i.e., quality teacher education programs assure that beginning teachers are fully proficient (and not deficient) on the first day of professional practice. Others argue that this is unrealistic and beyond the scope of teacher education programs because beginning teachers possess certain deficits that can only be remedied through actual practice. The resolution of this debate will involve public policymakers because it includes issues of extended programs, beginning teacher programs or internships, and provisionary certification. It also necessitates a common exploration of questions of governance and resources.

Central to change in teacher education are policymakers and others external to schools, colleges, and departments of education. Given the importance of these forces, professional educators must work to enhance their involvement in the accountability, control, and governance of preservice teacher education. Resolving the differences in perceptions between public participants and policymakers and professional educators is essential.

Accountability, Control, and Governance of Preservice Teacher Education

At the present time, teacher education is accountable to everyone and the responsibility of no one. As Kluender and Egbert (1983) note, "while legal authority rests with the state through legislatures, policy boards and administrative agencies, public and private institutions, education associations and accrediting agencies also attempt to exert major influences on the function and form of teacher education." As Bush and Enemark (1975) stated a decade ago, "control and responsibility in any successful enterprise should go hand in hand. They do not in teacher education which may be one reason why teacher education is perenially in trouble."

Higher education exerts enormous control over teacher education programs where, after all, preservice teacher education is housed and in which it is accountable to various academic committees, policies, and structures. Budgetary allocations, curricula, faculty appointments, promotion, and tenure are all controlled within the academy. At the same time, teacher education programs are accountable to the state through the teacher certification process and program approval procedures, to national and regional accrediting bodies, and to a variety of state mandates for the improvement of programs. One of the major problems with the governance of preservice teacher education is both the number and redundancy of checks and accountability mechanisms and the danger of the uniformity they produce. With so many points of control, teacher educators often find that their work is shaped by regulators in agencies who claim responsibility in setting directions and controls but who, in reality, impose constraints and limitations on program innovations. The public needs to appreciate the fact that teacher education is already regulated and needs deregulation to be more responsible and responsive.

Teacher education is also considerably different from the other professions because the states grant to other professions rights, privileges, responsibilities, and prerogatives with regard to professional sovereignty for training, testing, ethics, practices, and standards. In teacher education, on the other hand, the state retains these responsibilities, thus creating an uneasy relationship between professional educators and the public regarding state controls over teaching. The efforts of both teachers' and teacher-educators' organizations to establish professional standards boards through professional practices legislation have been thwarted by both those within the profession who seek dominance and power and those external to the profession who want to retain and strengthen their role in prescribing quality for teacher education.

Today, all fifty states have in place procedures for issuing teacher certificates to individuals who complete a set of prescribed minimum requirements. It is a system characterized by centralized state authority and a proliferation of certificates issued on the basis of type, field, and level. Currently there is a significant debate: some desire a move toward comprehensive certificates (Feistritzer, 1984), while others want to retain if not enlarge upon the types, levels, and fields certified. Those seeking reforms in certification will probably have to wait until there are basic curriculum reforms in elementary and secondary schools and a better definition of teacher roles in the future.

Conclusion: Problems Confronting Preservice Education

Given the alternative perceptions regarding the program, character, and quality of teacher education, perhaps the greatest danger confronting teacher education is that the public will expend its energy in trying to disestablish the system, the profession will give up trying to improve itself, and the system will continue to limp along virtually unchanged. Adding to this concern is the fact that many believe the system is simply too big and too complex to reform. A number of studies have suggested that teacher education does not warrant intervention by policymakers and others because it constitutes so little of the total education program as to have limited impact in terms of student achievement or school effectiveness (Kerr, 1983; Sykes, 1983). While others see teacher education as a critical point for intervention and urge that academic leaders, state policymakers, and teacher educators come together to reform teacher education (Sanders, 1983; Imig, 1982), this sentiment does not enjoy widespread support.

These concerns are compounded by emerging and persistent demographic changes in the society. An enrollment upsurge projected for the latter half of the 1980s in elementary schools will generate new demands for additional teachers (Darling-Hammond, 1984). That increase in enrollment is expected to reach the secondary schools by the 1990s; universities and colleges need to respond now to these anticipated demands. A severe teacher shortage is likely to precipitate new hostility between school officials, public policymakers, and teacher educators because adding course requirements and imposing higher admission standards and more rigorous exit or competency measures without magnets to attract increased numbers of students will exacerbate the teacher shortage.

Those in charge of teacher education programs have tried to be vigorous in their advocacy of excellence and their effort to promote reform. Thus, they have advocated public policy support for a) attracting more and better teacher candidates, b) screening candidates using a variety of standardized basic skills tests as well as other criteria, c) carefully monitoring students throughout the program, d) increasing the rigor and quality of each course in the program, e) adding a research dimension and infusing new knowledge, f) extending the direct and indirect experiential focus of the program using both multiple school sites and experiences and new forms of microteaching, g) adding computer literacy programs, h) bridging the transition from prospective teacher candidate to practicing professional through a series of beginning teacher programs, and i) evaluating teacher competence through performance assessments. These are not sufficient reform strategies. They are only basic reforms currently being employed to achieve an optimal base for significant reforms. The challenge before both public policymakers and teacher educators is to move beyond these minimums. A series of issues present themselves for consideration by both policymakers and professionals:

- We share a common need to define quality for schools, colleges, and departments of education, to work to strengthen those who meet such quality considerations, and to find ways to link the remaining institutions with one another to promote collaboration and quality.
- We share a common agenda to recruit and retain a diversified and high-quality faculty in pedagogy for both professional studies and field components of the program. To effect this, faculty and staff must be provided with development opportunities, including the option of returning to the elementary and secondary classroom; reward and tenure systems must be developed that accommodate the needs of the profession as a whole instead of just the academy's needs. Inexpensive and reliable information systems must be counted upon to reinforce significant staff development opportunities.
- We share a common concern to enhance the quality and quantity of the applicant pool, giving serious attention to the recruitment of talented women and minorities. To effect this, the public image of the role and importance of teachers and teacher education must be changed, and appropriate ways of assessing and evaluating beginning teachers must be found. Tremendous information needs are inherent in these efforts.
- We share a common need to develop professionally sound ways of addressing teacher shortages in numerous fields. To effect this, new staffing patterns for schools, new incentives for teachers, and new technologies for delivery must be explored.
- We share a common need to build more rigorous and realistic preparation programs that draw upon the expanding knowledge base and that give renewed attention to bilingual and multicultural issues and global awareness.
- We share a common interest to experiment with various structural reforms that provide for extended programs in teacher education, that facilitate the entry of beginning teachers into

school environments, integrate theory and practice, rely upon more and earlier clinical experiences, and are based on a firmer grounding in the arts and sciences.

- We share a common need to build new systems that promote quality inservice and staff development programs, continue to enhance delivery systems, and effect additional inservice and staff development incentives for practicing teachers.

John Dewey's great contribution to philosophy was that he helped move us beyond the nineteenth century's preoccupation with perception and object reality. He gave to philosophy a way of looking beyond these concepts. Dewey blurred the then-prevalent distinctions and introduced experimentalism as a way of reconciling those differences. Today, enabling policymakers and practitioners better to communicate about the realities and experiences of teaching and teacher education is an imperative. The profession must provide leadership and understanding for this task.

References and Bibliography

AACTE. 1984. 1984 report to the profession. *AACTE Briefs* 5(5): 1–11.

Adler, M. J. 1982. *The Paideia Proposal.* New York: Macmillan.

Allport, G. W. 1954. *The Nature of Prejudice.* Reading, Mass.: Addison-Wesley.

Andrews, T. E. 1984. Teacher competency testing: 1984. Draft report to the National Institute of Education.

Berliner, D. C. 1984. The half-full glass: A review of research on teaching. In *Teaching: Using What We Know,* 51–77. Washington: ASCD.

Borrowman, M. L. 1956. *The Liberal and Technical in Teacher Education: A Historical Survey of American Thought.* New York: Teachers College, Columbia University.

Boyer, E. 1983. *High School: A Report on Secondary Education in America.* New York: Harper and Row.

Bush, R. N., and P. Enemark. 1975. Control and responsibility in teacher education. In Kevin Ryan, ed., *Teacher Education: The Seventy-*

Fourth Yearbook of the National Society for the Study of Education, 265–294. Chicago: University of Chicago Press.

Clark, D. L. 1984. Transforming the contexture for the professional preparation of teachers. In Jim Raths and Lillian Katz, eds., *Advances in Teacher Education*. Forthcoming.

Clark, D. L., and E. G. Guba. 1976. *A Faculty Self Report on Knowledge Production and Utilization Activities in Schools, Colleges and Departments of Education*. Bloomington: Indiana University School of Education.

Clark, D. L., and G. Marker. 1975. The institutionalization of teacher education. In Kevin Ryan, ed., *Teacher Education: The Seventy-Fourth Yearbook of the National Society for the Study of Education*, 53–86. Chicago: University of Chicago Press.

Cohen, D. 1984. *A Study of the Academic Qualifications of Students Recommended for Basic Teaching Credentials*. Bakersfield: California State University.

College Board. 1983. *Academic Preparation for College: What Students Need to Know and Be Able To Do*.

Cremin, L. A. 1977. The education of the educating profession. 19th Annual Charles W. Hunt Lecture. Washington, D.C.: AACTE.

Cruickshank, D. R. 1984. Toward a model to guide inquiry in preservice teacher education. Prepared for the AACTE Task Force on Inquiry in Teacher Education, June 1984.

Daly, N., et al. 1983. *The Impact of Teacher Shortage and Surplus on Quality Issues in Teacher Education*. Report of a Task Force on Shortage/Surplus/Quality Issues in Teacher Education. Washington, D. C.: AACTE.

Darling-Hammond, L. 1984. *Beyond the Commission Reports: The Coming Crisis in Teaching*. Washington, D.C.: The Rand Corporation.

Denemark, G., and N. Nutter. 1980. *The Case for Extended Programs of Initial Teacher Preparation*. Washington, D.C.: Clearinghouse on Teacher Education.

Dilworth, M. E. 1984. *Teacher's Totter: A Report on Teacher Certification Issues*. Washington, D.C.: Institute for the Study of Educational Policy, Howard University.

Ducharme, E., and R. M. Agne. 1982. The education professoriate: A research based perspective. *Journal of Teacher Education* 33(6): 30–36.

Evertson, C., W. Hawley, and M. Zlotnik. 1984. *The Characteristics of Effective Teacher Preparation Programs: A Review of Research*. Draft report to the Education Analysis Center, Office of Planning, Budget and Evaluation, U.S. Department of Education. Nashville, Tenn.: Peabody College, Vanderbilt University.

Feistritzer, C. E. 1983. *The Condition of Teaching: A State by State Analysis*. Princeton, N.J.: The Carnegie Foundation for the Advancement of Teaching.

Feistritzer, C. E. 1984. *The Making of a Teacher: A Report on Teacher Education and Certification*. Washington, D.C.: National Center for Education Information.

Feinman-Nemser, S. 1983. Learning to teach. In *Handbook of Teaching and Policy*, 150–170. New York: Longman, Inc.

Finn, C., and D. Ravitch. 1984. *Against Mediocrity: Humanities in America's High Schools*. New York: Holmes & Meyer.

Fullan, M. 1982. *The Meaning of Educational Change*. Toronto: The Ontario Institute for Studies in Education.

Gardner, W. E., and J. R. Palmer. 1982. Certification and accreditation: Background, issue analysis and recommendations. Prepared for the NCEE.

Garrison, J. W., and C. J. B. Macmillan. 1984. A philosophical critique of process-product research on teaching. *Educational Theory* 34: 255–274.

Gideonse, H. 1982. The necessary revolution in teacher education. *Phi Delta Kappan* 63:15–18.

Gideonse, H. 1983. *In Search of Effective Service*. Cincinnati: S. Rosenthal & Co., Inc.

Gifford, B. R. 1984. *The Good School of Education: Linking Knowledge, Teaching and Learning*. Report prepared for the Education Review Committee, University of California Systemwide Administration. Berkeley: Graduate School of Education.

Glassberg, S., and N. A. Sprinthall. 1980. Student teaching: A developmental approach. *Journal of Teacher Education* 31(2):31–38.

Goodlad, J. 1984. *A Place Called School*. New York: McGraw-Hill.

Griffin, G. A., S. Barnes, R. Hughes, Jr., S. O'Neil, M. Defino, S. Edwards, and H. Hukill. 1983. *Clinical Preservice Teacher Education: Final Report of a Descriptive Study*. Report No. 9025. Austin, Tex.: University of Texas, R&D Center for Teacher Education.

Griffin, G. A. 1984. Why use research in preservice teacher education? A proposal. *Journal of Teacher Education* 35(4):36–40.

Haberman, M. 1974. Needed: New guidelines for teacher candidate selection. *Journal of Teacher Education* 25(3): 234–235.

Haberman, M. 1984. Teacher education in 2000: Implications of demographic and societal trends. *Education and Urban Society* 16(4): 497–509.

Harris, L., et al. 1984. *The Metropolitan Life Survey of the American Teacher*. New York: Metropolitan Life Insurance Company.

Heald, J. E. 1983. *Report to the Profession*. Washington, D.C.: AACTE.

Howsam, R. B., D. C. Corrigan, G. W. Denemark, and R. J. Nash. 1976. *Educating A Profession: Bicentennial Commission on Education for the Profession of Teaching*. Washington, D.C.: AACTE.

Imig, D. G. 1982. An examination of teacher education scope: An overview of the structure and form of teacher education. Paper prepared for the Airlie House Conference on Teacher Education and Special Education.

Ishler, R. 1984. The Dean's corner. In "The Red Letter," newsletter of the Texas Tech University College of Education 9(2): 1+.

Jantzen, J. M. 1981. Why college students choose to teach: A longitudinal study. *Journal of Teacher Education* 32(6): 45–48.

Jordan, K. F., and N. B. Borkow. 1984. *Federal Efforts to Improve America's Teaching Force*. Washington, D.C.: Congressional Research Service.

Joyce, B., and R. Clift. 1984. The Phoenix agenda: Essential reform in teacher education. *Educational Research* 13(4): 5–18.

Kauchak, D. 1984. Testing teachers in Louisiana: A closer look. *Phi Delta Kappan* 65(9): 626–628.

Kerr, D. H. 1983. Teaching competence and teacher education in the United States. In *Handbook of Teaching and Policy*, 126–149. New York: Longman, Inc.

Kluender, M. M. 1984. Teacher education programs in the 1980s: Some selected characteristics. *Journal of Teacher Education* 35(4): 33–35.

Kluender, M. M., and R. L. Egbert. 1983. The status of American teacher education. Draft report to the National Institute of Education.

Lanier, J. 1984. Quoted in J. L. Taylor, ed., *Teacher Shortage in Science and Mathematics*, 175–179. Washington, D.C.: National Institute of Education.

Lee, J. B. 1984. Tables prepared for meeting of the Forum of Education Organization Leaders. Washington, D.C.: Applied Systems Institute, Inc.

Miller, L. S. 1984. *Science Education in the United States: Essential Steps for Achieving Fundamental Improvement*. New York: The Exxon Education Foundation.

National Center for Educational Statistics. 1977. *The State of Teacher Education*. Report prepared for the National Survey of Preservice Preparation of Teachers by Lewin and Associates, Inc.

National Center for Educational Statistics. 1980. *The Condition of Education, 1980 Edition.* Washington, D.C.: Goverment Printing Office.

National Center for Educational Statistics. 1983. *The Condition of Education, 1983 Edition.* Washington, D.C.: Government Printing Office.

National Commission on Excellence in Education (NCEE). 1983. *A Nation At Risk: The Imperative for Educational Reform.* Washington, D.C.: United States Department of Education.

Nelli, E. 1981. Program redesign in teacher preparation. *Journal of Teacher Education* 32(6):39–42.

Peck, R. F., and J. A. Tucker. 1983. Research in teacher education. In R. Travers, ed., *Second Handbook of Research in Teaching,* 940–978. American Educational Research Association.

Peseau, B., and P. Orr. 1982. The outrageous underfunding for teacher education. *Phi Delta Kappan* 62(2):100–102.

Pickle, J. 1984. Relationships between knowledge and learning environments in teacher education. Unpublished manuscript.

Powell, A. G. 1976. University schools of education in the twentieth century. *Peabody Journal of Education* 54(1):3–20.

Ravitch, D. 1983. Scapegoating the teachers. *The New Republic,* November 7, 27–29.

Sandefur, J. T. 1984a. *Standards for Admission to Teacher Education Programs.* An Issue Paper Prepared for the Minnesota Higher Education Coordinating Board. Bowling Green: Western Kentucky University.

Sandefur, J. T. 1984b. State assessment trends. *AACTE Briefs* 5:17–19.

Sanders, T., et al. 1983. A national emergency—teaching: A report of the Council of Chief State School Officers Ad Hoc Committee on Teacher Certification, Preparation and Accreditation. Policy paper presented to Council of Chief State School Officers, Washington, D.C., October.

Scannell, D. P. 1983. *Educating a Profession: Profile of a Beginning Teacher.* Washington, D.C.: AACTE.

Schlechty, P. C., and V. S. Vance. 1983. Recruitment, selection and retention: The shape of the teaching force. *The Elementary School Journal* 83(4):469–487.

Sizer, T. R. 1984. *Horace's Compromise: The Dilemma of the American High School.* Boston: Houghton Mifflin.

Smith, B. O. 1980. *A Design for a School of Pedagogy.* Washington, D.C.: Government Printing Office.

Smith, D. C. 1984. *Essential Knowledge for Beginning Teachers.* Washington, D.C.: Clearinghouse on Teacher Education.

Smith, G. P. 1984. *The Impact of Competency Tests on Teacher Education: Ethical and Legal Issues in Selecting and Certifying Teachers.* Hawkins, Tex.: Jarvis Christian College.

Smith, P. L., and R. Traver. 1983. Program and prophecy: The fate of general studies in teacher education. *Educational Theory* 33(2):73−77.

Stoddart, T., D. J. Losk, and C. S. Benson. 1984. *Some Reflections on the Honorable Profession of Teaching (A Policy Analysis for California Education).* Berkeley: University of California.

Sykes, G. 1983. Teacher education and the professional project: An account of its predicaments. Forthcoming.

Task Force on Education for Economic Growth. 1983. *Action for Excellence.* Denver: Education Commission of the States.

Task Force on Federal Elementary and Secondary Policy. 1983. *Making the Grade: Report of the Twentieth Century Fund Task Force.* New York: Twentieth Century Fund.

Tucker, A., and R. A. Mautz. 1984. Solving the teacher education problem: A university-wide obligation. *Educational Record* 65(2):34−37.

Vance, V. S., and P. C. Schlechty. 1982. The distribution of academic ability in the teaching force: Policy implications. *Phi Delta Kappan* 64:22−27.

Vaughn, J. C. 1984. Knowledge resources for improving the content of teacher education. *Journal of Teacher Education* 35(4):3−8.

Wilson, G. W. 1984. Teacher education program evaluation: A new direction. Prepared for the NASDTEC Annual Meeting.

Wright, D. 1983. Survey of teacher education: Perceptions of methods for improvement. *National Center for Education Statistics Bulletin.* Washington, D.C.: NCES.

Zeichner, K. M. 1980. Myths and realities: Field based experiences in preservice teacher education. *Journal of Teacher Education* 31(6):45−55.

Zeichner, K. M. 1983. Alternative paradigms of teacher education. *Journal of Teacher Education* 34(3):3−9.

Leadership Issues

Richard S. Podemski

Educational historians may well regard the decade of the 1980s as one of the most significant times for educational reform that the United States has ever known. Although other periods of reform have helped to shape the structure of education, few have been accompanied by the widespread public and political interest which is so characteristic of this current examination.

Multiple factors have brought about such focused attention on educational reform at this time. Perhaps the genesis of the current movement has been the general public dissatisfaction with the quality of education, caused by steady declines in scores on standardized tests. An increase in the nation's unemployment rate due to a general downturn in the economy, competition from other countries, and the emergence of vast new technologies have also raised questions about whether American schools are providing appropriate training for the workers of the future.

Although historically there have been other instances of public concern about education, the character of the current examination is different because of two additional developments: the publication of a series of related research studies regarding the characteristics of "effective schools" and the recommendations of numerous state and national commission reports regarding excellence in education. The report of the National Commission on Excellence in Education, more commonly referred to as *A Nation at Risk* (1983), followed shortly thereafter by numerous other reports, provided grist for the political mill and spawned similar examinations of educational practices along with recommendations for improvement in virtually every state. It is, however, the effective schools research which has been unique; it has provided a broad research base for examining recommendations to improve the structure of schools, a research base which has never before been so rich and descriptive. The fact that public concern for education, recommendations from educational authorities, and the recognition of significant research on the nature of school effectiveness have now converged is cause for considerable trepidation and optimism for educators—trepidation for those who have a vested interest in maintaining the status quo and optimism for those who see a crisis as the opportunity for change and improvement.

Probably no group of educators should be more concerned and interested in these educational reforms than school administrators. On the one hand, administrators are designated as educational leaders who by virtue of their positions must help the schools respond to changes in society and meet the goals which society has for the educational system. On the other hand, the current recommendations for educational improvement focus clearly on the role which school administrators can and must play in helping schools achieve excellence. Although the mosaic regarding the role of the administrator in fostering school improvement is not as yet completely clear, recognizable elements have begun to indicate the larger picture of the administrator's role in educational excellence.

The term administrator in most cases refers here equally to the school superintendent and principal. Individuals in both of these positions must respond to the challenge for excellence, and although the specific activities they use in meeting that challenge may differ according to the level within the school organization at which they exercise their authority, it is most likely that their general strategies will be similar. Administrators who occupy more specialized positions should be able to readily infer implications for their own behavior.

Problems Affecting Administrative Excellence

In a sense, every issue which affects education affects the administrator. The administrator is the executive leader of the school: the one who attempts to help the school identify and achieve the purposes for which it exists; the boundary spanner who bridges the gaps between the school and its constituent groups; the organizer who designs human and physical structures; the monitor of societal, legislative, legal, and professional changes; and the change agent who helps identify and implement needed educational changes. As a generalist the administrator must keep abreast of trends in many societal and educational arenas and must help the school respond in an appropriate manner. Several issues directly affect the administrator's ability to promote excellence in education.

Education as an Open System

Although our nation's founding fathers didn't view education as a right to be provided for the masses, public education in the United States has evolved into a system which is open to all and which seeks to give each child the opportunity to become all that he or she is capable of being. This view has developed slowly in practice but has been reinforced by a variety of recent court decisions and federal mandates pertaining to the civil rights of citizens. Not only did *Brown v. Board of Education* (1954) establish that every child has the right to an equal education which is not structured on the basis of race, but this egalitarian view has been restated for different populations of children by Public Law 94-142 and the Civil Rights Act of 1965, as well as Title VII of that act and Title IX of the Education Amendments of 1972. Although each of these mandates dealt with a specific "minority" group, their joint impact stresses the fact that the American public school is open to all and will be judged by the degree to which it provides a suitable program for every child who enters its doors.

Further, our instructional technology has traditionally been geared to allow parents and children open access to the type of curriculum which they believe is appropriate. Because of this belief we have not instituted the various tracking systems common in Russia, Japan, and Europe which give the school more control over educational processes, number of students enrolled, and student accountability.

Although open access is philosophically compatible with our American ideals of freedom of choice and as such is a desirable goal, one must recognize that such a goal creates tremendous pressures for the administrator who must manage the diverse instructional, personnel, and organizational systems which are needed to fulfill that goal. The school administrator does not have the luxury of narrowly defining statements of philosophy or goals, restructuring the scope of clients who will be served, or barring children from school because their instructional needs require programs which are difficult to implement and costly to continue. Although the business literature might suggest that organizational effectiveness is enhanced by clearly defining the nature of one's product and limiting the scope of the product line to only as many different products as can be easily managed, such a closed philosophy is not possible in education.

The school administrator must believe in a free, public education which is available to all and which provides maximum opportunities for all children. Further, the administrator must attempt to design and implement an instructional program which is consistent with that philosophy regardless of fiscal constraints, community and parental attitudes, the competence of available staff, and student abilities and interests. Although making education a truly open system may seem a tall order, it is a philosophy to which most educators subscribe. However, the implications of that philosophy often place the administrator in a no-win situation, especially in fulfilling the expectations of parents and community members, for often the school does not have the resources to be all things to all people.

The Nature of Excellence

Issues related to the open systems view of education are the multiple instructional expectations which are held for the educational system and confusion about how to measure the educational product.

Although an earlier chapter by Mangieri has documented well the aspirations which educators and the public have for the educational product, the expectations of legislators, business leaders, students, and other reference groups are confusing and often conflicting. It is important to recognize that the administrator lives in the very center of the maelstrom created by that confusion and is the one who must help bring organizational clarity out of this potential chaos.

The diverse expectations created by sex education, computer education, back to basics, and the many other "educations," make it difficult for the school to identify clear goals and to know when it has accomplished those goals. Everyone seems to have a personal opinion about precisely what type of education the school should provide; everyone is also willing to criticize the school when it fails to live up to those expectations. Since these various views of education are not always clearly stated nor compatible, it is difficult for the administrator to develop a simple, efficient organizational and instructional structure. The administrator is challenged at one and the same time to design programs by which the school can address the community's needs for a basic curriculum, gifted and talented programs, college preparatory programs, remedial programs, vocational education, special education, and special interest curricula. All of these programs must be excellent, yet it is not always easy to develop precise definitions nor criteria for measuring that excellence.

Governance

The governance system for education has evolved into something quite complex. During our nation's first hundred years, public education was not very complicated. Public schools were not available to all children, yet where there were schools, educational goals were established by the board of directors. The board hired one or more teachers and closely supervised their work. The goals for education were easily monitored since they usually consisted simply of basic reading, writing, and computational skills (Cubberley, 1919).

With the widespread interest in and availability of education came fiscal problems for local communities without the resources necessary to offer more diverse and comprehensive instructional programs. Appeals to state governments for financial assistance resulted in formal state regulation and control of education. State control has increased in recent years to the point where the state now exercises plenary control, as can be attested by the current fury with which the majority of states have recently passed sweeping educational reform measures.

The United States Constitution does not mention education as a federal right but, by virtue of the Tenth Amendment, reserves that right to the states. Federal involvement in education, although evident through the land grants in the 1800s and various programs for veterans and the unemployed at the turn of this century, did not achieve its zenith until the Elementary and Secondary Education Act of 1965 and other legislation designed to help a post–World War II and Korean War society deal with economic prosperity, increased social consciousness, and economic and technological threats from other countries. Backed by this legislation and the impact of the liberal civil rights decisions of the Warren Court, the federal government has sought to influence the character of American education. Schools increasingly feel the federal presence through the regulations accompanying federal fiscal support.

The governance of schools has also become increasingly complex on the local scene. Citizen groups representing diverse publics seek to influence board of education decisions as well as operations in individual schools. Board of education elections themselves have become the battleground for community controversy and have often resulted in single-issue board members being unable to view the complex needs of the total school organization or to compromise with board members who represent different points of view. Furthermore, local teacher and administrator associations have organized to protect the rights of their constituent groups (Lieberman, 1984).

These federal, state, community, professional association, and local board of education attempts at influence have made it difficult for the administrator to develop a clear set of school goals as well as manage the means by which all of these groups can participate in the educational decision-making process. Although the board of education must also confront the complexities created within this potentially diverse arena, it is the administrator who must advise the board regarding wise educational practices, implement the board's organizational and instructional policies, and maintain the day to day symbolic and actual contact with representatives from each of these groups. Furthermore, the administrator must forge a consensus among these groups while helping them and the school itself understand their legal and ethical obligations.

Bureaucracy vs. Professionalism

As education has become more complex, it has also become more standardized. The development of formal rules and regulations, functional specializations, and hierarchies of command has increasingly bureaucratized education. Although the formalization which accompanies complexity is to some extent desirable, it has affected the degree to which individual principals and teachers can make independent decisions that tailor the educational process to the individual needs of children (Hoy and Miskel, 1982). This results in a rigid organization which cannot adapt as needs change, and a disgruntled and ineffective staff who believe that their professionalism and related self-worth are not being recognized.

Many of the premises underlying standardization in education discount the competence of the individual teacher and the degree of freedom which the teacher needs to make instructional decisions in the classroom. These reforms seek to remove the locus of educational decision making from the individual classroom and establish it at a board of education or even state department of education level (Cramer, 1984; Sizer, 1984). Initiatives such as teacher testing, standardized supervision, and evaluation systems with narrowly defined performance criteria are based on an assumption of teacher incompetence. Yet teachers now are better trained than ever and continuously seek to improve their competence through district-offered staff development and other means such as university courses. Further, research suggests that in order to handle the diversity of students in the typical classroom, teachers need greater flexibility in making instructional decisions which affect them; achievement increases when teachers have helped establish instructional goals and there is consensus regarding those goals (Good, Biddle, and Brophy, 1975).

Educational professionalism is further complicated by the activities of teacher unions. These developed to allow their constituent group some say in the decision process, a factor which is directly associated with teacher professional status. However, the union model is a labor model which clearly differentiates between management and workers (Lieberman, 1984), and this designation of teacher as worker admits to subordinate status in the organization. The issue of whether teaching can become a profession is quite complicated and owes as much to the historical development of education in the United States, governance issues at the state and local level, salary levels, and public sentiment, as it does to the teacher's desire to act as a professional.

The administrator is faced with the dilemma of recognizing teacher initiative and competence yet providing for state and locally mandated standardization. The administrator must realize that education is a labor intensive industry which relies on the professional competence of a staff to accomplish the goals of the organization. Every principal, for example, soon learns that he or she cannot teach all of the children in the building personally, and each teacher must share the goal of effective instruction so that the school's overall goals can be achieved. The administrative challenge, then, is to determine the most appropriate balance between that tight coupling necessary for standardization and the loose coupling that allows each teacher to make an independent professional contribution.

Changing Demographics and Economics

Educational reform during the 1980s must take into account a variety of demographic and economic variables which will affect the available reform options. The "management of decline" has been a much-discussed topic within educational administration literature since the mid-1970s (Divoky, 1979). School districts throughout the country have dealt with declining student enrollments by closing buildings, reducing the teaching staff, and curtailing programs. During the decade of the 1980s, elementary school enrollments may decline as much as 18 percent while secondary enrollments will drop approximately 25 percent when compared to enrollment figures for the previous decade. Declines in enrollment have been most severe in the North and Northeast, especially in urban areas, while states throughout the Sun Belt have actually experienced some increase in their student populations. These increases, however, have been due more to the southern migration of families than to increases in the birth rate.

A slight overall increase in student population, especially at the secondary level, is expected during the early 1990s due to the recent trend toward women waiting longer to have children. The overall population is also getting older, and in 1984 the median age of the American population was almost thirty-three years of age. Demographers predict an increase of 50 percent in the thirty-five to sixty-four age group by the year 2000 and an increase of 35 percent of those over sixty-five years of age (Hoyle and McMurrin, 1982).

These demographic trends affect a wide variety of administrative functions including facility planning, staffing, fiscal management, curriculum development, school-community relations, ratio of students to teacher, curriculum scope, transportation, and school district size and organization. Although demographic projections are not always accurate, administrators need to be aware of scenarios which may occur in the near future and anticipate their consequences (Mackett and Steele, 1982). For example, the teacher shortage in the early 1950s caught many administrators unprepared. Today there are evident shortages of teachers in specialty areas such as mathematics, science, and special education. During the early 1990s an overall teacher shortage is again expected. It remains to be seen whether teacher training institutions and public schools will be able to respond effectively to prevent this projected shortage.

The management of decline has also been associated with a decrease in available funds for public education. Rising energy costs, inflation, economic recession in many sectors of industry, a decline in the number of families with school age children, reduced federal aid to education, demands by teachers for increased salary and benefits, and increased competition for students from private schools have made it more difficult for schools to balance their budgets (Mackett and Steele, 1982). Enrollment decreases have exacerbated the impact of these economic variables. The public, however, finds it difficult to understand how school costs can increase when student enrollments drop, failing to realize that all schools have relatively fixed costs for personnel, utilities, and maintenance.

Administrators will be challenged in the decades ahead to bring about educational reforms without the windfall of additional monies which were characteristic of the post–World War II era and the 1960s. Recent educational reforms suggested by the various states have not been accompanied by dramatic increases in state or local funds. In fact, the cost estimated for these reforms is truly staggering and most likely precludes their full implementation (Odden, 1984).

Technology

Much has been written about the educational implications of emergent technology, especially through the use of microcomputers. Indeed microcomputers can be a boon for the management of education as well as for instruction itself. Administrators need to be aware of the implications of this technology for their own role as educational managers. Computers can facilitate scheduling, grade reporting, test scoring, fiscal accountability, record keeping, communications, research, and countless other organizational functions. Their implications for instruction also continue to unfold.

The current vision about the implications of this technology for education, however, is very naive (Podemski, 1984). Computers, and the full range of electronic learning technology, have the potential to supplant many forms of instruction which are currently used in schools. If, as Goodlad's (1984) data describe, teachers spend the majority of their teaching time achieving objectives at the knowledge and comprehension levels of Bloom's (1956) taxonomy, then we are making ill use of this valuable human resource. Learning objectives at this level are ideally suited to electronic learning technology, which can provide for true individualization and can be designed to use a wider variety of learning theory than is available to any one teacher (Meyer, 1984).

With the incorporation of this technology-based curriculum, teachers could alter their role and concentrate more on student diagnosis, remediation, motivation, instructional planning, and other skills which are more consistent with the role of a professional (Pogrow, 1983). The availability of a full range of high quality instructional software, which would duplicate much of what is currently taught in schools, could have tremendous implications for the teacher's role, school governance, the home-school interface, school finance, and other instructional and organizational factors, factors about which the administrator must be aware and over which he or she has control.

Educational Reform vs. Research

Most of the recommendations found in the current educational reform manifestoes are not based on either theory or research (Kirst, 1983). For example, *A Nation at Risk* was the result of discussion by members of a special presidential commission on education. Even the recommendations found in the Boyer (1983) and Sizer (1984) reports on the status of high schools were based merely on survey research and some on-site interviews as well as the informed wisdom of their authors. However, these national reports serve as the basis for the majority of reform measures which the various states have now adopted.

In contrast, some of the state reforms have used the "effective schools" research as their basis, attempting to translate the findings of this research into policy recommendations. Even though the effective schools research, surely not without its own methodological problems, was based on a more rigorous research methodology, mere implementation of its major findings will not necessarily improve school achievement or effectiveness. As Kirst (1983, 237) states, the very broad nature of these findings means that "many of the effective schools variables were difficult to operationalize at school sites or incorporate into state statutes or district regulations."

The fact that the educational reform recommendations are not based on theory or research places the school administrator in the precarious position of having to implement these state mandates without being sure that they will improve school effectiveness (Finn, 1984). Attempts by the administrator to blame external sources for lack of progress is a strategy which at best can only be marginally successful. However, the effective schools research and other studies do provide some specific guidance for excellence in administrative practice, even though we are a long way from having any valid predictive models for success.

Administrator Training

The last major problem area for excellence in administrative practice is the selection and training of school administrators. The last thirty years have seen great strides in the preparation of school administrators, including strengthened certification requirements, substantive developments in the scope and content of university preparation programs, and initiation of staff development programs by local districts (Silver and Spuck, 1978). Several major problems still remain, so the best people in education do not always find their way into administrative positions, and those who are selected may not have the full range of requisite skills.

The selection of administrators in many parts of the country is still based upon the "good-old-boy" system where one's experience in athletics is more relevant than one's knowledge of curriculum and instruction. As a result, many excellent teachers, among them competent women and minorities, still find the doors to school administration closed (Biklen and Brannigan, 1980). Shapiro (1984) reports figures from the American Association of School Administrators indicating that only 16 percent of principals and between 1.8 percent and 4.2 percent of superintendents in the United States are women.

Further, university training for many principals is inadequate. Because of the ever-expanding areas of expertise needed to be an effective adminstrator, many university programs have begun to overemphasize content courses and have failed to give students the opportunity to develop and improve their administrative skills. School-site observation experiences and internships are becoming more difficult to arrange. On-campus residence, when students can participate in more intensive training, has become less frequent, even for doctoral programs. Further, the widespread emergence of off-campus centers, where training is delivered without the benefit of adequate library and research facilities and where there is little time for meaningful dialogue and follow-up between professor and students, further dilutes the quality of administrator training.

Achieving Excellence in Administration

The Research Base

The systematic study of school organizations and educational administration is a relatively young science. Most of the early literature consists of descriptions of actual school practices along with recommendations for the administrator. In the 1950s the theory movement sought to apply concepts from the social and behavioral sciences to the study of educational administration. Although the theory movement has provided substantial insights into the nature of schools and administrative practice, it has not resulted in as comprehensive an understanding of educational administration as the movement's founding fathers had intended (Culbertson, 1983). It is possible that researchers within the theory movement held expectations which were unrealistic for such a new arena of inquiry. More than likely, however, their success is limited because wholesale application of social and behavioral science concepts to the study of administration does not take into account the nature of education as a unique social system and organizational entity. The challenge for the theory movement during the next decades may well be to redefine borrowed concepts in terms of their specific relevance to educational administration or to develop new paradigms which apply uniquely to education (Mackett and Steele, 1982).

During the last decade, some educational researchers have taken a different approach to the study of schools. Numerous studies have focused upon the school or classroom as the unit of analysis in an attempt to understand the instructional and social environment as well as identify effective instructional practices. In addition, a variety of studies, now known as the "effective schools" research, used detailed interview and observation techniques to provide rich descriptions of actual practices found in high-achieving schools. Conclusions based on this research provide some insight into the nature of effective administrative, instructional, and organizational practices.

Of all of the studies, the effective schools research has gained the most attention. Although this research, done largely in elementary schools, focuses only on achievement of basic skills competencies and contains some methodological problems (Purkey and Smith, 1982; Cuban, 1983), its findings have become the center of widespread interest among educators considering reform. Basically this research suggests that effective schools have:

- Strong administrative leadership by the school principal, especially in regard to instructional matters.
- An orderly, though not rigid, school climate that facilitates instruction.
- School-wide emphasis on basic skills instruction and agreement among professional staff that instruction is the primary goal of the school.
- Teacher expectations that students can reach high levels of achievement, regardless of pupil background.
- A system for monitoring and assessing the performance of students in relation to instructional goals (Cohen, 1982).

The effective schools research is of interest to school administrators for several reasons. First, it highlights the important role that the administrator plays in creating the school climate necessary for student achievement. Secondly, as Kirst (1983, 237) has pointed out, these studies "were instrumental in helping educational policy makers focus on 'in school' versus socioeconomic status variables." Prior to this time, considerable attention was paid to nonschool variables and their impact upon instruction. The advantage of the effective schools findings is that they identify alterable variables which are under the control of most school administrators and teachers. Lastly, this research provides suggestions for administrators to consider in developing their own strategies for improving organizational effectiveness, especially in their interactions with teachers in instructional matters. Regarding this latter point, administrators must understand that these research findings have only been inferred from observational studies but have not been fully tested in controlled settings. That is to say, we know that these are characteristics found in effective schools, but we do not yet know if implementing these findings in an ineffective school will turn it around. Nonetheless, until more controlled research is done in this area, the current recommendations of the effective schools research, along with the findings from other studies of classroom instructional practices, are provocative enough to give every superintendent and principal a basis for personal reflection.

Creating Symbolic Meaning

Peters and Waterman (1982, 280) quote an executive of one of America's best-run companies:

> I firmly believe that any organization, in order to survive and achieve success, must have a sound set of beliefs on which it premises all its policies and actions. Next, I believe that the most important single factor in corporate success is faithful adherence to those beliefs. And finally, I believe that if an organization is to meet the challenge of a changing world, it must be prepared to change everything about itself except those beliefs as it moves through corporate life. In other words, the basic philosophy, spirit, and drive of an organization have far more to do with its relative achievements than do technological or economic resources, organizational structure, innovation, and timing. All of these things weigh heavily in success. But they are, I think, transcended by how strongly the people in the organization believe in its basic precepts and how faithfully they are carried out.

This statement is just as valid, if not more so, for education. As Weick (1976) has pointed out, educational organizations, although they have the trappings of a bureaucratic structure, are not as tightly coupled as one might think. Tight coupling is the degree to which the various elements of the organization are closely integrated and respond together to help the organization accomplish its goals. Factors such as the professional status of teachers, diversification in technology, a broad-based goal-setting and decision-making structure, the teacher's ability to make independent decisions behind the closed classroom door, as well as geographical separation of school buildings from the central office, break down the integrating forces within the organization. In the absence of tight coupling, the administrator must seek alternate ways to help the organization generally, and more specifically the staff, make decisions which complement each other. Weick (1982) believes that the administrator can achieve this goal-directed activity through symbolic management, creating and using symbols which describe the true values of the organization to help members know what the organization stands for and assess whether their own actions are consistent with those values.

Since education is labor intensive, it is important that teachers, students, parents, and the general public understand the key values of the local school. Cohen (1983a, 5) states that schools need to develop a sense of "community" and that this "requires the creation of a moral order, which entails respect for authority, genuine and pervasive caring about individuals, respect for their feelings and attitudes, mutual trust, and the consistent enforcement of norms which define and delimit acceptable behavior. . . . [Schools] cannot rely simply on coercive power to bring about order. Rather, schools are normative organizations which must rely on the internalization of goals, the legitimate use of authority, and the manipulation of symbols, as means of controlling and directing the behavior of participants."

The administrator must understand that schools are social systems. Although each teacher independently decides to become an educator and work in a particular school, all want to feel that they are part of something bigger than themselves and that they are contributing to the accomplishment of organizational as well as personal goals. This transcendent meaning is important to both the organization and its individual participants because it unites and directs activities toward the attainment of goals, helps each individual assess personal behavior in relationship to transcendent organizational values, and further helps the organization determine whether each individual is a contributing member (Manasse, 1984).

The creation of symbolic meaning within the organization is clearly an administrative responsibility. Sergiovanni (1984) differentiates between administrative actions which he believes result in competent schools and those which are necessary for achieving excellence. The competent school is characterized by technical leadership, through which the administrator attempts to effectively plan, organize, coordinate, and schedule organizational activities; human leadership, by which the administrator emphasizes morale building and participatory decision making; and educational leadership, by which the administrator manages instruction-related processes such as curriculum development, supervision, and staff development.

In order to achieve educational excellence, however, the administrator must also demonstrate symbolic and cultural leadership. Through modeling, the symbolic leader attempts to communicate behaviors consistent with the goals of the school. "Touring the school; visiting classrooms; seeking out and visibly spending time with students; downplaying management concerns in favor of educational ones; presiding over ceremonies, rituals, and other important occasions; and providing a unified vision of the school through proper use of words and actions are examples of leader activities associated with [symbolic leadership]" (Sergiovanni, 1984, 7).

Through cultural leadership the administrator creates and maintains the core values and beliefs of the school, thereby establishing a unique identity for the school with which both those within and outside the school can relate. "Leader activities associated with the cultural force include articulating school purposes and mission; socializing new members to the culture; telling stories and maintaining or reinforcing myths, traditions, and beliefs; explaining 'the way things operate around here'; developing and displaying a system of symbols over time; and rewarding those who reflect this culture" (Sergiovanni, 1984, 9).

Through symbolic and cultural leadership, the administrator creates a shared meaning among everyone in the school, which bonds them together and helps to unite their activities in accomplishing the school's goals. Further, staff members are more motivated and satisfied because they believe that they are contributing to something unique and special and because the school has helped them develop a sense of personal worth.

The effective schools literature emphatically concludes that the central goal of the school must be instruction and that all other goals must be compatible with and subservient to that primary goal (Dwyer, 1984). Given the current national confusion in defining excellence in education and the lack of specific criteria by which excellence should be assessed, it is imperative that the school administrator understand the importance of and create symbolic meanings which are relevant and unique to his or her local school. In other words, the current discussions of alternative approaches to defining and achieving excellence in education may be healthy for the profession at large, but the local administrator must seek to develop clearly articulated and commonly shared descriptions of the specific values, philosophy, and goals of the local school.

The superintendent must work with members of the board of education and involve the community in developing and fostering this symbolic meaning. Once developed, this symbolic meaning, focused on instructional goals, must be clearly articulated throughout the school and community. Principals should also attempt to give symbolic expression to the values unique to their school while focusing upon how local school values are consistent with those at the district level. Administrators at all levels should examine their own behavior and the procedures associated with the systems they administer to determine if they are consistent with key organizational values. Further, administrators should help teachers and students interpret their own behavior in terms of the organizational value structure, rewarding individuals whose behavior is consistent with those values while helping others change behavior patterns which are inconsistent with organizational values and philosophy.

Instructional Leadership
Probably no concept to emerge from the effective schools research has captured the current attention of educational administrators as

much as the principal's instructional leadership role. Indeed, since the earliest superintendents and principals were viewed as master teachers, it is disappointing that the various attributes associated with instructional leadership "for so long, have been neglected in the literature of educational administration" (Sergiovanni, 1984, 7). In spite of the positive impact of management and human sciences on the study and training of school administrators since the 1950s, it is refreshing that the administrator's central role in instruction is once again receiving the attention it rightfully deserves.

Instructional leadership describes the principal's personal knowledge of curriculum and instruction as well as actions which enable individual teachers and the school as a whole to accomplish instructional goals (De Bevoise, 1984). Framing school goals and objectives, developing and promoting expectations and standards, assessing and monitoring student performance, protecting instructional time, having a personal knowledge of curriculum and instruction, promoting curricular coordination, promoting and supervising instructional improvement, supervising and evaluating instruction, and creating a productive work environment are aspects of instructional leadership mentioned by Murphy et al. (1983).

When instructional excellence is articulated as the key symbolic value in which the school believes, then the principal's implementation of these general functions is more sharply focused (Lipham, 1981). Through the use of decision-making processes the principal can help the staff develop a clear goal. Principals can help teachers and students understand the importance of setting and achieving high yet realistic instructional objectives. Further, the principal controls many factors, such as the scheduling process, staff allocations, school policies on class attendance, class size, student groupings, authorization of extracurricular activities, and direct interruptions of class time for housekeeping functions which affect instructional time and its use (Hallinger et al., 1983).

In effective schools, the curriculum structure is more tightly coupled than in less effective schools (Cohen, 1983b). Effective schools have curricula which are more clearly defined, tied to the overall school goals, integrated among grade levels and across subject areas, and clearly measured in terms of student performance.

Only the principal is in the position to help the staff coordinate these various aspects of the curriculum. Further, through interviews with teachers as well as by direct observation, the principal is responsible for determining if the curriculum is appropriately designed and is being correctly taught. The principal must also have sufficient knowledge of effective teaching techniques to be able to help ineffective teachers.

This view of instructional leadership places a great responsibility on the principal. However, it also highlights the fact that each principal, in cooperation with the staff, needs a great deal of flexibility in determining the procedures used to develop instructional design (Dwyer, 1984; Goodlad, 1984). In discussing current trends in educational research, Bloom (1980) used the term "alterable variables" to describe a shift from the study of nonschool factors over which educators have no control to factors which the educator can manipulate. Bossert et al. (1982) suggest that time-on-task; class size and composition; student instructional grouping; pacing, sequencing, and coverage of curriculum; types and methods of instructional feedback; and complexity of instructional objectives and tasks are all variables affecting student achievement which educators can control and, therefore, alter. The principal must be aware of research describing the effects of these variables, help teachers to become aware of the research's implications for their own teaching, and monitor teachers to determine if they are making wise classroom decisions.

Not all principals will implement their leadership role in the same fashion (Hall et al., 1984). Indeed, a variety of styles have been described in the literature. Some principals actively visit classrooms and conduct model lessons, while others are rarely in the classroom but prefer to coordinate instructional improvement programs through department chairpersons, committees, or other administrators (Dwyer et al., 1983). The factor which is common to all of these leadership styles is that effective principals personally believe in the importance of instruction, use the criterion of instructional goal accomplishment as the focus of their decisions, and clearly articulate their stance regarding the central role of instruction to staff and others.

Although the effective schools research does not specifically discuss the instructional leadership role of the superintendent, it is obvious that achieving excellence must first be a recognized district goal before it can be meaningfully addressed at the building level (Stabile, 1984). The superintendent must assure that the board and district understand the importance of this emphasis and its superordinate status as a district goal. Then the superintendent must realign district policies and procedures to support the attainment of instructional goals first. There will always be pressure to bend the rules to accommodate other programs or activities, such as athletics, but the superintendent must not succumb to such pressure lest he or she send harmful messages to principals and other staff about the "real" goals of the system. Finally, the superintendent's instructional leadership role finds expression in the development of the district's budget and the allocation of funds. The budget must facilitate the achievement of the district's instructional goals and thus provide money for facilities, supplies and materials, competent staff, staff development, and staff rewards which are necessary to achieve excellence.

Organizational Management

Because of the tension between bureaucracy (standardization and tight coupling) and professionalism (autonomy and loose coupling), it is important to consider the type of organizational structure appropriate for achieving excellence in education. Many recommendations of the national educational commissions as well as reforms by the various states support more standardization of educational practices, while the research on effective instruction indicates that principals and teachers need more flexibility to handle the diverse situations with which they must deal (Finn, 1984). Another way to phrase this is to ask, "To what extent should the organization be tightly coupled or loosely coupled?" Although further research is needed, the answer most consistent with currently available studies is, "Some of both" (Manasse, 1984; Sergiovanni, 1984).

Tight coupling should be achieved through the establishment and use of symbols and goals as well as the design and integration of the personnel, instructional, and fiscal support systems necessary to carry out the work of the schools. It is important that the key instructional values and symbols of the organization be central to all of its functions. All procedures must be designed to help the school achieve its instructional goals, especially in secondary schools which are less tightly coupled than their elementary counterparts (Firestone and Herriott, 1982). Further, administrative support systems must be designed so that their procedures complement each other.

This latter point is especially important with the increased specialization of administrative staffs and functions and an associated tendency for each administrative system to be independent of and unrelated to other support systems. Not only is it important that these all help the school achieve its instructional goals, but it is also crucial that the procedures for each of these systems be integrated. For example, the supervision, teacher evaluation, and staff development systems should each be designed so that together they help the administrator achieve district and building goals. Output data from each of these systems should also be used as input for each other system. Data about teacher deficiencies obtained through evaluation should be plugged into the staff development system. Staff development should be considered a vital tool in remediating curriculum design problems which become evident through the supervision system. Other possible interrelationships exist between personnel recruitment, selection, and orientation; staff development; supervision of instruction; personnel evaluation; curriculum development; scheduling; budgeting; student management; and school-community relations.

On the other hand, there must be sufficient flexibility in the organization to allow individual principals and teachers to address local problems in unique ways. Unless this autonomy is available, individual initiative and creative problem solving are reduced or eliminated altogether. Principals in effective schools sometimes create a "buffer" between teachers and the demands from central office and community (Bossert et al., 1982). The importance of symbolic management is highlighted when one ponders the complexities of trying to assure tight coupling throughout the many aspects of the school organization and among the activities of each individ-

174

ual. Close supervision, the natural procedure for achieving standardization in a bureaucracy, is administratively burdensome and costly as well as incompatible with the concept of teacher professionalism. If, however, staff members subscribe to the clearly articulated instructional philosophy and values of the organization, they will automatically base their behavior on those values without the need for external monitoring and yet retain the flexibility to adapt those behaviors to the unique requirements of the situation at hand.

With the increased popularity of site-based management, school superintendents must be careful to decentralize control over the resources needed to accomplish a task along with the responsibility to carry out that task. Boyer (1983) recommends that principals be given more direct control over budget, procedures for rewarding good teachers, and staff selection procedures.

Human Resource Management

School administrators must realize that their staff is the most important resource they have to assist them in achieving educational excellence. The concept of human resource management describes a set of processes by which administrators can make maximum use of that staff resource. Principals in effective schools recognize the importance of good human relations. They attempt to help teachers fulfill personal needs through the organization and recognize the contributions teachers make to the accomplishment of school goals (Austin, 1979). Staff morale is a precious commodity which is difficult to develop but easy to lose. Effective principals recognize this and do everything possible to ensure that staff is motivated and satisfied (Gross and Herriott, 1965). Along with emphasizing high standards, these principals encourage and recognize good work. The result is that teachers appear to be more committed to effective principals and have a sense of pride in their school and their work.

Another instructional leadership skill which both superintendents and principals must possess is effective communication (Pitner and Ogawa, 1981). Through communication the administrator clarifies organizational goals, forges consensus, provides feedback about performance, interprets organizational behavior, and facilitates countless other organizational tasks (Murphy et al., 1983). Effective communication strengthens the coupling among individuals within the organization and between individuals and the organization itself. Effective principals are able to resolve conflicts between themselves and staff on a wide variety of issues (Anderson, 1982), thereby achieving consensus regarding goals and procedures for their attainment.

Effective principals were observed to use shared decision-making techniques with teachers to accomplish a variety of organizational tasks, although the type and amount of involvement varied with the nature of the task (Rutter et al., 1979). It is not necessary that principals decentralize the decision-making process to allow teachers to make the final decision, but sincere consultation is expected (Greenblatt, Cooper, and Muth, 1984). This team approach reinforces the status of the teacher, makes use of the unique talents of each staff member, and helps to assure the teacher's commitment to the decision (Gersten and Carnine, 1981). Although the team approach is compatible with the collegial atmosphere found in elementary schools, it may also be effective at secondary levels for different reasons, since the principal's lack of specific subject expertise limits his or her "expert" power (Glatthorn and Newberg, 1984). The caveat regarding the coupling of authority with responsibility also applies as the administrator attempts to decentralize decision making, organizational tasks, and accountability to the teacher level.

Creating Climate

One characteristic of an effective school is a positive climate which supports instruction. The principal has much to do with the development and maintenance of that climate. Although individuals can usually identify the existence of a positive school climate, specific descriptions of its elements are problematic (Bossert et al., 1982). Climate may refer to the effects of the physical school environment; the norms, beliefs, and attitudes which pervade the school; or informal social patterns between or among teachers and students. Hallinger et al. (1983) believe that the administrator influences school climate by maintaining high expectations for students, establishing academic standards and incentives for learning, protecting instructional time, and promoting instructional improvement and professional development. In spite of the nebulous definition of this concept, effective principals view climate as a factor which influences student achievement and as a factor which they can develop and nurture (Bossert et al., 1982). The school's climate communicates to students and staff the core values of the school and indicates whether the school is a "good" place to be and a supportive environment in which to learn.

Personal Traits

In summarizing the Far West Laboratory studies of effective principals, Dwyer (1984, 35) states, "Personal traits, experience, training, and beliefs were discussed by principals as influential factors affecting their decisions and activities as instructional leaders. To a large extent, our observations bore out their claims." Principals who espoused certain values such as democracy and shared power tended to practice those values in their dealings with teachers. Other studies suggest that effective principals have a personal vision of what the school should be and then seek support among school staff for that vision. Further, such principals have well-developed analytic, interpersonal, and intellectual skills which they use to identify problems, seek information, and resolve problems.

In addition to those traditionally recognized administrative skills such as setting goals and defining purposes, planning, organizing, communicating and managing information, and building trust, Cunningham and Pyzant (1983) believe that the administrator must possess the following additional leadership skills: focusing on the present and future simultaneously; bridging between and among many sectors of interest; scanning, monitoring, and interpreting events; appraising; adapting; using intuition; developing decision-making policy; and managing symbols.

The importance of addressing personal attitudes, knowledge, and skills in the achievement of excellence cannot be minimized. Since education is relatively insulated from society, lasting change must be internally generated and sustained (Carlson, 1964). External demands from study commissions, state boards of education, and the local community can be imposed, but the success with which they become an integral part of the school will largely depend upon whether the administrator and teachers support and fully implement them. This is why personal characteristics such as the principal's vision of excellence in education and his or her ethical posture are such vital elements in bringing about these changes (Dwyer, 1984; Sergiovanni, 1984).

The nature of administrative personal traits has grave implications for the training and selection of administrators. Many administrators complain that their university training inadequately prepared them for their job (Goor and Farris, 1978). University training programs need to focus more on the leadership functions of the administrator, provide more opportunities for administrators-in-training to develop and test their skills as well as their knowledge, and evaluate the success of their students prior to completion of the degree (Silver and Spuck, 1978). School districts need to be sensitive to the nature of job performance skills associated with administrative excellence and use diverse ways of determining if applicants possess those skills (Goodlad, 1984). In-district training academies, extended internships (Boyer, 1983), and simulation training approaches may need to be explored. Research suggests that women may make better principals (McQuigg and Carlton, 1980), and that neither years of experience nor age are predictors of administrative success (Sarason, 1971). Boards of education and superintendents need to be more receptive to hiring women and minorities. Further, districts and communities "must be prepared for principals who may be 'boat rockers,' not satisfied to keep a low profile and maintain the status quo. Furthermore, to be effective, these principals will require a fair measure of building autonomy. They must be allowed the opportunity to use their information sensing skills, set appropriate agendas, and develop strategies for their particular circumstances" (Manasse, 1984, 451).

One must be cautious in developing too prescriptive a view of the personal characteristics of effective principals, since the studies which have addressed this issue are few and aspects of their methodology have been criticized (Bossert et al., 1982). Nonetheless, the effects of the administrator's personal traits cannot be ignored and should be the focus of continued research.

One Caveat

Since school districts are political and social institutions, they must respond to political and social pressures. Counts (1932) discussed the classic tension created between the societal expectation for educators to maintain the status quo and the educator's professional obligation to change society. Since education's decision-making structure is decentralized to the point where there is considerable local influence, the willingness of the community and board of education to allow or even promote change is very important. This willingness may be expressed in terms of the community's willingness to provide more financial support, in the degree to which they complain about school consolidation, the deemphasis of athletics and extracurricular activities, or similar problems. There is a point beyond which even the most astute and progressive administrator cannot lead a reluctant community or board toward change. The administrator faces the political reality that once that magic point is passed, he or she risks being fired and thereby forfeits all opportunity to bring about any change in that district.

This tension can also be felt at the building level, where the principal's attempts at change must be supported by the superintendent and board. Consider the case of a competent principal who was transferred to another school after its principal was removed because of poor performance. The previous principal rarely supervised teachers and generally gave them adequate or even glowing written evaluations. The new principal took the challenge of instructional leadership seriously and visited classes often. He placed several teachers on remediation plans, instituted termination procedures for one teacher who was extremely deficient, and gave all teachers more honest evaluations, which for many resulted in their receiving lower marks on the evaluation forms. As a result, several teachers filed grievances complaining of harassment, and the teacher who was recommended for termination filed suit claiming racial discrimination.

Bossert et al. (1982) found that effective principals are sensitive to community expectations yet find ways to bring about innovation. However, without the active support of the superintendent and even the board of education, the principal's efforts at change will be thwarted. School administrators must recognize these political and social realities and display a personal and professional integrity whereby they attempt to alter those community and organizational forces which hinder achievement of educational excellence.

Summary

The current discussions in the literature regarding educational excellence and administrator effectiveness would fill volumes. Further, this research is relatively new and as yet has not been subjected to full scrutiny. This chapter has attempted to provide a general framework for reviewing problem areas which affect the practice of excellence by school administrators and to further propose some strategies which the current literature suggests may promote that goal.

Problems which affect the administrator's pursuit of excellence include the nature of education as an open system, confusion regarding the purpose of education and the definition of excellence, the broad base of educational governance, tension between the need for standardization within the bureaucratic nature of schools and for autonomy by principals and teachers, the changing nature of educational demographics and economics, the emergence of new instructional technology, discrepancies between the recommendations of various reform movements and the recommendations from current research, and the inadequacies of administrator training. Current thinking and research reflect several ways through which administrators can achieve excellence in education. Of prime importance is the creation of symbolic meaning through which the administrator identifies key values for the school and then guides staff and student behavior in ways consistent with those values.

Administrators today should rejoice in the fact that current research reinforces the significance of their role and gives guidance for them to assist the school in achieving excellence. More research needs to be conducted regarding administrator effectiveness, but until it is completed the current literature gives administrators a focus for self-reflection and organizational diagnosis. Reforms in the training and selection of school administrators as well as improvements in organizational design and administrative behavior will, when coupled with other recommendations, surely provide an appropriate and plausible agenda for any school district interested in the pursuit of educational excellence.

References and Bibliography

Anderson, C. S. 1982. The search for school climate: A review of the research. *Review of Educational Research* 52:368−420.

Austin, G. R. 1979. Exemplary school and the search for effectiveness. *Educational Leadership* 37:10−14.

Biklen, S. K., and M. B. Brannigan, eds. 1980. *Women and Educational Leadership*. Lexington, Mass.: D. C. Heath.

Bloom, B. S., ed. 1956. *Taxonomy of Educational Objectives*. New York: David McKay Co.

Bloom, B. S. 1980. The new direction in educational research: Alterable variables. *Phi Delta Kappan* 61:382−385.

Bossert, S. T., D. C. Dwyer, B. Rowan, and G. V. Lee. 1982. The instructional management role of the principal. *Educational Administration Quarterly* 18(3):34−36.

Boyer, E. L. 1983. *High School: A Report on Secondary Education in America*. New York: Harper and Row.

Brown v. Board of Education, 347 U.S. 483 (1954).

Carlson, R. O. 1964. Environmental constraints and organizational consequences: The public school and its clients. In *Behavioral Science and Educational Administration*, Sixty-third Yearbook of the National Society for the Study of Education, Part II. Chicago: University of Chicago Press.

Cohen, M. 1982. Effective schools: Accumulating research findings. *American Education* 18(1):13−16.

Cohen, M. 1983a. *Instructional Management in Effective Schools*. Washington, D.C.: National Institute for Education.

Cohen, M. 1983b. Instructional, management, and social conditions in effective schools. In A. Odden and D. Webb, eds., *School Finance and School Improvement: Linkages for the 1980s.* Cambridge, Mass.: Ballinger.

Counts, G. S. 1932. *Dare the School Build a New Social Order.* New York: John Day.

Cramer, J. 1984. Quick fixes carved in stone: Some state commandments of excellence ignore reality and undercut local control. *American School Board Journal* 171(9): 25–28, 44.

Cuban, L. 1983. Effective schools: A friendly but cautionary note. *Phi Delta Kappan* 61: 695–696.

Cubberley, E. P. 1919. *Public Education in the United States.* New York: Houghton Mifflin Co.

Culbertson, J. A. 1983. Theory in educational administration: Echoes from critical thinkers. *Educational Researcher* 12: 15–21.

Cunningham, L. L., and T. W. Payzant. 1983. *Understandings, Attitudes, Skills, and Symbols: Leadership in the Future.* Columbus, Ohio: University Council for Educational Administration.

De Bevoise, W. 1984. Synthesis of research on the principal as instructional leader. *Educational Leadership* 41(5): 14–20.

Divoky, D. 1979. Burden of the seventies: The management of decline. *Phi Delta Kappan* 61: 87–91.

Dwyer, D. C. 1984. The search for instructional leadership: Routine and subtleties in the principal's role. *Educational Leadership* 41(5): 32–37.

Dwyer, D. C., G. V. Lee, B. Rowan, and S. T. Bossert. 1983. *Five Principals in Action: Perspectives on Instructional Management.* San Francisco: Far West Laboratory for Educational Research and Development.

Finn, C. E. 1984. Toward strategic independence: Nine commandments for enhancing school effectiveness. *Phi Delta Kappan* 65: 518–524.

Firestone, W. A., and R. E. Herriott. 1982. Prescriptions for effective elementary schools don't fit secondary schools. *Educational Leadership* 40: 51–53.

Gersten, R., and D. Carnine. 1981. *Administrative and Supervisory Support Functions for the Implementation of Effective Educational Programs for Low Income Students.* Eugene, Oregon: Center for Educational Policy and Management, University of Oregon.

Glatthorn, A. A., and N. A. Newberg. 1984. A team approach to instructional leadership. *Educational Leadership* 41(5): 60–63.

Good, T. L., B. J. Biddle, and J. E. Brophy. 1975. *Teachers Make a Difference.* Washington, D.C.: University Press of America.

Goodlad, J. I. 1984. *A Place Called School: Prospects for the Future.* New York: McGraw-Hill Book Co.

Goor, J., and E. Farris. 1978. *Training Needs of Public School Administrators: A Survey of Local School Districts.* FRSS Report No. 5. Washington, D.C.: National Center for Educational Statistics.

Greenblatt, R. B., B. S. Cooper, and R. Muth. 1984. Managing for effective teaching. *Educational Leadership* 41(5):57–59.

Gross, N., and R. E. Herriott. 1965. *Staff Leadership in Public Schools: A Sociological Study.* New York: Wiley.

Hall, C., W. L. Rutherford, S. M. Hord, and L. L. Huling. 1984. Effects of three principal styles on school improvement. *Educational Leadership* 41(5):22–29.

Hallinger, P., J. Murphy, M. Weil, R. P. Mesa, and A. Mitman. 1983. School effectiveness: Identifying the specific practices, behaviors for principals. *National Association of Secondary School Principals Bulletin* 67(463):83–91.

Hoy, W. K., and C. G. Miskel. 1982. *Educational Administration: Theory, Research, and Practice.* 2d ed. New York: Random House.

Hoyle, J. R., and L. E. McMurrin. 1982. *Critical Challenges for Leaders Who Anticipate and Manage the Future.* Columbus, Ohio: University Council for Educational Administration.

Kirst, N. W. 1983. Effective schools: Political environment and education policy. *Planning and Changing* 14:234–244.

Lieberman, M. 1984. Here's why the key recommendations of the excellence commissions never will become reality in most local school systems. *American School Board Journal* 171(2):32–33.

Lipham, J. A. 1981. *Effective Principal, Effective School.* Reston, Va.: National Association of Secondary School Principals.

Mackett, M., and D. Steele. 1982. *Society and Education: Educational Management for the 1980s and Beyond.* Columbus, Ohio: University Council for Educational Administration.

Manasse, A. L. 1984. Principals as leaders of high performing systems. *Educational Leadership* 41(5):42–46.

McQuigg, B. D., and P. W. Carlton. 1980. Women administrators and America's schools: A national dilemma. *High School Journal* 64(2):50–54.

Meyer, R. 1984. Borrow this new military technology, and help win the war for kids' minds. *American School Board Journal* 171(6):23–28.

Murphy, J., P. Hallinger, M. Weil, and A. Mitman. 1983. Instructional leadership: A conceptual framework. *Planning and Changing* 14(3): 137–149.

National Commission on Excellence in Education (David P. Gardner, Chair). 1983. *A Nation at Risk*. Washington, D.C.: U.S. Government Printing Office.

Odden, A. 1984. Financing educational excellence. *Phi Delta Kappan* 65:311–318.

Peters, T. J., and R. H. Waterman. 1982. *In Search of Excellence*. New York: Harper and Row.

Pitner, N., and R. Ogawa. 1981. Organizational leadership: The case of the school superintendent. *Educational Administration Quarterly* 17: 45–65.

Podemski, R. S. 1984. Implications of electronic learning technology: The future is now! *Technological Horizons in Education (T.H.E.) Journal* 11(8):18–20.

Pogrow, S. 1983. *Education in the Computer Age: Issues of Policy, Practice, and Reform*. Beverly Hills, Calif.: Sage.

Purkey, S. C., and M. S. Smith. 1982. Too soon to cheer? Synthesis of research on effective schools. *Educational Leadership* 40(3):64–69.

Rutter, M., D. Maughan, P. Mortimore, J. Ouston, and A. Smith. 1979. *Fifteen Thousand Hours: Secondary Schools and Their Effects on Children*. Cambridge, Mass.: Harvard University Press.

Sarason, S. 1971. *The Culture of the School and the Problem of Change*. Boston: Allyn and Bacon.

Sergiovanni, T. J. 1984. Leadership and excellence in schooling. *Educational Leadership* 41(5):4 –13.

Shapiro, C. 1984. We'll sue to win equity, say women administrators. *American School Board Journal* 171(3):43–45, 47.

Silver, P. F., and D. W. Spuck. 1978. *Preparation Programs for Educational Administrators in the United States*. Columbus, Ohio: University Council for Educational Administration.

Sizer, T. R. 1984. *Horace's Compromise: The Dilemma of the American High School*. Boston: Houghton Mifflin Co.

Stabile, R. G. 1984. Take this map on the long, lonely journey to excellence. *American School Board Journal* 171(2):25–26, 40.

Weick, K. E. 1976. Educational organizations as loosely coupled systems. *Administrative Science Quarterly* 21:1–19.

Weick, K. E. 1982. Administering education in loosely coupled schools. *Phi Delta Kappan* 63:673–676.

The School Board

Luvern L. Cunningham

here are more than 15,000 school boards in the United States and nearly 100,000 citizens serving as school board members. Within such numbers there are many different patterns of practice and experience. Some boards operate effectively. They have worked out their responsibilities satisfactorily, and the quality of their service is commendable. At the other extreme are school boards wracked with conflict and internal dissension, resulting in low productivity. Their decisions are arrived at in frenetic surroundings with little attention given to quality or wisdom. In between is a broad spectrum of school board performance.

Over the years, patterns of behavior within individual boards have gone through transitions. There are school districts in the United States that in the past had reputations for the quality of their board's work but now are marked by extraordinary conflict and low productivity. The chemistry of intraboard relationships as well as interactions between superintendents and boards ebb and flow over time. Often the change of a single board member can lead to improvement or to radical deterioration in board performance. Given America's commitment to democratic processes and the open invitation for anyone to run for boards of education, it is likely that either pattern of behavior can and will occur.

Local Control and Local Boards in Historical Perspective

The school board is a distinctively American governmental form. Although there are laymen involved in shaping local educational policy in other nations, no other countries have endowed local school communities so generously with substantial power over educational affairs. Despite recent calling into question of most forms of authority and often frenetic atmospheres in which educational issues are examined in many places, school boards persist.

The origins of lay control of education in America are embedded in the early history of the colonies, as Campbell et al. (1985, ch. 8) have pointed out. There is little evidence that the founding fathers of the New England towns possessed gifted political insights or philosophical sensitivities that caused them to establish school committees and eventually school districts. School committees were an obvious response to the growing burden of government thrust upon the selectmen, the forerunners of today's city councilmen (Reeves, 1954, 17). There was simply too much for the selectmen to do. They were part-time officials struggling for survival in primitive surroundings; they hardly had time to manage the affairs of the town, let alone run the schools. It was simply a sensible move for selectmen to create school committees, endow them with some authority, and encourage them to be about the business of supervising local schools. Much had to be done; education was important. The tasks of governance had to be shared among a larger group of citizens. In fact, as Gilland (1935, 8–14) has observed, similar conditions—too much work, need for special knowledge, rapid increase in enrollments, and growing recognition of the importance of education to an industrialized society—subsequently led to the establishment of the superintendency.

In Massachusetts in the early colonial period, two levels of educational government emerged simultaneously, and each affected the development of the other in fundamental ways (Campbell et al., 1985, ch. 8). One of these was the town meeting and the other, the

General Court. The earliest law requiring schools was passed by the General Court in 1647. However, public schools preceded this act by decades in some towns, where citizens established schools through the instrument of the local town meeting. The inhabitants of the towns assembled and voted on such questions as whether or not to have a school, the levy to support it, and even the teacher. Despite local procedural differences, the general religious and cultural homogeneity of the predominantly English population produced remarkable similarities among the town schools that were launched. The 1647 order of the General Court had the effect of endorsing emerging practices in some towns and requiring them in others. All towns were directed to establish schools but were permitted considerable discretion in how it was to be done.

For nearly fifty years the General Court continued the town's responsibility for educational government through the town meeting. In 1693, however, the selectmen were singled out for the first time as local officials with special responsibility for education. Their role gradually evolved within the towns. Fewer decisions were made in town meetings; more were assumed by the selectmen (Campbell et al., 1985, ch. 8). Whether these growing responsibilities were formally delegated at town meetings or simply assumed by selectmen is not clear. Probably the simple imperative of efficiency caused the gravitation of management and supervision away from the town meeting to selectmen.

An interesting circularity was at work. Practices emerged within the towns; they were recognized, endorsed, and reinforced by the General Court; local practices were extended even further; and the General Court legitimated those and added new regulation of its own.

The appearance of school committees, forerunners of school boards, was first noted in the eighteenth century. Once again, practice preceded legislation. Selectmen began assigning responsibility for certain school affairs to special groups. Early school committees were of several stripes: special purpose, temporary, term, elected, appointed, large, and small. Special school committees were assigned a variety of tasks such as visiting schools, selecting teachers and headmasters, providing school housing, and certifying teachers. As characterizes most acts of delegation, selectmen were often reluctant to relinquish complete responsibility to school committees and consequently developed some misgivings about them. In 1826 the General Court gave every town a school committee as a definite body charged with the care of schools. This left little for selectmen or town meetings to do in regard to schooling (Campbell et al., 1985, ch. 8).

Schools, over two centuries, had become complicated enterprises, their functions, numbers, and levels expanded. They eventually had outstripped the supervisory capacity of the town meeting, surpassed the governance ability of the selectmen, and were established as new units of local government. The growth of local school government was a rather natural, evolutionary process in the New England area. In fact the total structure of educational government which evolved in New England was imitated in many sections of the country. School committees became governing bodies and school districts became units of government in the territories and states of the expanding nation during the nineteenth century.

Eventually the school board became a sacred thing—a symbol of all that is good and right and virtuous. We thought it important to shelter most school boards, until recently at least, from the rough-and-tumble of legislative life common to city councils and state legislatures. Most Americans still believe in school boards, even though they may fail to comprehend in definitive terms their functions or social significance. (For further development of such issues as evolution of local school districts, the simultaneous specification of school board responsibilities, and the federal, state, and local statutes and constitutional provisions affecting the everyday performance of school boards, see Campbell et al., 1985, Chs. 1–4, 8).

The School Board Ideology
The ideology of educational governance appears strikingly similar in small towns, common school districts, cities, and other local units of educational government. (Nystrand and Cunningham (1974) dis-

cuss ideology at length.) The dominant pattern is that a group of laymen, chosen in a manner compatible with local interest and state mandate, is responsible for local education. The theory is that laymen can best represent the public interest in this institutional sector. Historically there has been reluctance to relinquish all responsibility for formulation of administration to professionals. Even after the appointment of superintendents, school boards overtly and covertly tried to retain many executive responsibilities (Gilland, 1935).

The school board ideology permeates the language used to describe school boards and school board service. The guides prepared for orienting school board members to their responsibilities, the literature of educational administration, the books on school boards, the hundreds of field studies of school district problems are steeped in ideological sentimentality. School boards *should* be comprised of good people, intelligent people, in fact the best people. They *should* be community leaders, civic oriented, compassionate, understanding—persons dedicated to children. Boards *must* stay out of politics, are best if they are small, elected at large, and allow the administrators and teachers to run the schools. It is *sinful* for board members to cross the policy line into the arena of administration. In fact administrators are to *resist* forcefully all board encroachments on the sanctity of their domains. And similarly boards are to protect their preserves—the enactment of wise and insightful local educational policy.

Current and Emerging Issues of Consequence

Although individual states are at liberty constitutionally to choose their own pattern of educational governance, there are remarkable similarities between and among states in their structures and forms. All states, with the exception of Hawaii, are decentralized. Several types of local districts, special districts, county units, or intermediate structures have responsibility for schools. Superintendents move from one state to another with ease. Furthermore, there are persons who have served on school boards in more than one state. Despite rhetoric to the contrary, the United States has a national system of education, at least structurally. Consequently, the enduring as well as emerging issues confronting school boards are common across the country.

The day-to-day problems of local district administration have not gone unnoticed (Campbell et al., 1985, ch. 8; Cunningham, 1980; Callahan, 1975). Those in a position to observe and analyze school boards in action are aware of serious problems that boards and board members encounter. Many have to do with role, function, and scope of responsibility. In the mid-1970s, I observed a large city board of education for twelve months. Many problems were noted, but among the most prominent was confusion about the roles and scope of responsibility (Carol, 1975). The board was titled "board of education," but most of its energy was addressed to noneducation matters, most of them dealing with adults. Seldom were the educational interests of children in evidence. The questions before the board were those of finance and personnel as well as contracts for school facility maintenance and improvements. Certainly these were far from trivial, but often they engendered extensive debates involving the special interests of individual board members. The relationship between board member discourse and educational policy relevant to learners was remote to nonexistent. That board could have been properly titled a "board of educational personnel and finance" rather than a "board of education."

There is a need, therefore, to consider the central function of local boards. Is it educational policy development and oversight? Or is the central function fiscal stewardship and personnel control? Or is it mediating between the general citizenry and the professionals who operate the schools, as well as the state which imposes its will on local interests (James, 1982)? Some would agree that these are inseparable, that educational policy is inextricably intertwined with issues of finance and personnel and that finance and personnel questions have educational policy implications. The board stands too in judgment of state policy regarding such matters as bilingual education, either facilitating its implementation or blunting its impact if state policy appears to be at odds with locally defined needs. Unfortunately many boards become preoccupied with a part rather than the whole. Their destinies often rise or fall on narrowly based controversies ignoring the basic educational needs of children (Cunningham, 1980).

School Board Member Recruitment and Selection

Many citizens have fuzzy views of school boards, their roles and functions, as well as the responsibilities of school board members. The images that citizens have of boards and board members are the products of a curious blend of disinterest, lack of information, and a faith that in a democracy things just seem to be cared for by somebody, somewhere. Other citizens, on the other hand, have made it their business to learn about school boards and school board members. Such persons develop an information base which allows them to affect local district decisions in substantial ways. Informed citizens are unfortunately few; thus only a limited number of persons can assume school board positions effectively or lobby for educational change or reform.

At midcentury several systems were devised to encourage citizens to consider school board service. Some of the large cities used blue ribbon committees to recruit and screen persons who would later be appointed to the school board. That practice in Chicago drifted into disuse only to be revived in the early 1980s. Caucuses were used extensively in several states to identify, persuade, and eventually sponsor slates of candidates for election in local communities. Occasionally opposition arose from other individuals or groups to challenge the slates, but this occurred infrequently. In fact, a small number of citizens guided the caucus system and were responsible for those who eventually were elected to the board (Campbell et al., 1985, ch. 8).

Such screening devices have had both positive and negative consequences. On the positive side, it is argued that persons with higher educational qualifications, broader community insights, and a trustee ideology toward board service are selected. The negative argument is elitism. Persons chosen for the board are often relatively homogeneous in terms of social class. Individuals who become board members under the caucus system by and large share the values of persons already on the board. Minorities are selected less often than caucasians. Thus, the dominant values are those of white middle- and upper-middle-class persons who often emphasize college preparatory curricula and do what they can to perpetuate that emphasis.

School board service in recent years has become very demanding. Consequently, it may be time to consider some new qualifications for service on school boards. First, persons have to have enough time to invest in this form of public service. Boards spend varying amounts of time on their responsibilities, but it appears that the numbers of meetings are increasing. For example, a prominent superintendent noted that he attended ninety school board meetings during his first year as superintendent in a large school district. Although this figure is unusually high, many board members and superintendents complain about the time given to attending board meetings and preparing for them.

Not only do board members meet more often per month in regular session and stay in session longer than in the past, but there are committees, both continuing and *ad hoc*, that encroach upon citizens' time. Obviously time is money for many people. Thus there may be substantial personal and financial sacrifice involved. We invest modestly in policy development in the United States and expect extensive contributed service, especially at the local government level. It may be time to reconsider district policy regarding stipends for board members. Two approaches could be considered. One would be an extension of present practice of some districts which provide a modest per diem directly to board members for attendance at school board meetings. Another method of payment would be to have these monies go to board members' employers, if the members are employed, to compensate in part for employee time that individuals give to school board work. Using the latter concept, employers may be more enthusiastic about their employees running for boards of education, viewing such service as a public contribution. Such policy in some measure may lead to more heterogeneous patterns of school board composition, representative of the diversity of community values that are found in classrooms. It is time to pay attention to this problem and to find adequate solutions.

School Board/Superintendent Relationships

The relationship between policy and executive levels is hardly a new topic. It has been analyzed and described over and over again. Despite the attention that this nexus has attracted, it is still saturated with difficulty and often misunderstanding (Cunningham and Hentges, 1984, 13–20). It is frequently argued that administrators should stay out of policy and that board members should refrain from intervening in administrative affairs. On the surface at least, there is need to retain some clarity in defining these responsibilities. In its simplest form, administrators should tend to administrative matters and policymakers should attend to policy matters. In the day-to-day welter of management, however, those lines become blurred. Some critics maintain that where there is encroachment in either direction, difficulties arise. Others believe that board members can participate substantially in the administrative activities of a district without harm and that administrators may cross into the policy domain without undue negative consequences. It is in error therefore to suggest absolute separation of responsibilities. There can be settings and conditions where violation of the rule produces not negative but positive results. A few scenarios help make the point.

Scenario A: Administrative Encroachment upon the Policy Domain

The superintendent in this district is in his early sixties. He has served as a school superintendent for twenty-eight years in five districts and three states. He has a fine reputation as a manager, and seldom has he encountered difficulty in working with boards of education. He knows education inside out, has earned the respect of staff members, union representatives, community leaders, and even students in districts where he has served. He has a unique capacity to keep his ear to the ground, sense problems before they become conspicuous, and communicate effectively with boards of education. He keeps board members informed, works well with the chairperson, and provides detailed information coupled with executive summaries so that board members can do their homework efficiently and quickly.

Board members in the several districts with whom he has worked acquire a sense of confidence in his performance and, over time, confidence in their own responsibilities. Much of the policy preparation is handled by the superintendent and his staff. Board members, as a consequence of their confidence in the chief executive, are not uneasy about the central role the superintendent plays in policy development. They seem to think that is the way it ought to be. Consequently, both policy development and administration appear to be in good order. Most, if not all, policy initiatives originate with the superintendent. Board members edit, ratify, and usually support the policy recommendations which issue from the superintendent's office. This pattern of behavior violates the textbook definition of separation of policy and administrative functions but appears to work satisfactorily.

Scenario B: Board Encroachment upon the Administrative Domain

In this school district, the school board historically has run the district. The board member role has been defined so that members take active and sustained interest in the management of schools. This interest includes management activity at the central office and extends through the building level as well. No one knows when this pattern of behavior became prominent. It has become, however, an established pattern, acceptable to the community. Here, as in Scenario A, it dictates the traditional and expected way for board members to perform their duties. They relate directly to principals and central office staff persons. They seldom if ever take their interests through the superintendent's office. Most policy initiatives come from individual board members.

Superintendents in this district have had relatively short tenure. They are stewards expected to do the bidding of the board and of

individual board members who may often make idiosyncratic demands on school personnel, demands unrelated to the board's collective responsibility. Issues related to personnel and finance command most of the board members' attention. Occasionally a board
member is elected with expressed interest in education, but by and
large educational questions have low priority. Superintendents come
to understand "how things are done in this district," fall back, re-
lax, and try to do what they can to benefit children, while they scout
around for another job.

Scenario C: Encroachments in Both Directions

Occasionally there are districts where superintendents control much
of the policymaking function and boards inject themselves heavily
into the management of the district. It is often hard to determine
where initiatives come from without close observation of the interaction between superintendent and board. When this occurs, it appears that there can be reasonable satisfaction on the part of the
board, the superintendent, and the broader community. Again, an
ethos which supports such patterns of behavior develops over time.
In such situations, substantial bargaining and trade-offs must have
occurred in the past. For example, a superintendent may have to
accept a particular administrative appointment advocated by the
board if he or she is to achieve support for policy proposals regarding discipline. As long as everyone plays by these informal rules and
no one violates the norms, such situations seem to be satisfactory. If
board members have substantial confidence in their superintendents
and if superintendents think well of their board members, such re-
versals of the classic definition of responsibility seem to serve the
public interest. Since the pattern does not follow the textbook definition, it begs the question of whether or not clarification of administrative and policy responsibility would improve matters.

Scenario D: Clear, Distinct Separation of Function

This example satisfies the textbook definition of the separation of
functions. Here clear understanding of policy roles and management roles has been achieved. The behavior of administrators and

board members is consistent with this belief system. Board members focus their attention on policy, especially educational policy, and depend upon the superintendent and staff for support services. On the executive side, superintendents depend upon board members for policy initiatives and then provide assistance in policy development. In the meantime, administrators are stewards of the district and manage its affairs without board member interference. Board members hold the management staff accountable for the general welfare of the district. Each participant knows what is expected, abides by those understandings, and in theory as well as in practice, sustains the general welfare of the district.

These brief scenarios describe school district experiences in the United States. They are overly simplistic to make a point. None exists in pure form. But they do offer a basis for comparing and contrasting a broad range of school districts. Hentges's (1985) research provides additional insights into the complexities of these relationships. He emphasizes the importance of trust in determining how effectively superintendents and boards can work together. Hentges notes that school boards permit their chief executives to dominate the decision process 1) when a trust relationship has been established, 2) when the board and superintendent have shared expectations about role behaviors, and 3) as long as the superintendent operates within a zone of tolerance that respects the values and expectations of the board members. From Hentges's work, one can conclude that the superintendent's power is fairly secure on internal, especially technical, matters where educational expertise is required and respected. The executive's power is much less secure on external issues where educational expertise is less germane and board members sense that their community knowledge gives them the edge in the power relationship.

Competition for Visibility Between the Board and the Executive

In recent years, it has become more and more apparent that there is an inherent competitiveness between the board, individual members of the board, and the superintendent. This may be more widespread in large districts than in those of smaller size, but it is always a matter of serious consequence. More than one example could be cited where such competition has led to serious trouble, sometimes even to a superintendent's departure.

Some board members appear to have a lot at stake in regard to this matter, especially those that have further political ambitions or wish, at the least, to be reelected or reappointed to the board. If the superintendent is always seen on TV or sought out by the press, board members become anxious. They develop resentments regarding the popularity of their chief executive. This seems to occur even when board members admire and respect their superintendent. Consequently, the issue becomes how properly to share in both the applause for a job well done and the criticism which inevitably accompanies both policy and executive responsibilities in education.

At the overt level, the problem can be approached forthrightly and, over time, solved. If not attacked in this way, it is likely to lead to trouble. Board member discomfort will lead to resentments and, if unattended, to severe hostility ending in the firing of the superintendent. The needs of children may get lost in the adult problems and concerns. The consistent tension between adult needs, as reflected in school board and superintendent issues, and the genuine, enduring requirements of children and youth are at the heart of policy and executive dilemmas.

Servicing the Policy Needs of the Board

Earlier, reference was made to servicing the policy needs of the board, an important dimension of the superintendent's responsibility. Much of the literature, until recently at least, focused on the superintendent's managerial duties in regard to the school system. The precise responsibilities of superintendents in relation to policy development, the central board function, has been treated sparsely. Moreover, preparation programs for administrators have not singled out the superintendent's policy services to board members as a distinct and major responsibility for chief executives.

Central to this function is assisting the board with creation of a policy development calendar, delegating specific staff assistance to the board in regard to policy arenas under consideration, offering professional consultation about those matters where the superintendent has particular expertise, expediting the movement of policy deliberations through a time sequence, and assisting the board in crystallizing and settling upon final policy statements. After a board has adopted policy, responsibility for implementation is lodged firmly with the chief executive.

Policy development is an evolutionary process. Staff persons servicing the board need to think through the particular points in a policy development sequence where information sharing and the participation of board members are most important. The division of responsibility between staff and board members must be understood. In the absence of such clarity, confusion and even conflict can arise.

A useful framework for delineating the executive's responsibility in working on policy development is Harold Lasswell's *decision phase analysis*, in which the superintendent's function is described in relation to each of several phases of the decision and policy process (Lasswell, 1971; Cunningham, 1979, 1981).

Intelligence Phase. Educational policy should be judged in terms of its quality. For policy to have quality, substantial data gathering must accompany its development. In Lasswell's terms (1975a, 1975b), this is the *intelligence phase* and comes first. Consistent with today's complexity, the range of data sources for policy development extends well beyond what we may have thought it to be in the past. Consequently, staff persons who service the policymaking needs of boards must understand the importance of consulting diverse sources of information, some of which may seem remote. Obviously, school boards can enact policy without examining data. Board members can propose policy changes based solely upon whimsy or caprice, but the application of systematic policy development processes is a higher order of responsibility.

Take the area of discipline and classroom control as an example. Most districts have policies and procedures in place in regard to this area. But these were probably developed over many years and in response to changing needs. Such policies may be perfectly adequate and should be sustained. On the other hand, school boards and administrators, to be confident about policy relating to behavior, may wish to do an extensive analysis of existing policy to determine its adequacy. Identifying the sources of content or knowledge that should be explored is a first step. Once these are known and available, a comprehensive policy development process can begin. Thus staff members assigned to policy development should always be aware that new domains of knowledge may generate fresh insights and therefore better-quality policy.

Returning to the example of discipline and behavior, there are many sources of expertise in most communities that can enhance board members' understanding of issues in this policy area. Persons who work with young people in areas other than schools have experience and insight that might be useful. Clinical psychologists work with children in nonschool settings; family counselors see children's relationships with their parents in ways not available to workers in schools; ministers, rabbis, and priests have associations of a primary nature with young people; psychiatrists possess knowledge that may be applicable, as do persons who work with juvenile justice systems.

Intelligence gathering is exciting in many respects. It must be disciplined, however, and approached with efficiency. The intelligence phase involves staff in gathering and sifting information, synthesizing salient insights, and using those insights as backdrop for potential policy to be prescribed by the board. Although much of the day-to-day intelligence gathering is done by staff, it is important to provide progress reports to board members who eventually must make the ultimate policy determinations. Therefore, the policy development process should not be separate from board oversight and knowledge.

Promotion Phase. Superintendents and staff, trained in policy development, seem to acquire a sixth sense in regard to integrating the intelligence function with *promotion* and *prescription*, the next two phases. These Lasswellian terms are both general and specific. The promotion phase, which primarily involves staff, should not move forward without the board's knowledge and participation. Substantial promotion is required prior to *prescription* (phase three). Board members must be involved in *promotion* if there is likelihood that policy and procedure may need to be enacted by other policy-makers, e.g., the state board of education or the legislature. In regard to discipline and classroom behavior, it is conceivable that the intelligence-gathering phase may lead to the conclusion that there should be changes in the juvenile justice system or the mental health system joined by policy change in school systems. Collaborative changes in three institutional governance structures may be required to enhance opportunities for children and improve their life chances.

Prescription Phase. Prescription is a relatively simple phase. It involves the board, with the help of administrative personnel, arriving at a policy determination. Board members at this point have been informed of relevant data, presented with alternate policy formulations, and given the benefit of a preferred policy alternative hammered out through intensive analysis of comprehensive and complex data. Prescription requires only a motion and an affirmative vote.

There may be important concurrent, ancillary, or supportive policies to be enacted within other policy-making domains, as indicated earlier. Thus the total pattern of *prescription* may not reside only with the school board. Once a board has finished its prescriptive task, the new policy should be analyzed to determine what other procedural changes are needed for it to be consistent with existing policy and procedures. Administrative staff who are policy development specialists are best equipped to do much of this work, and this function rests entirely with administrators in many districts. On the other hand, some boards require a thorough review of procedures essential to implementation and will in fact pass upon those as a matter of board interest.

Invocation Phase. The most underrated and underdeveloped phase in policy activity within most governments is the *invocation* phase. It is preparation for implementation and requires promotional activity largely within the bureaucracy in support of the policy. After the board has completed its work, including oversight regarding implementation procedures (*application*, in Lasswell's terms), preparation for implementation is to begin. Considerable preparatory work must be done to ensure that the inherent quality of the policy will be reflected through effective implementation. Persons responsible for policy application must understand the policy as clearly as the board members who have prescribed it. Thus there is an informing function in addition to a learning responsibility for employees charged with implementation. Those expected to implement policy are often reluctant to do so unless they understand the policy, including its rationale. Education, therefore, is at the heart of preparation for implementation. This is a big order in large districts where there are hundreds of teachers and many, many administrators and other staff who will have a role in carrying out the policy. Boards are wise to allow reasonable time for invocation before expecting implementation to take place and should invest monies in preparation activities.

Implementation simply does not emerge full-blown. It is the result of substantial organized activity. *Invocation* implies acceptance of the policy; acceptance leads to stakeholding, which in turn leads to effective *implementation* or application. Responsibility for invocation rests essentially with the administrative staff, although the board has responsibility for supporting its policy within the community.

Application Phase. Lasswell preferred the term application to implementation, although the two are synonyms. Application is by and large the professionals' responsibility. Implementation means that the policy has been accepted and is now in force. Changes in practice or behavior on the part of professionals or nonprofessionals in the system have taken place. In the example of classroom discipline, the new policies and procedures governing students are in force.

Termination Phase. The application phase extends until some change is required. Lasswell noted that some policies should be terminated early when it is evident that the results are negative. Judgments about *termination* rest ultimately with school boards, but administrators have a responsibility to provide data from which termination decisions can be made.

Appraisal Phase. Ideally, policy warrants systematic review. Few districts, however, approach the ideal. Ongoing policy appraisal falls within the oversight expectation of school boards. Oversight, however, is dependent upon data regarding the effects of policy, and such data are most efficiently provided by administrative staff. Boards can enunciate the range and kind of information they believe necessary to appraise existing policy. Staff must follow through and collect the data requested. Occasionally boards may have outside appraisals made to augment, enrich, or even challenge appraisals made by staff.

The Oversight Function of School Boards

One of the most difficult responsibilities of school boards is to monitor school district activities. Historically the most conspicuous area of oversight has been finance. Stewardship over the fiscal resources of districts has occupied a substantial amount of board member attention, and fiscal reporting has become refined, even routine. Board members who are interested usually get an adequate overview of expenditures as well as revenues on a systematic and regular basis.

Oversight of personnel, educational programs, student achievement, and school facilities is another matter. Board members are less well-prepared to respond to inquiries from citizens about these areas. Summaries and evaluations for oversight purposes of these areas are irregular and less systematic. Often they are done only after board members have made requests for specific data. School facilities, once a focus of substantial interest, have in recent years become less a topic of sustained interest, except for school closings. Consequently studies of school facilities for maintenance, repair, or expansion purposes are requested by board members only now and then. Evaluations of personnel, programs, and achievement are more frequent but seem not to satisfy oversight needs of board members.

Because the regular auditing and oversight mechanisms for these areas are less well developed, stresses and strains can result between administrators and board members. Administrators have become accustomed to providing fiscal data on a regular basis but are not as experienced in their reporting in other areas.

In the future more attention should be given to problems of oversight in the governance and management of local districts. The escalation of public interest in education leads inevitably to community pressures for board accountability. Boards respond by escalating their requests for information from the superintendent and staff. In turn staff members spend more and more time generating data for board members. The production of oversight information encroaches heavily upon the time of administrators, thereby threatening their managerial effectiveness. Somehow balance must be achieved.

Selection of Superintendents

School boards periodically are confronted with the task of choosing a new chief executive. The average tenure of a superintendent in the United States is about five or six years, although turnover rates have ebbed and flowed through the decades. Obviously superintendent selection is an important action. It is a time for reappraisal in many districts, for clarifying the definition and description of the superintendent's role and allowing boards to examine their own functions in regard to the executive.

In the past three decades, school boards have increasingly employed consultants to help in the search process, although the ultimate choice (and legal responsibility) rests with the board. Some board members, as well as citizens of local districts, reject hiring consultants on at least two bases: people feel that the board or the community can carry out a successful search, and the costs involved are viewed as unnecessary expenditures of public monies.

The sequence of selection begins with a vacancy in the superintendency. The school board considers how it will proceed in its search for a successor. If consultants will be involved, they are identified, screened, and employed. They assist the board in refining the criteria to be used in the selection process. Jointly they develop a description of the superintendency and announce the vacancy in several ways, through regional and national newspapers, placement offices, newsletters of state associations of school boards, and other superintendents. Getting the word out that a given school district is searching for a new superintendent is important. Consultants also

announce vacancies through their professional networks of contacts. Their networks include leading practitioners, professors of
educational administration, and other administrative officers in colleges and universities across the country, who nominate candidates
for the post. These nominees are then invited to apply should they
be interested. Other people apply on their own, whether or not they
have been nominated for the post. Eventually a pool of applicants is
acquired. Consultants then examine the applications, contact references, sift and sort those who apply, and choose a small number of
persons who appear to be most highly qualified for the superintendency. Those candidates are then recommended to the board for
interviews.

Embedded in this sequence is an important opportunity for
school boards to understand their role, function, and responsibility
more clearly. The departure of a superintendent may produce a division within a school board. This is particularly true when superintendents are fired or pressured to leave. Most superintendents have
some support on school boards and although, over time, their support may be reduced, a few board members retain their respect and
affection for the incumbent. If the previous person has been fired,
the search process is an opportunity to bring new cohesiveness to a
divided body.

Evaluation of the Superintendent

One aspect of the selection process not discussed to this point is
proposing an evaluation procedure for the new superintendent. Detailed and intensive discussion of evaluation at the time of selection
can be a healthy investment of time and effort on the part of the
board and the superintendent-to-be.

Recent research (Sonedecker, 1984; Carol, 1972) has revealed
several patterns of superintendent evaluation. Some boards never
evaluate their superintendents formally. Others, over the years, have
developed refined procedures for assessing their superintendents'
performance. In between, there is a range of partially formal and
partially informal practices. Where attention is focused on superintendent evaluation, there is a higher degree of satisfaction with the

chief executive and school board roles than in those districts where evaluation is casual, intermittent, and not carefully designed.

Substantial progress in formalizing evaluation has occurred in recent years. Much of it has been stimulated by the work of state school board associations. Illinois, for example, has developed detailed procedures which are rational and feasible and can easily be adopted by local school districts. Evaluation of superintendents is now mandatory in some school districts as a point of law. The thesis is that evaluation is important and can be a factor in improving the quality of local school districts.

Trustee and Representative Orientation

Hentges (1984) has concluded that board members' orientation regarding their school board service contributes either to harmony or discord within the board or between the board and the superintendent. The trustee orientation is similar to the perspective that corporation boards or college trustees hold regarding their responsibilities. Trustees hold their executives responsible for management of the enterprise, and they supervise within clearly defined boundaries and expectations. Individuals with a constituency perspective, on the other hand, believe their primary responsibility is to their constituents, those who have either elected or appointed them. They often find it difficult to place the collective board ahead of what they define as a constituent interest. Their allegiances are outward to the community and not inward to the board or the superintendent.

When some members of the board are trustees and others have a constituency perspective, conflict will arise. And that circumstance will, in the long run, increase the power of the superintendent (Hentges, 1984). As time moves along, the representative board members become increasingly frustrated as trustee types support the superintendent in his executive behaviors. If the board membership is tipped toward the trustee perspective, the superintendent is likely to sustain his power position. On the other hand, if the balance is in favor of the representative orientation, the superintendent's power is increasingly vulnerable.

Boards might examine their membership in terms of orientation. When the realization that there are differences is acknowledged, everyone has a better chance of understanding those differences and openly responding to them. Second, the superintendent who is confronted with such circumstances can choose an approach to working more intelligently with the board. Third, if it appears that the frequency of nonconstructive conflict growing out of such situations is high, state legislatures may choose to change methods of board member selection to favor board majorities with one orientation or the other. Obviously, change in state policy of this sort would be controversial, engendering widespread debate which in itself could be constructive.

Strengthening the Governance and Management of Local School Districts

Citizens have been inclined to take the American educational system as a given. Seldom, if ever, are questions raised about other patterns of organization and control. The belief in local control is deeply embedded in the minds of most school board members as well as professional educators, even though the scope of local control appears to be diminished (James, 1982; Campbell, 1959). Yet, there are alternative forms of educational governance which offer suggestions for fine tuning our existing system.

Turning the Responsibility Over to Professionals

One alternative is to place both the means and the ends of education in the hands of professional educators with a minimum of lay participation. Health policy, for example, is argued essentially by professionals from the health care professions at the state and federal levels. With the exception of some mental health policy matters, most health policy is centralized. Although the Congress and state legislative bodies are responsible ultimately for policy determinations, they are influenced strongly by the health professional interest groups. Only recently have other public interest groups become active participants in the development of health care policy, for example policy related to the uninterrupted escalation of health costs. With the exception of health care costs, professional domination of health care development has contributed to extraordinary advances to health care science and technology. Similar advances have not occurred in education. Schooling seems to be linked to the least common intellectual denominator, while improvements in health care are tied to breakthrough ideas advanced through research. Generous research funding from public and private sources enhances medical science. If one system of control fits one human service area well, it stands to reason that another field, such as education, could study its neighbor. In Ohio, for example, eight professions are joined in a structure which permits them to affect human services policy, including education, by producing policy analysis services and documents for policymaking bodies.

Today, the United States is intensively involved with other nations of the world in technological competition of economic consequence. Each breakthrough, either in basic science or technology, has immediate impact on the U.S. economy and subsequently upon employment. The competition is so intense that established industries such as automobile manufacturing cannot depend upon their own research and development capability to keep pace with competitors. Major American corporations such as Ford and General Motors rely upon consulting specialty firms to develop advanced laser-based technologies directed toward the product refinements and quality control which permit them to remain competitive.

Education is in the same race in its own way. The achievement of American students compares unfavorably with that of youngsters from several other nations. If American students continue to fall behind, local discretion may have to give way to additional centralized decision making for the U.S. to remain competitive in education. Pressure may grow in the years ahead to reduce further local policy prerogatives, even to the point of discontinuing local school boards. Should that occur, education professionals would have a more central role in educational policy determination.

Boards of Educational Finance

Observers of boards of education have often noted that school boards are preoccupied with finance issues. This is understandable since many school districts depend heavily upon local revenue sources for fiscal support. Historically many boards also became involved in personnel appointments, and patronage, once widespread in American education, is reappearing in some districts. As a result of these influences, little time may be allocated or available for educational policymaking. Educational policy goes by default, is enunciated at the state level, or becomes the province of administrators.

An alternative is to create local boards of educational finance with powers and responsibilities limited to that domain. Educational policy would be the responsibility of state boards of education, and state policies would be applicable to all local educational units. There are advantages and disadvantages to this proposal. Some would be fearful of too much centralization in regard to curriculum and instruction. Others would resent this encroachment upon local control. On the other hand, some board members would find it attractive to concentrate on finance and its attendant problems rather than to carry the additional burden of educational policy development, an area which is often alien to board member interests and competencies, and as noted earlier, is the area where board members relinquish power to their superintendent.

Another argument for making this change is to bring state and local policy into conformance with practice. Since, as a matter of fact, local boards make relatively few educational policies and spend much, if not most, of their time on finance and personnel-related matters, it makes sense to clear the air and address board member attention and energy completely to these issues. Many educational policies of long standing have already been enunciated by either state legislatures or state boards of education. Since we have found this acceptable over a long time, formal responsibility for educational policy might well be placed at the state level.

Local Boards of Education with Central Fiscal Support

Another alternative would be to clear the agendas for local boards and to allow them to focus completely on educational policy. The function of local boards could be confined to educational policymaking without attendant concerns for finance; financial support would be centralized. This would preserve traditional beliefs in local control and allow educational policy to adjust to local needs. In fact, local control would be enhanced since boards would have time to examine educational needs, refine and develop sound educational policy, and engage in educational oversight activities that would be meaningful.

Centralizing state education fiscal policy is consistent with state responsibility for education. The state's welfare, which is intrinsically linked to education, would be more visible and politically conspicuous. Bargaining of teacher contracts would consistently bring educational needs before the people on a statewide basis. The primary arenas for political activity affecting eduation would be shifted in some measure, but these could very well be constructive changes.

As the general citizenry becomes more aware of the interdependency between education, economic growth, and high technology, for example, it may be possible to develop policies at the state level which are fashioned after intensive thought about the impact of these areas upon one another. It can be argued that it would be more efficient and effective for such policies to be made on a state-wide basis rather than district by district.

Fine Tuning the Present System

These three alternatives are useful if for no other reason than that they allow us to see our present structure in a fresh light. There are some modifications in existing governance structures and mechanisms that could improve the quality of educational policy and the effectiveness of management. Dror (1968, 299–300) has noted that American governments at all levels spend very little for policy development. This is especially true at local levels and applies to most state boards of education too. School boards not only fail to invest in policy development and policy oversight but also seldom have clear definitions of how policy is to be determined, who is to be involved, what staff roles and responsibilities are, and when new policy is to be developed or present policy reviewed (i.e., having a policy calendar to guide their work). Several suggestions might be considered:

1) That local boards of education develop discrete and definitive policies about policy, some of which are implied by the subsequent proposals for change in the governance and management of local school districts.

2) That educational policy become the primary and continuing focus of school officials, as distinct from personnel, business, and physical facilities, for example.

3) That school boards meet four times per year for extended periods of time (two or three days) in order to gain full command of policy-related data and knowledge and have time to reflect and consider the views of citizens in regard to policies under consideration.

4) That policymaking agendas be prepared two to three years in advance to frame the work of the board, administrative staff, professional organization leaders, student leaders, and citizen groups.

5) That superintendents be given long-term contracts (three to five years) with clear-cut guidelines to surround their performance as well as the freedom to administer schools within those boundaries.

6) That the form and substance of the superintendent's evaluation be clearly defined and understood at the outset of the contractual period and that data be accumulated and organized to allow the board as the employing agency to pass adequate judgment about the superintendent's performance.

7) That the employee salary and wage determination prerogative now retained by boards of education of local school districts be moved to the state level.

8) That representatives of professional groups (teachers' and administrators' organizations) for local school districts become members of the local boards of education

and assume policy and accountability responsibilities equivalent to that office.

9) That boards of education utilize a disciplined framework for policy enunciation and employ that framework within a facility especially designed for that activity, one which emphasizes the efficient use of data retrieval and display technology.

10) That school board members and the executive staffs of school districts be trained to handle policy development activity for their enterprises.

11) That one or more states pass special legislation allowing school districts to suspend (for a period of time) current statutes, rules, and regulations for the governance and management of school districts in order to test alternative approaches to governance and management.

12) That processes of policy development and their enunciation, as well as the processes of management, be designed to include genuine, sustained student, parent, citizen, and professional educator involvement (Cunningham, 1980).

Implications for These Proposals

It is clear that one set of implications relates to policy development itself. From my perspective, it is evident that the *policy development process* is an important concept and should be addressed to broad sectors of educational policy. It is also clear that policy development needs to be a disciplined and organized process requiring extensive time, conducted in settings conducive to concentration and reflection, and incorporating participation of laymen and professionals. Similarly intensive thought needs to be given to the *policy needs* of school districts, including public and professional involvement in policy identification, preparation of policy development agendas and calendars, provisions for the training of school officials in their respective roles and responsibilities in the *policy development process*, and incorporation of policy technologies and support capabilities to enhance the quality of policy products.

It is also clear that the policy requirements of an institution, once understood, defined, and listed on a calendar, are manageable and can be met. In chaotic circumstances, many decisions are made but few well-developed policies are produced. Actually only a few basic policies need to be developed each year. Thus what may appear to be an overwhelming problem is not so intimidating when it is broken into policy sectors and fitted into a rational agenda of review and development. The segmenting of intensive work on policy permits a staff to have reasonable time to perform policy development services for school boards. Much of the current frenzy could be reduced, and information which results from within-district research as well as new knowledge acquired from other sources can be incorporated into the policy development process. This is the intelligence work so strongly advocated by Harold Lasswell.

It *is not* the intent of these proposals to depoliticize education. It *is* the intent to make the policy process more open and accessible, less vulnerable to the machinations of policy elites, and more yielding to the best policy science intelligence. Implementation of the proposals would compartmentalize a bit more clearly the work of board members and executive staffs. But it would also lead to the integration of these two functions in order to produce an improved institutional performance. The power and influence of neither the governors nor the managers would be reduced. Both would be enhanced.

Implementation of these proposals would, in my judgment, create a setting where the idealized "creative experience" so wisely articulated by Mary Parker Follett in the mid-1920s could be realized. It would be possible for integrative behavior to occur, reducing the occasions for compromise and stalemate.

There are problems associated with the proposals. If taken seriously, they may lead to general reexamination of the constitutional and statutory provisions for the governance and management of local districts. For example, many current school board responsibilities may need to be managed in other ways. Determining salaries and wages of school personnel, constructing and even naming school buildings, authorizing the issuance of bonds, setting school tax elections or referenda of other sorts, approving applications for federal funding, and other such decisions may be designated as responsibilities of other governments. Removing the collective bargaining function from local districts would clear out underbrush and permit boards of education and top school officials to focus more directly upon pedagogical and learning policy. State-level bargaining may lead to a clearer, more uniform delineation of the scope of bargaining and to the identification of educational program costs distinct from those of personnel.

If these proposals were adopted, much of the current trivia which occupies board member time and energy would fall away. The energies of the administrative staff would be devoted to the effective administration of policies enunciated by the board. As a consequence of longer contracts for superintendents, the period for judging the effectiveness of administrative leadership and performance would be extended. At the same time, school district planning would fall within longer time frames, and some sanity could be restored to the administration of many school districts where chaos is now the rule.

Incorporating High Technology into Policy Development
Discussions of high technology take place in all aspects of institutional and personal life. We are interested here in its meaning for policy development at the board level. Computers have been incorporated into management for nearly forty years. Although applications within educational institutions have varied, they nevertheless have had substantial meaning for administration. Computers have been used for financial accounting and pupil accounting, payrolls, inventory and warehousing. Computer-assisted instruction has been the subject of widespread application, research, and analysis.

Teledemocracy is attracting attention in some arenas of government (Danziger, 1982). Through television linked with computers, it is possible to involve the electorate more frequently and fundamentally in governance issues. Experiments such as QUBE in Columbus, Ohio have demonstrated the technical efficiency of taking the public's pulse on local issues through interactive television. Local school boards in the future may choose this method to take straw votes of the public on policy issues. Or they may change election laws to allow taxpayers to vote electronically from their living rooms on specific issues, thus relieving boards of that responsibility. Boards would retain the responsibility of developing educational policy proposals, but the voters would ultimately vote for or against the proposed policy. Obviously such utilization of technology for policy purposes would follow substantial changes in state law as well as local district policies and procedures. The full use of teledemocracy would bring districts full circle. The town meetings that generated the tradition of lay control of public education would return, with living room push buttons as proxies for a show of hands.

New policy questions will surface in school districts in response to teledemocracy. New questions of data ownership and school board access have already arisen. Traditionally, board members have had considerable information about finance provided by the staff. But financial data lend themselves to quantification and relatively inexpensive storage and retrieval. Some types of personnel data fall into this category, too. Allowing board members access to personnel data files immediately raises the complex issue of privacy and confidentiality. Do school board members have the right to personnel data on individuals? There seems to be little question about board member rights to aggregate personnel data from data storage systems, but information about individuals is another matter. Similarly, there are questions about the ownership of data relative to individual pupils. Who owns the personnel data about individual children? Are such data the property of the board? The parents? Again there appears to be little problem with aggregate data. But other questions arise when records of individual students are opened for professional or other use. School boards need to develop policy about data storage and retrieval, access rights and privileges, and data ownership.

Thoughts in Closing

Several major questions have been left unaddressed. One is the impact of collective negotiations upon the policy process. Obviously collective bargaining has narrowed the range of discretion that local boards possess. The impact of bargaining imposes itself in other ways. For example, much staff and board time is given over to items on the bargaining table, creating an enormous drain on policy development resources. Such is the nature of things today, and unless there is a move to elevate bargaining to the state level, these circumstances will continue.

Another prominent need is for improved board member orientation and preparation. In a September 1984 issue of *School Board News*, the president of the National School Boards Association argued forcefully for school board training. He indicated that this was the number one need for board members in the United States. Serving on school boards is an exceptionally difficult public service. The time requirements are extensive, and even more important than time is the amount of knowledge that board members must acquire if they are to be effective. Requiring board members to go through several months of preparation before they begin to take active parts in policy determinations would likely narrow the field of candidates; few would have the time and interest to devote to school board membership.

As we move further towards the year 2000, issues facing school boards will be even more complex. For example, public responsibility for the first five years of life will confront boards soon. Local school districts may have to assume responsibility for providing educational and custodial services for children below the age of five. The nation slowly has become aware of the great significance of those formative years upon later development. Bloom's (1964) book, *Stability and Change in Human Characteristics*, documents unequivocally the need for thoughtful attention to child development before the age of five. Kindergarten teachers note the differences among children in terms of maturation and emotional and cognitive development, depending upon the nature and quality of their preschool experience. Educational, social, economic, and political questions abound in this area. Before districts attempt to conclude what their policy should be, exhaustive studies should be made. And this is only one policy arena that promises to be more difficult in the future.

The ideas advanced in this chapter are offered in the hope that they will stimulate thought and discussion leading to more effective educational governance. Widespread recognition of the importance of education to the national interest and elevated expectations for school systems reveal the significance of the governance and management functions at all levels. Thus it behooves laymen and professional educators to join in the search for the best ways to perform their functions.

Bibliography and References

Bloom, B. 1964. *Stability and Change in Human Characteristics.* New York: John Wiley.

Callahan, R. E. 1975. The American board of education 1789–1960. In Peter C. Cistone, ed., *Understanding School Boards*, 19–46. Lexington, Mass.: Lexington Books.

Campbell, R. F. 1959. The folklore of local school control. *The School Review* 67 (Spring): 1–15.

Campbell, R. F., L. L. Cunningham, R. O. Nystrand, and M. D. Usdan. 1985. *The Organization and Control of American Schools.* Columbus, Ohio: Charles E. Merrill Publishing Company.

Carol, L. N. 1972. *A Study of Methods for Evaluating Chief School Officers.* Trenton: New Jersey School Boards Association.

Carol, L. N. 1975. School board/superintendent relationships. Unpublished paper presented to Third Party Education Network, San Francisco, California.

Cunningham, L. L. 1979. Policy sciences in the field: 1973–78. *Quarterly Report.* Columbus, Ohio: The Mershon Center.

Cunningham, L. L. 1980. Policy about policy: Some thoughts and projections. *The Executive Review* 1 (November). Institute for School Executives, The University of Iowa, Iowa City.

Cunningham, L. L. 1981. Applying Lasswell's concepts in field situations: Diagnostic and prescriptive values. *Educational Administration Quarterly* 17 (Spring): 21–43.

Cunningham, L. L., and J. T. Hentges. 1984. *The American School Superintendency, 1982: A Full Report.* Arlington, Va.: American Association of School Administrators.

216

Danziger, J. N. 1982. Computers in the policy process. In *Computers and Politics*. New York: Columbia University Press.

Dror, Y. 1968. *Public Policymaking Reexamined*. San Francisco: Chandler Publishing Company.

Follett, M. P. 1924. *Creative Experience*. New York: Longmans, Green and Co., Inc.

Gilland, T. M. 1935. *The Origin and Development of the Power and Duties of the City-School Superintendent*. Chicago: The University of Chicago Press.

Hentges, J. T. 1984. The politics of superintendent-school board linkages: A study of power, participation, and control. Ph.D. dissertation, The Ohio State University.

Hentges, J. T. 1985. The politics of superintendent-school board relationships. Paper presented at the February 1985 convention of the American Association of School Board Members, Dallas, Texas.

James, H. T. 1982. Educational administration and organization: A 40-year perspective. *Educational Researcher* 2 (February): 14–18.

Lasswell, H. D. 1971. *A Pre-View of Policy Sciences*. New York: American Elsevier Publishing Company.

Lasswell, H. D. 1975a. The future of government and politics in the United States. In Louis Rubin, ed., *The Future of Public Education: Perspectives on Tomorrow's Schooling*. Boston: Allyn and Bacon, Inc., 1–30.

Lasswell, H. D. 1975b. Research in policy analysis: The intelligence and appraisal functions. In Fred J. Greenstein and Nelson Polsby, eds., *The Handbook of Political Science*, Vol. 6: *Policies and Policymaking*, 1–22. Reading, Mass.: Addison-Wesley.

National Commission on Excellence in Education. 1983. *A Nation at Risk: The Imperatives of Educational Reform*. Washington, D.C.: U.S. Department of Education.

Nystrand, R. O., and L. L. Cunningham. 1974. *Dynamics of Local School Control*. ERIC Documents Reproduction Service.

Reeves, C. E. 1954. *School Boards, Their Status, Functions, and Activities*. Englewood Cliffs, N.J.: Prentice-Hall.

Sonedecker, J. 1984. Evaluation of the American public school superintendent. Ph.D. dissertation, The Ohio State University.

Zuhlke, D. J. 1984. Use of the decision seminar as an enabling convention for problem-solving and policy development in the Seattle public schools. Ph.D. dissertation, The Ohio State University.

The School
and the Community

John W. Arnn, Jr.

he fact that public schools have recently been placed under the scrutiny of the American public is not a revelation. Indeed, one can hardly escape some sort of encounter with a topic concerning public education. However, too often the American school is dealt with by the media and professional reports as an entity or institution that is somehow isolated from its setting, the American community. If one is to study the public school, then one must also consider the milieu in which it functions and which to a large degree it reflects.

Communities in which public education exists have undergone dramatic changes during the last three decades. The neighborhood or community of the 1950s was significantly different from today's. In most parts of the country, the neighborhood population was much more stable. People tended to reside for a longer period of time in a given community, and one was much more likely to encounter second- and third-generation families in the same locale. The country's population dispersion was also more stable. Many areas in the country had higher densities of racial and cultural mixes, but even those areas remained rather static, with little shifting.

The family unit was more likely to include both the mother and father. The father usually was employed in the same area in which he lived, and he was less likely to change jobs than today's father. The mother was far less likely to be employed outside the home even after children completed their schooling.

The church was a prominent institution in development of and activity within the community. Children and parents tended to spend a greater amount of time in church-related activities than to-day's families.

Schools and teachers had a better-defined role and status in the community of thirty years ago. Schools were not only the community hub for education but were also centrally involved with community activities. Teachers tended to become long-term residents of a community, often teaching three generations of the same family during their career. Generally speaking, the teacher was held at a higher level of esteem by students and the community. There was a high degree of satisfaction among teachers regarding their profession and more significant involvement in professional organizations (Oliva, 1976).

Three decades ago, there was a higher degree of formal and informal collaboration among schools, churches, and families within a community. The child was a strong focal point of concern and attention. Commonly understood and shared values promoted mutual support and reinforcement of learning and behavior. The overall stability of the community and its residents provided consistency and continuity in the pursuit of education.

Attitudes concerning education began to alter during the mid-1950s. Teachers no longer felt the same about their profession as they once had. Parents became more isolated from schools and had less time or incentive to remain involved. Certainly, student attitudes about school changed. School encountered a different student than ever before. Learning was not as much a goal as it was an interruption to the stimulation provided by a technologically enhanced age.

The goal of education has remained the same. However, the role of the school and its personnel has changed dramatically. During the last thirty years, the school has been used by society as a vehicle to eradicate racial injustice, poverty, crime, and poor nutrition as well as illiteracy and ignorance. Education has been called upon to support values no longer supported in the home and to foster traditions that are little valued by the community.

The responsibilities assigned to public education are monumental, but what is equally awesome is that schools have *accepted* these responsibilities rather than sharing them.

Several factors were catalytic in forming the current school-community relationship. These factors include desegregation, changing social conditions, teacher attitudes, and community attitudes.

Desegregation

Desegregation was a significant factor in its impact on schools and communities. Beginning with the 1954 *Brown vs. Board of Education* case, educational activity shifted from pedagogical development to social change.

Gerard and Miller (1975), in their study of school desegregation, identified eleven assumptions underlying the predicted impact of desegregation on schools, teachers, students, and parents:

1) The achievement gap is not due to a difference in native ability between blacks and whites.
3) Any achievement gap is due to a difference in orientation and expectation toward education by black and white communities.
3) Deficits in orientation and attainment are reversible and are easier to reverse in the younger child.
4) Social influence will occur in any group and the behavior, attitudes, and values of the majority will influence the minority.
5) There are no significant obstacles to communication and interaction.
6) Teachers' influences will balance achievement.
7) Competition is good and will lead to improved performance.
8) If a performance standard is raised, a person will improve to meet the new standard.

9) Teachers will treat students the same regardless of their race.
10) Desegregation will improve a minority child's self-esteem.
11) Higher esteem will generate higher levels of achievement.

Time has not been kind in validating the underlying assumptions of desegregation. In fact, many of the obstacles which have emerged in school-community relations have clear ties to the assumptions delineated by Gerard and Miller. What school desegregation has proven is the folly of pinning all of society's hopes on a single institution—schools—to precipitate change.

Changing Social Conditions

The family unit of today has changed significantly. By 1980, approximately 55 percent of mothers of school-age children were employed outside the home. Nearly half of the children born today can expect to live with a single parent by the time they finish high school, and there is a much higher incidence of complex family units formed by remarriage. It is becoming increasingly rare for a child to start and finish public education within the same community. In fact, over forty million people move annually in the United States.

According to the recent Carnegie Foundation technical report on *The Condition of Teaching*, today's population dispersion is dramatically different than it was twenty years ago (Feistritzer, 1983). Large population shifts are occurring from the Northeast and North Central states to the Sunbelt. Six of the ten states that grew most in the last decade showed the greatest increase in individuals aged sixty-five and older. This population brings with it many implications for public education.

As John Goodlad (1984) has indicated, the relationship between school and community is also different today. Actions and activities once initiated at school were, in all likelihood, supported at home thirty years ago. However, today's response to disciplinary actions at school is far more likely to be adversarial in nature. The issue of *in loco parentis* has ceased being a major school-community issue. Paradoxically, however, there has probably never been a time when the school has been asked to provide more support for children in light of the changing family unit. Parents often leave their children at school early and pick them up late.

The double-income family has added a new child to society, the "latchkey" child. This child sometimes leaves an empty house in the morning and almost always returns to an empty house. The emotional and educational impact on these children is just now beginning to be addressed and investigated. Latchkey children comprise a significant portion of the population. Some communities have begun to establish telephone hot lines so that the children can call to talk with someone or to ask for help in an emergency.

Schools have always been considered ethnic melting pots. However, today's mobile population, combined with immigrants fleeing from strife-ridden countries around the world, provides additional challenges to schools and communities alike. In the last twelve years, the Hispanic population, the fastest growing ethnic group in America, has increased by more than 60 percent, creating a young population whose impact is immediately felt in the public school classroom. It has been projected that by the year 2000, the United States will become the fifth largest Spanish-speaking country in the world.

In many areas of the country today, the terms "neighborhood" and "community" have lost their traditional meanings (Boyer, 1983). Economic conditions and changing lifestyles have replaced the traditional neighborhood scene of thirty years ago with massive apartment complexes, shopping malls, vast supermarkets, emergency clinics, and entertainment centers. People today may well identify with a geographic area but are less likely to think of it as a neighborhood or "their" community. As a by-product of increased mobility, people may not stay long enough in a place to develop any identification with it.

Another factor that complicates the sense of community, both educationally and socially, is that many individuals neither work in nor play in the area in which they live. The children may have closer ties to the school and community than do their parents. Suburbia usually supports no major vocational industry where adults invest the major part of their time and energy each day. Many individuals seek no additional involvement or emotional investment in their residential community.

Changing social conditions are not necessarily good or bad. But they are occurring. Traditional strategies simply have not effectively met changing times and needs.

Teacher Attitudes

It should come as no surprise that teachers' attitudes have also changed somewhat during the past decades, even though many teachers still enter the profession for the same reasons they did twenty-plus years ago:

1) the desire to teach a specific subject or just to teach in general,
2) the desire to be of service to others, and
3) the value of teaching as an ideal (Goodlad, 1984).

Salary has never been a major factor in attracting teachers to the profession, except perhaps as a second family income. Regretfully, in terms of real dollars today's teachers make less than they did twenty years ago (Feistritzer, 1983). Recent legislation in many states, however, has greatly improved the salary incentive available to teachers and may provide the impetus to bring teachers' salaries in line with other professions.

In a recent study of student attitudes about entering the teaching profession, Mangieri and Kemper (1984) found that in order to make the profession more attractive, prestige of teachers and teaching careers, which suffered in the changing community, also needs to be enhanced.

As a result of changing family structures and parental roles, teachers often have little to no actual contact with parents. Parents often are simply not available during school hours and perhaps are

224

working in a city or community over thirty miles distant. Teachers are confronted with parents who are too tired or too distracted to contribute the requested time and energy in educational support.

Teachers in many states have found themselves responsible for implementing an increasing number of state-mandated requirements in addition to teaching their content specialties. In many areas around the country, teacher credibility has been questioned, tested, and found lacking. Many teachers have found themselves ill-prepared to confront the realities of overcrowded and underfunded classrooms. As a result, community perceptions have deteriorated and existing support diminished. Shortages in critical teaching fields have also generated temporary and emergency measures which have sometimes adversely affected teacher morale.

These conditions, combined with the daily demands associated with the teaching act and the teaching profession, can often generate strong feelings, ranging from frustration to despair, in teachers.

Community Attitudes

Individuals in communities or neighborhoods tend to have three different responses to school issues. The first is from their own experience as students in the educational system. Since American education has been highly successful in insuring that the majority of the native citizenry has passed through its doors, most have had personal experiences through which current information, situations, and proposals are filtered.

Secondly, individual response to schools may reflect some personal encounter as parents with children in the system. All too often, that encounter is problem- or crisis-oriented and leaves a lasting impact which is not always objective or positive.

The third response involves a reaction to comparative data, for example, when one reads in a newspaper about local ACT or SAT scores compared to a regional or national norm, or about a drop in achievement scores over the last two years, or about some percentage of teachers who have failed to achieve a minimum cutoff score in a state competency test.

A recent study by Kappa Delta Pi (Frymier, 1984), surveying over one hundred schools in the United States, revealed the following teacher beliefs concerning parent commitment to schools:

1) Only at the middle and high school levels were parents rated as being "often" supportive by more than 50 percent of the teachers.
2) Thirty-seven percent of high school teachers indicated that parents seldom or never come to school to discuss their children's problems.
3) Twenty-one percent of high school teachers indicated that parents seldom or never encourage and support their efforts.
4) Sixty-two percent of high school teachers indicated that parents seldom or never make sure that their children do their homework.

Community attitudes about education change more slowly than teachers' attitudes (Frymier, 1984). Once the public forms a specific perception, it is difficult to change that perception in a short time. For example, a 1984 Gallup Poll of Public Attitudes Toward the Public Schools showed no change over a five-year period in the public's ranking of discipline as the number one school problem. However, high school teachers, who had ranked discipline as the number two school problem five years ago, currently rank it as tenth.

Communities have been fairly consistent across the country in giving their schools and school personnel low grades as educators. On the other hand, teachers criticize parents for not assisting their children in homework assignments, failing to respond to requests for teacher-parent conferences, and being totally unaware of the impact of nonschool-related activities on academic progress. A teacher interviewed during a study by Ernest Boyer (1983) made one of the more generous assessments of parent attitudes toward teachers: about 50 percent supported teachers, 10 percent always supported their children, and 40 percent wanted teachers to handle everything and not bother them.

In another study, when parents were asked what they really understood about the roles of various school personnel, the responses indicated a sharp decline in understanding between elementary school and high school (Arnn, Strickland, and Miller, 1983). The parent responses also paralleled a familiar decline in parent-school involvement from elementary to high school.

Growing complexities in both the school and society precipitated modifications in traditional school organization and administration and in lines of communication with the community. As responsibilities and purposes increased in the public schools, so did the administrative superstructure. Nowhere was this more obvious than in urban America. As early as 1968, there were assertions that, in the large schools, service to students and the community was often secondary to career considerations of school officials and that officials' emphasis on professional autonomy isolated them from their students and the changing needs of their clients (Rogers, 1968).

Unfortunately, many smaller school districts began to emulate the organization of larger districts. Seeley and Schwartz (1981) offer a rationale: when communities pressure schools for higher levels of accountability, an increase of bureaucratic control at the top is not unusual, and additional administrative positions are created to monitor progress. Too often, the individuals who fill the new positions are drawn from the classroom, and in many instances these are the most effective teachers, thereby further diminishing quality classroom instruction. In another study cited by Seeley and Schwartz, the higher the proportion of administrators to teachers, the lower the academic achievement.

Strategies for Developing School-Community Relations

Attempts to deal effectively with the growing dissonance between communities and their schools have been well documented under a variety of models such as decentralization, community control, shared power, and advisory committee structures. Today, most of these attempts are viewed as failures, not because they were tried and did not work but because they failed to be fully used (Seeley and Schwartz, 1981).

Too often, the models were viewed as strategies to meet ends, such as civil rights, rather than as attempts to build a more productive relationship between schools and the community. Developing a better school-community relationship as a step toward quality education was somehow lost in the ensuing turmoil and debate.

Schools frequently create administrative organizations in an attempt to respond to concerns of the community; however, in actuality, this frequently causes an interesting dichotomy to emerge. Schools attempt to work with communities toward goals and principles that at times differ from the administrative goals of the larger institution. Schools and communities tend to work toward *developmental* goals and principles, while administrators are concerned with *maintenance* goals.

The following is a modification of an illustration developed by Julius Menacker (1974), that illustrates this dichotomy:

School-Community Educational Goals	*School-Community Administrative Goals*
Assisting student in optimal personal development; includes social, emotional, vocational, and educational components (the whole person).	Promoting maximum organizational efficiency.
Assisting student to make appropriate personal plans, interpretations, and judgments.	Organizational maintenance and self-perpetuation.
Assisting in understanding of self.	Legitimizing and justifying existence of the organization.

228

Helping student utilize opportunities and resources to best advantage.	Achieving the stated objectives of the organization.

Principles	*Principles*
Stress on individual worth and dignity.	Stress on group integration and function.
Recognition of individual's right to choose.	Predetermined organizational and individual objectives.
Cooperative as well as competitive orientation involving student, parent, teachers, and all significant others.	Hierarchical organization, with advancement based on competition.
Continuous, sequential educational process.	Division of function, authority, and responsibility.
Individualizing, personalizing, and socializing element in education.	Task- or performance-related relationships.
Concern with all areas of student's life and environment.	Specialization of function based on technical competence, backed by certification or credentials.
Support of self-discovery and self-development.	Submergence of individual needs and desires in favor of organizational needs and goals.
Responsible to the changing interactive needs of the individual, school, community.	Adherence to organizational rules and regulations, often for their own sake.
Support for self-expanding relationships.	Enforced rules of normative behavior.

229

Although the dichotomies may be overdrawn, they highlight potential inconsistencies in policy and operation that can thwart even the most determined collaboration between schools and communities. When overdeveloped administrations define educational goals for schools (providers) and communities (consumers), the gap can widen further.

A potential bridge in the gap between schools and communities involves administrative decentralization combined with collaborative local or site-based community involvement. In the cycle of educational concern, previously developed models can now be revamped and used for their original purposes.

It should be clear at this point that there is a strong rationale supporting school-community interaction and relationship-building strategies. The focus of such strategies, however, should be clearly identified and maintained so as not to be confused, used, or supplanted by additional agendas.

Action Plans

During the last thirty years, educational reforms affecting schools and communities have utilized most, if not all, methods attempted throughout history (Ryan, 1976):

1) *Revolution.* Do away with the old and begin anew. Fortunately, the institution of education is so entrenched and large that it is less susceptible to this type of reform than in the past.

2) *Change in the balance of power.* Many reforms of this type would shift the decision-making power to lay groups other than school boards. It is usually forced change which lasts only as long as the initial "force" is intact.

3) *Adversary action.* Usually this method concentrates on specific agendas. Too often the reaction generated is counterproductive to the original goal or aim. It is difficult to focus this method on the whole of education.

4) *Advocacy.* As a reform strategy, advocacy appears to work best for the advocate and not necessarily for the

group or issue being supported. Advocacy too often becomes its own institution.

5) *Negotiation.* As negotiation has evolved in education, it has moved toward an advocacy model. Negotiation is usually a reactive strategy undertaken after polarization on an issue has occurred. Often, by that time, attitudes are so strong that win-win outcomes are impossible and even compromise is viewed as either a win or a loss.

6) *Collaboration or partnership.* Of the six reform strategies mentioned, collaboration or partnership is the only one which is developmental rather than reactive. It is also the only strategy which has high potential for effectiveness continuing beyond the developmental stage into the maintenance stage. Collaboration in its truest form anticipates those issues which lead to polarization and provides strategies to lead to win-win results.

The negotiation and collaboration models, in terms of strategies for school-community improvement, are perhaps the most common in the current literature (Rutherford and Edgar, 1979; Gordon and Breivogel, 1976; Saxe, 1975; Bushkin, 1975).

As indicated earlier, many decentralized models appear promising for current difficulties between schools and communities. Schools preparing large populations of students for college admission have different priorities from those preparing many students for job entry. No specific set of priorities appears totally acceptable to all schools. A site-based approach seems imperative because of the diversity of populations in different sections of a district. Generic guidelines for a school-community collaborative effort are:

1) *Team concept expansion.* The team concept is too often limited to interaction between service providers (administrators, counselors, and teachers) in many district action plans. While there will always be some differences in perception between providers and consumers (parents, students, and community representatives), parents and

students must, in some way, be viewed as active team members, and the concept of teamwork must include their concerns and opinions.

2) *Communication network development.* Effective communication is one of the most difficult goals to achieve in any organization or community. It seems apparent that the communication between teachers and community must be improved. Each must have access to other team members if important needs are to be fulfilled. Communication networks must be developed and maintained effectively all the way from the superintendent of schools to the parents of students preparing for school entry.

3) *Counselor role modification.* Counselors are not trained to perform many of the registrar activities currently included either officially or unofficially in their duties. Counselors are, or should be, prepared to perform much more significant roles which place them in the mainstream of the school-community process. Rather than being consumed with clerical responsibilities, counselors should be valuable resources in areas such as team building, communication network development, and evaluation, to name a few. Counselors can offer invaluable services to school personnel; assisting teachers and administrators with stress management, burnout prevention, and human relations skill building are areas in which counselors should possess strong skills.

The role modification proposed is of a more developmental than traditional nature. As such, it must evolve through cooperative efforts. The change in role for counselors would utilize school personnel who already possess, by virtue of training and experience, many of the skills necessary for productive community work. It recognizes that the counselor should already be knowledgeable about the local community and many of its students, and it assumes that counselors and school personnel either currently possess developmental skills or will develop such skills.

It should be emphasized that the role definition being proposed for counselors must be put into practice in the school. It is not merely a role description on paper, but an actual practice which must evolve through the co-operative efforts of school personnel and the community.

4) *Community research.* The dissonance between schools and communities suggests that educational personnel, and particularly those in school leadership positions, should be more aware of the needs of those they serve. More attention must be given to research to determine the effectiveness of current interactions between school and community and any need for modification and improvement.

Several characteristics are essential to a program designed to enhance the relationships between school and community. The program should:

a) be developed gradually and specifically rather than abruptly superimposed on school and community,

b) foster continuous communication among all affected populations,

c) interweave itself with the instructional program,

d) play a key role in the school's public relations efforts,

e) offer access to all and not just to those who are most vocal,

f) be constantly evaluated with relation to all affected populations within the school and community, and

g) have the commitment of appropriate resources and key district and community leadership.

From Plan to Practice

In order for any improvements or suggestions to be taken seriously, at least two conditions must be present. First, the changes must be given visible support by those in positions of power. Improvements must be supported verbally and by demonstrations of "released" time, access, and other requirements necessary to make these new efforts successful. Providers and consumers will believe only what they can see and experience in terms of key school and community support. If there is no support, no real change or improvement will occur.

Second, both school and community must have some responsibility in determining whatever positive modifications are made. People tend not to support new endeavors which they have had no hand in developing. Those who must implement the suggested changes must be responsible for developing strategies to make them occur.

Assuming that the necessary support and representation exist, several strategies seem appropriate:

1) *Steering committee appointment.* Each school must have a representative unit, consisting of school personnel, students, and citizens, which will provide direction and continuity for change. The name of the unit (i.e., steering committee, task force, etc.) does not matter as long as its function is clear and its representation balanced. The unit will determine the structure for improvement, beginning with an on-site needs assessment and continuing through program evaluation and modificaton.

2) *Planning and implementation.* The actual model to be employed must be determined by the steering committee at each site. The following plan is suggested because it encourages team building.

   a) *Needs assessment and priority identification.* Some form of needs assessment must be employed so that providers and consumers can express their needs and concerns. An open forum model is recommended, accompanied by the same form of priority identification.

   b) *Obstacle identification.* Once priorities are identified, potential obstacles to attaining them must also be identified. This step usually is critical in effective change and is too often ignored until after implementation.

   c) *Strategy development.* Another key to effective change is the development of strategies to overcome obstacles and attain priorities. Strategy development, like all other steps, must be a team effort.

234

d) *Implementation*. Specific individuals or groups should be identified and assigned clear responsibilities in the action phase.

e) *Evaluation and modification*. Continuous monitoring should be the goal at every phase of this or any model utilized.

3) *Role definition or development*. As providers and consumers assume responsibility for delivering specific services or implementing strategies, their roles must be developed cooperatively, not in isolation or by any single representative, and must be thoroughly understood by all involved.

4) *Performance appraisal*. Effective role performance requires a high level of delivery by each provider and consumer. The performance of *each* must be appraised regularly if the quality of delivery is to be maintained. The vehicle for performance appraisal must be developed through representative input and consensus.

Since change is a prerequisite for improvement, it is imperative to consider some associated realities:

1) Many providers and consumers will consider any model in operation as archaic and will respond to changes enthusiastically and supportively. They should become key actors in plan development.

2) Some providers and consumers will view any proposed change apprehensively and will need everything from support to retraining.

3) Some providers and consumers will either overtly or covertly attempt to block all efforts to modify the existing model. Again, all ranks may be represented. The only viable alternative available to the district may be to replace these personnel.

The proposed model requires *maximum* participation by on-site providers and consumers and *minimum* intervention by external consultants. External consultants can be helpful as low-visibility resource people to offer suggestions and alternatives, but such consultants must not occupy positions of responsibility in the process of improvement. The specific interventions employed must be determined by the on-site providers and consumers.

Building the School-Community Process On-Site

Building the partnership between school and community initially is based on two important principles (Ryan, 1976). The first is that of open membership: the collaborative process must include everyone who wishes to participate. The second principle is equal membership. There is no doubt that some members feel more equal than others because of a greater knowledge of relevant issues, position in the school or community, previous service on other groups, or stature generated from unrelated situations or activities. Provisions should be made to establish equality in the membership, not only to broaden the potential input and solutions but also to maintain continuity in the membership as time reveals additional issues and agendas.

The First Step

Initial meetings of school and community representatives should focus on goals rather than problems. Goals are developmental, action-oriented, and progressive, while problem solving often leads to more problem solving and generates a negative or reactive mind set. Problem solving is part of attaining goals but should remain a means rather than an end in itself.

It is ultimately more productive to describe what the situation is than to explain the why behind it. The focus should remain on the present and the future rather than on the past. Analyzing the past too often leads to assigning blame, which generates reaction and defensiveness. In any event, the time and energy consumed is counterproductive to moving beyond the present.

Establish Collaborative Representation

It is very important that everyone who realistically should be involved in the planning effort is represented. Beginning a process without including key representatives is potentially more counter-productive than not beginning the process at all. If, after the initial session, it is discovered that others should be represented, review sessions should be planned and held for them so as not to impede the momentum of the larger group.

Develop Expectations for Involvement

Defining the role and expectations of involvement, as well as invest-ment, is extremely important. Participants need to know the specific charge to the group, what kind of involvement is expected, and the individual accountability associated with their involvement. Any in-volvement should be tied directly to accountability; assessment and feedback on performance are vital to individual effectiveness as well as to the overall productivity of the process.

Assign Responsibilities

Usually, more information is needed than is originally available. Teams or task groups of balanced representation can collect the needed materials and information. However, the assignments, whether voluntary or directed, need to be specific and understood by all. Too often assignments of responsibility are incomplete, vague, or misunderstood. This can add to misunderstanding and generate frustration, which impedes progress and detracts from the partici-pants' image of themselves as an effective group.

Decide on Action

Consensus is a key activity in developing school-community collab-oration. Unfortunately, it is more likely to be supported as a concept than as an activity. To many individuals and groups, it is an ideal only. When one considers many of the administrative models of effi-ciency and productivity, consensus does not fare well: it is not viewed as effective from a time-management perspective.

However, consensus is very consistent with collaborative en-deavors. Collaboration by its very nature is process-oriented rather than event-oriented, and consensus provides a strong thread of in-ternal consistency to such efforts.

The following steps for decision making, provided by Ryan (1976), illustrate the consensus process:

1) Points to be resolved are distinguished and taken in order of emerging or preestablished priority.
2) Emerging proposals are superimposed on previous agreements as successive approximations move toward a final decision.
3) Reality testing against previous disagreements or obstacles is necessary for any current group support.
4) The final decision should be supported by all members to the greatest degree possible and in light of fully explored possible solutions.
5) Unwillingness to come to an action decision may occur and should be considered a part of the collaborative process rather than as failure.

We Americans usually want a quick, efficient, effective solution. In many ways, Americans have been taught that is the "best" way to deal with change. Realistically, though, the quick strategy for change is totally inconsistent with the long-term growth of conditions necessitating change and is more appropriate for dismantling than for enhancement.

The ability and commitment of people to work together toward a goal, instead of identifying with separate camps or factions who win or lose, is at the heart of the school-community process. The following interactive behaviors are listed in terms of their impact on building or damaging collaborative endeavors (NCPT, 1971):

Building Behaviors	*Damaging Behaviors*
1) Assisting	1) Indoctrinating
2) Building others	2) Building self
3) Working to improve present practice	3) Working for change for change's sake
4) Facilitating decision making	4) Interfering with decision making

5) Increasing sense of group

5) Taking public credit

6) Showing appreciation of challenges faced

6) Deprecating the position of leadership

7) Facilitating communication by listening, feedback, skillful questioning.

7) Blocking communications with inflammatory remarks, ultimatums, and zingers.

Although the school-community picture may appear somewhat bleak viewed from a national perspective, there are many successful programs scattered about the country which utilize the facets described or some variation thereof.

The private sector also is becoming increasingly involved in school partnership programs. Throughout the country, programs are specifically designed around community needs and resources. Representative examples of collaborative efforts include the following:

1) In Atlanta, 50 different schools have been adopted by 103 private organizations who comprise the Atlanta Partnership of Business and Education, Inc.
2) In Granite City, Illinois, more than ninety local businesses have worked together with the local school board in the Linkages Education/Employment Exploration Project.
3) In Seattle, Private Initiatives in Public Education was founded with the ultimate goal of pairing businesses with schools to meet existing needs.
4) In Boston, the Boston Compact commits community businesses to hiring local young people.
5) In Florida, the Florida School Volunteer Program provides school districts with resources of several different types in order to increase the private sector's involvement with education (Moran, 1983).

Another successful program which began in Delaware and had spread to eight other states by 1983 is Jobs for America's Graduates (McManus, 1983). The program was based on the assumption that it is less costly to prevent unemployment than to solve it after the fact. Basically the program worked at placing and monitoring high school graduates, primarily through an advisory committee structure.

In spite of past failures of various advisory structures, citizens' committees can be very successful. School trustees of Fort Worth Independent School District appointed eleven members to a citizens' committee to study Fort Worth's school system. The Fort Worth Citizens' Committee, the school board, and the school system worked together successfully through the implementation phase of the program. Everyone connected with the effort maintained the goal of quality education throughout the process.

In a recent copy of *Education Week*, a parent was asked to respond to a three-hour television special on ABC. The parent commented that the institution of education is "expected to work miracles" (Shriner, 1984). She went on to say that this cannot be accomplished apart from the society in which schools exist. Collaboration is the essence of the symbiotic relationship between America and its educational ideal.

The school-community relationship cannot be dissolved. Its connections are too numerous and tied to the core of each institution. In effect, the relationship can only be damaged, enhanced, or maintained. America has been through many different cycles of the relationship and should, at this point, reflect on the lessons learned and the models and strategies developed or implemented to improve and maintain positive relationships between schools and communities.

As in every symbiotic relationship, change is a part of the natural process. Unless productive strategies can be developed that include both partners in the relationship, the relationship may be lost. If that happens, it is usually to the detriment of both partners and ultimately to the larger milieu in which they function. Certainly, this is the situation with the school and community.

References and Bibliography

Arnn, John W., Ben R. Strickland, and Patrick Miller. 1983. External audit of an urban guidance program. Unpublished district assessment contracted by the Center for Organization Research and Evaluation Studies, Texas Christian University.

Boyer, Ernest L. 1983. *High School: A Report on Secondary Education in America*. New York: Harper & Row Publishers.

Bushkin, Martin. 1975. *The Open Partnership*. New York: McGraw-Hill Book Company.

Feistritzer, C. Emily. 1983. *The Condition of Teaching: A State by State Analysis*. Carnegie Foundation for the Advancement of Teaching. Princeton, N.J.: Princeton University Press.

Frymier, J., and others. 1984. *One Hundred Good Schools*. West Lafayette, Ind.: Kappa Delta Pi Press.

Gerard, Harold B., and Norman Miller. 1975. *School Desegregation*. New York: Plenum Press.

Goodlad, John I. 1984. *A Place Called School*. New York: McGraw-Hill Book Company.

Gordon, Ira J., and William F. Breivogel. 1976. *Building Effective Home-School Relationships*. Boston: Allyn and Bacon, Inc.

Mangieri, John N., and Richard E. Kemper. 1984. Factors related to high school students' interest in teaching as a profession. Study supported in part by a grant from the Research Fund of Texas Christian University.

McManus, Michael J. 1983. They help kids to get jobs. *New Castle News*, March 21.

Menacker, Julius. 1974. *Vitalizing Guidance in Urban Schools*. New York: Mead & Company.

Moran, Mary E. 1983. Improving schools through private sector partnerships. *American Education* (January-February), 5–8.

National Congress of Parents and Teachers (NCPT) and the North Dakota Congress of Parents and Teachers. 1971. *A Tool Kit for Project ADAPTA*. Findings of meeting in Chicago.

Oliva, Peter F. 1976. *The Secondary School Today*. New York: World Publishing Company.

Ponce, Linda. 1982. Citizens' committee pressing for changes in Fort Worth schools. *Fort Worth Star-Telegram*, December 7.

Rogers, David. 1968. *110 Livingston Street*. New York: Random House.

Rutherford, Robert B., and Eugene Edgar. 1979. *Teachers and Parents*. Boston: Allyn and Bacon, Inc.

Ryan, Charlotte. 1976. *The Open Partnership*. New York: McGraw-Hill Book Company.

Saxe, Richard W. 1975. *School-Community Interaction*. Berkeley, Calif.: McCutchan Publishing Company.

Seeley, David, and Robert Schwartz. 1981. Debureaucratizing public education: The experience of New York and Boston. In Don Davies, ed., *Communities and Their Schools*. New York: McGraw-Hill Book Company.

Shriner, Elizabeth. 1984. Parents' negligence: Can't we do better? *Education Week* 4 (September 19): 20.

Contributors

M. Carol Allen, Associate Superintendent of the New Orleans Public Schools, has been a classroom teacher of elementary, junior, and senior high school students, an elementary school principal, an assistant professor in education administration at the University of South Carolina, and an assistant superintendent for curriculum and instruction. She has published several articles and technical papers and has given numerous lectures on curriculum development and evaluation, administrator training and evaluation, and school-community relations. She is widely travelled and has reviewed educational programs in several foreign countries. Currently she is the area superintendent for forty elementary schools in New Orleans.

John W. Arnn, Jr., Assistant Dean, School of Education, Texas Christian University, is the author of numerous articles as well as co-author of two handbooks and instructional manuals. As an associate professor of counselor education, Dr. Arnn has served as a human relations consultant to several school districts, human service organizations, and business and industry.

Ernest L. Boyer is president of the Carnegie Foundation for the Advancement of Teaching and Senior Fellow of the Woodrow Wilson School, Princeton University. His most recent publication is the widely acclaimed book *High School*, a report on secondary education in America. In 1983 Dr. Boyer, in a national survey, was selected by his peers as the leading educator in the nation. Before joining the Carnegie Foundation in 1980, he served as the twenty-third United States Commissioner of Education. From 1970–77 Dr. Boyer was chancellor of the State University of New York. Prior to 1970, he served as academic dean of a small college in California and director of the Center for Coordinated Education at the University of California at Santa Barbara. Dr. Boyer is the recipient of sixty honorary degrees and many awards, among them the President's Medal from Tel Aviv University. In 1984 he received a Fulbright Distinguished Lectureship Award.

Luvern L. Cunningham, Novice G. Fawcett Professor of Educational Administration at The Ohio State University, has been a student of school boards for more than a quarter century. His interest in the control of education is reflected in several publications including *Governing Schools: New Approaches to Old Issues, The Organization and Control of American Schools* (co-authored and in its fifth edition), *Leadership: The Science and Art Today,* and numerous other monographs and articles. Professor Cunningham is chairperson of the Ohio Commission on Interprofessional Education and Practice as well as Special Master-Commissioner in the Columbus school desegregation case. He has lectured and consulted in several countries. For several years he has worked with school districts and state departments in the incorporation of the decision seminar problem-solving technique at state and local levels. Currently he is co-editing a volume for the National Society for the Study of Education on educational technology.

C. Emily Feistritzer, Director of the National Center for Education Information, has been writing and publishing works about teaching and teacher education through her own private sector organizations in Washington, D.C. since 1979. She directed the Teacher Corps program at the University of South Carolina from 1974 to 1976 and coordinated the National Teacher Development Initiative for the U.S. Office of Education in 1977–78. She publishes the newsletters *Teacher Education Reports, NCEI Reports, Health Education Reports,* and *White House Weekly.* She has authored four major reports since 1983: *Cheating Our Children: Why We Need School Reform; The Making of a Teacher: A Report on Teacher Education and Certification; The Condition of Teaching: A State-By-State Analysis;* and *The American Teacher.* She is called upon frequently to testify before Congress and state legislatures and to speak on the teaching profession. Dr. Feistritzer has received various honors and recognition for her work, including the Distinguished Woman's Scholar Lecturer Award of the Delta Kappa Gamma Society in Virginia and the Distinguished Alumni Award from Indiana University, both in 1985.

David G. Imig, Executive Director of the American Association of Colleges for Teacher Education, has been working for fifteen years to promote reform and innovation in American teacher education. He has served the association in a number of capacities since 1970: as director of governmental relations, special assistant to the executive director, and project director for international education. He has been instrumental in producing numerous studies and reports on teacher education and is currently part of a major national study of teacher education being completed for the U.S. Department of Education. Prior to his work in Washington, Dr. Imig was associated with the Agency for International Development in Sierra Leone and Liberia and before that taught in a secondary boys' school in Tanzania.

John N. Mangieri, Dean of the School of Education at Texas Christian University, is the author of three books and more than seventy professional articles, chapters, or papers on teacher education, reading, and administration. A former Teacher Corps director at Ohio University (1974–78), Dr. Mangieri has served as a consultant to numerous school districts throughout the United States and has conducted seminars and professional presentations at several institutions of higher education. In 1983, he was awarded the "Alumni Achievement Citation for Professional Accomplishments" by Westminster College. Dr. Mangieri has spoken at over thirty national professional meetings. He has served on several special commissions, including the National Task Force on Urban Education (1974–75) sponsored by the United States Department of Health, Education, and Welfare, as well as the American Association of Colleges for Teacher Education's Quality in Teacher Education Task Force.

Richard S. Podemski, Professor of Educational Administration at the University of Arkansas, Fayetteville, is the senior author of *Comprehensive Administration of Special Education* and over forty book chapters and articles in professional publications, and is currently working on a text which deals with the principal's instructional leadership role. He is a member of the Executive Committee of the University Council for Educational Administration and has served as a consultant to school districts, state departments of education, and professional associations. Dr. Podemski's current areas of interest include the implications of electronic technology for the structure of education and the nature of teaching, the professionalization of education, and the relationship between organizational health and school effectiveness. This chapter was written while he was in residence at Texas Christian University as the recipient of the Cecil H. and Ida Green Honors Professorship.

Kevin J. Swick, Professor of Early Childhood Education at the University of South Carolina, Columbia, is the author or editor of eight books and more than two hundred professional papers, journal articles, and monographs on early childhood education, early learning, family-school relationships, teacher education, and classroom discipline. A past president of the South Carolina Association on Children Under Six, Dr. Swick has received many honors for his work, among them the Service Award of the Association for Childhood Education International. He recently was elected president of the Southern Association on Children Under Six and is in *Who's*

Who in the South. He has served as a member of *Childhood Education*'s editorial board for six years and was editor of the Southern Association on Children Under Six's recent position statement on developmentally appropriate programs for young children. Dr. Swick has been a leading researcher in the area of parent involvement in early childhood and recently published his fourth book on the subject: *Inviting Parents into the Young Child's World*.

Typesetting by *G & S Typesetters, Inc., Austin*
Printing and binding by *Edwards Brothers, Ann Arbor*
Design by *Whitehead & Whitehead, Austin*